PHalarope Books

PHalarope Books are designed specifically for the amateur naturalist. These volumes represent excellence in natural history publishing. Most books in the PHalarope series are based on a nature course or program at the college or adult education level or are sponsored by a museum or nature center. Each PHalarope Book reflects the author's teaching ability as well as writing ability. Among the books:

The Western Bird Watcher

AN INTRODUCTION TO BIRDING IN THE AMERICAN WEST

KEVIN J. ZIMMER

A SPECTRUM BOOK

Prentice-Hall, Inc., Englewood Cliffs, New Jersey 07632

Library of Congress Cataloging in Publication Data

Zimmer, Kevin J.
  The western bird watcher.

  (PHalarope books)
  "A Spectrum Book."
  Bibliography: p.
  Includes index.
  1. Bird watching—West (U.S.) I. Title.
  QL683.W4Z56 1985   598'.07'23478   85– 3716
  ISBN 0–13–950825–2
  ISBN 0–13–950817–1 (pbk.)

10 9 8 7 6 5 4 3 2 1

ISBN 0-13-950817-1 (PBK.)

ISBN 0-13-950825-2

Editorial/production supervision by Joe O'Donnell Jr. and Rhonda K. Mirabella
Cover design by Hal Siegel
Cover illustration by Adelaide Murphy
Book design by Maria Carella
Manufacturing buyer: Carol Bystrom

This book is available at a special discount when ordered in
bulk quantities. Contact Prentice-Hall, Inc., General
Publishing Division, Special Sales, Englewood Cliffs, N.J. 07632.

Prentice-Hall International (UK) Limited, London
Prentice-Hall of Australia Pty. Limited, Sydney
Prentice-Hall Canada Inc., Toronto
Prentice-Hall Hispanoamericana, S.A., Mexico
Prentice-Hall of India Private Limited, New Delhi
Prentice-Hall of Japan, Inc., Tokyo
Prentice-Hall of Southeast Asia Pte. Ltd., Singapore
Whitehall Books Limited, Wellington, New Zealand
Editora Prentice-Hall do Brasil Ltda., Rio de Janeiro

Contents

Preface

This book is an introduction to finding and identifying birds in the American West. It is aimed primarily at beginning and intermediate level birders, but it should prove helpful even to those with many years of experience. The area covered is that which falls between the Canadian border on the north, the Mexican border on the south, and the Mississippi River on the east.

The first three chapters deal with finding western birds, first in generalities, then in specifics. Chapter 1 is an introduction to the exciting and varied habitats and birding opportunities to be found in the West. Chapter 2 deals with concepts of bird finding—everything from habitat recognition to pelagic trips, to Rare Bird Alerts (RBAs). Chapter 3 provides specific information on when and where to go to find more than 200 species that are uniquely western.

Finding the birds is only half the battle. You must also be able to identify the birds encountered. Accordingly, Chapter 4 treats the basics of bird identification, dwelling in particular on concepts that have been largely ignored until recent years—gestalt birding, the study of molt patterns, more intensive study of geographic variation, and so on.

Chapter 5 builds upon the foundation laid by Chapter 4 by applying many of the techniques to detailed treatments of some of our hardest to identify birds. These treatments go beyond the information found in most field guides by synthesizing a growing but scattered body of literature on advances in the field recognition of birds. As such, it is this chapter that will be of most interest to more advanced birders.

Chapter 6 serves as a guide to keeping field notes, a desirable practice that will enhance both the pleasure and the importance of your birding activities. The book concludes with a short glossary of technical terms and a bibliography. The latter will provide you with avenues for further study.

Finally, although the focus of this book is on the West, I hope that eastern birders will find it of equal value. The general concepts of finding

and identifying birds apply across the continent, and many of the specific identification problems treated are also of concern in the East. Also, it is inevitable
that active eastern birders will eventually want to head west to experience
the fascination of the country and its birds.

ACKNOWLEDGMENTS

To paraphrase Roger Tory Peterson, this book has been written *by* the birders
of North America as much as *for* them. The advances in knowledge of bird
identification and distribution that have come about in the last decade are
the product of the efforts of hundreds of individuals. I am more the synthesizer
of this knowledge than an author. Jon Dunn has been a special inspiration,
not only because of his numerous contributions to our knowledge of identification, but also because of his willingness to share them with America's birders
by means of the written word.

A number of people were of direct help in the production of this book.
Mary Kennan, Laura Likely, and the rest of the staff at Prentice-Hall were of
inestimable help in all phases of the endeavor. The artwork provided by Janet
Rucci, Mimi Hoppe Wolf, and Dale A. Zimmerman has contributed greatly
to the finished product, as have the fine photos of Richard E. Webster and
Alan Wormington. Paul Lehman and Jon Dunn reviewed Chapter 5 prior to
publication, and offered much constructive advice on difficult identification
problems. Diana Burke lent her word processing skills and typed the entire
final draft.

The chapter on identification problems required that I photograph museum specimens for comparative purposes. Tom Huels and Sharon Goldwasser
arranged my access to the bird collection at the University of Arizona (Tucson),
as did Susan Breisch and Phil Unitt at the Natural History Museum in San
Diego. I am most grateful to them and to their institutions.

Richard Selinfreund (New Mexico State University) did the custom print-
ing of the museum photos, and his considerable technical skills greatly enhanced
the finished product. Brian Locke provided additional advice on technical mat-
ters.

Conversations with other birders have proven invaluable in sharpening
my own field skills by introducing me to subtle field marks long before they
appeared in print. Chief among these contributors is Paul Lehman, who has
freely shared his knowledge. Barry Zimmer, my brother and constant field companion over the years, has likewise been of invaluable help. Others who have
shared information include Jon Dunn, Victor Emanuel, Kenn Kaufman, Jim
Lane, Van Remsen, Don Roberson, David Wolf, and Dale and Marian Zimmerman.

I would be remiss if I did not mention some of the many field companions
who have shared countless birding experiences over the years. My thanks to

Beth Anderson, Carol Anderson, Joe DiPasquale, Jeff Donaldson, Richard Gilliland, Lorraine Hartshorne, Randy Hill, Charlie Jensen, Dan Jones, Sherry Nelson, Jorge Nocedal, Bill Principe, Ken Seyffert, Barbara and Bernie Steinau, Steve West, Deanne White, Geth and Ed White, Nat Whitney, Scott Wilson, Eleanor Wootten, and Jim Zimmer.

Special thanks go to my major professor, Ralph J. Raitt, who has inspired my keen interest in avian ecology. My in-laws, Alfred and Margeret Rucci, have provided much support as well as a thoroughly stimulating environment for my working holidays. My wife, Susan, has gone above and beyond the call of duty in providing every kind of support and encouragement. Final thanks go to my parents, Bernie and Mary Zimmer, whose encouragement and support over the years have truly made this book possible.

Kevin J. Zimmer formerly taught biology and bird identification at New Mexico State University, where he did graduate work. He is now based in California and leads birding tours throughout North America. He has written many articles on birdfinding and identification, as well as a book on finding birds in North Dakota.

For my wife, Susan, and my daughter, Marina,
my constant sources of joy and inspiration.

·1·

Birding the West

This chapter is an introduction to the wealth of birding opportunities available in the American West. It is not a bird-finding guide in the sense of giving detailed directions to specific spots. That task is left to the numerous state and regional finding guides that are available. It is, instead, a series of short vignettes covering a cross section of the more notable biotic communities and the birds to be found in each one. My purpose is to give you a feel for the birding possibilities in each region and, at the same time, to whet your appetite for more detailed investigations of your own.

For the most part I have adopted a habitat approach, and as such, many of the vignettes deal with the generalities of birding a particular habitat (for example, chaparral, desert, alpine tundra, conifer forest). In some of these cases I have talked only in generalities. In others I have used one or two outstanding specific spots to illustrate the potential of the habitat in general. In a few instances I have been more specific regarding particular locations. This treatment has been given only where an excessively large number of specialty birds are present, and/or when the habitat type is restricted to a few discrete spots (for example, south Texas).

Each account also generally restricts itself to the breeding birds to be seen, because they would be the most characteristic of any given locale. Exceptions are to be found in the West Coast and Gulf Coast write-ups, where much of the emphasis has been placed on migratory species.

THE LOWER RIO GRANDE VALLEY

Sooner or later, most gung-ho birders gravitate to the lower Rio Grande Valley of Texas. "The Valley" (as it is called by Texas birders) stretches from about Laredo on the west to Brownsville and the Gulf of Mexico on the east. Its northern boundaries are more nebulous but could be fairly stated to stretch north to about Raymondville. This land is a mecca for birds and for birders! The biggest lure is the promise of some thirty specialty birds, most of which are Mexican and/or neotropical species at the northern limit of their ranges, and most of which cannot be found elsewhere in this country.

The Valley is a mixture of highly agriculturalized land (complete with citrus groves, cotton, vegetable fields, and palm trees lining the highways) and dense, subtropical brush that is composed mostly of mesquite, acacia, and huisache. Unfortunately, the scales are tipped heavily toward agriculture, and little of the original vegetation remains. Fortunately, a few prime tracts of native vegetation have been preserved as parks and refuges, and these remnants rank among the best birding spots in the country.

One such tract is the Santa Ana National Wildlife Refuge located slightly south and east of McAllen. This refuge (comprising about 2000 acres) is nestled along the banks of the Rio Grande. It is covered by a dense, subtropical woodland of ash, ebony, elm, tepeguje, hackberry, mesquite, acacia, and huisache. The

FIGURE 1.1. Subtropical south Texas forest (Santa Ana National Wildlife Refuge). Artwork by Mimi Hoppe Wolf.

larger trees are covered with moss (*Tillandsia*), lending a surrealistic quality to the surroundings that is evident only when you walk one of the many trails that penetrate the woods.

A walk around Willow Lake (one of three small lakes in the refuge) will generally provide the best birding. Birds are everywhere, appearing and disappearing rapidly in the thorny, vinaceous undergrowth. Your first view of the incredible Green Jay flashing across the trail will be unforgettable, and the glimpse of a White-tipped Dove or Plain Chachalaca slipping silently into the underbrush will further whet your appetite. From all sides come the sounds of birds that are generally invisible in the closed canopy and thick understory: the eerie bottle-blowing calls of the White-tipped Doves, the endless bickering of the Couch's Kingbirds and Golden-fronted Woodpeckers, and the sporadic raucous cacophonies of groups of Plain Chachalacas.

You would do well to search the noisy roving bands of "Black-crested" Titmice, for they often harbor wintering or transient warblers, vireos, and kinglets among their ranks. The screeches and squeals of dozens of Great-tailed Grackles disturbed from their roosts will lend a strong tropical flair and, at the same time, remind you that you are approaching the lake. From the various observation points you will be treated to leisurely views of a variety of birds. Throughout the year there will be Least Grebes, Olivaceous Cormorants, and Common Gallinules on the water, Black-shouldered Kites and Harris' Hawks wheeling overhead, and flashy Great Kiskadees hawking insects and minnows from the water's edge. In summer there will also be a few Least Bitterns and numbers of colorful Black-bellied Whistling Ducks, and in winter and during migration a variety of ducks, shorebirds, and waders.

Continuing along the trail, you will stop many times for such specialties as Groove-billed Ani, Brown-crested Flycatcher, and Long-billed Thrasher. Near the trail's end, a side trail leads to a photo blind where suet feeders, sugarwater feeders, and scattered seed attract a number of birds. You may have to push aside the incredibly tame Chachalacas from your path before entering the blind. This blind is a paradise for birders and photographers. From the cover of the blind you can see and photograph such Valley specialties as Plain Chachalaca, White-tipped Dove, Golden-fronted Woodpecker, Green Jay, "Black-crested" Titmouse, Altamira Oriole, and Olive Sparrow, all from a few feet away. The flower gardens at the end of the trail (near the old headquarters) are a good place to watch for Buff-bellied Hummingbirds.

Although the trail around Willow Lake is a great introduction to Valley birding, it is still only a beginning. You will want to explore the other trails of the refuge to search for such exciting rarities as the Hook-billed Kite, Red-billed Pigeon, Rose-throated Becard, Northern Beardless Tyrannulet, Tropical Parula, and Audubon's Oriole.

Farther upriver (near the town of Mission) is the Bentsen–Rio Grande Valley State Park. This park has much of the same vegetation and birds as Santa Ana, but it is generally less productive for birding because of the large numbers of people, the dense forest with fewer trails, and the absence of lakes. In spite of this, the birding is good, and the park offers certain advantages not found at the refuge. Among these are campgrounds with hot (or cold, if your visit is in summer) showers, and accessibility at night for nocturnal birding. Indeed, if you are camping, Bentsen is a great base for exploring the Valley.

As mentioned, the birdlife is nearly identical to that of Santa Ana, but the open area around the main campground provides more opportunities for good viewing of many of the area's specialties. Altamira Orioles are particularly easy to see here and often suspend their incredible nests from trees right in the campground. Bronzed Cowbirds are constantly strolling about the lawn, and the Chachalacas will wake you up each morning at dawn. Wherever you see concentrations of tree snails in the forest, be alert for Hook-billed Kites, which prey on them.

The nocturnal birding at Bentsen is particularly good and can be carried out safely by walking the paved loop through the park. The most sought-after bird is the Common Pauraque, whose loud "go-wheeer" call is perhaps the dominant night sound. Pauraques can be effectively spotlighted as they sit calling in the road. One of the best methods is to drive slowly along the road and watch for their bright orange eyes as they reflect your headlight beam. Other nocturnals of interest include the Eastern Screech Owl, Elf Owl, and Armadillo.

The hottest birding spot in the Valley is the area below Falcon Dam, reached by traveling west from McAllen on U.S. Highway 83. Roadside birding through the mesquite brushlands along the way is good, with numerous Harris' Hawks and possibly a Crested Caracara or two to draw your attention. In summer, Scissor-tailed Flycatchers and Painted Buntings adorn the wires. Cassin's Sparrows skylark from the more open mesquite grasslands along the road into the dam, and Common Bobwhite frequent the roadside.

After parking your car at the spillway overlook below the dam, walk downstream along the trail to the old primitive camp. Work your way down to the river bank, where the birding is best.

Black Vultures will be circling overhead, but your primary quarry are the Ringed and Green Kingfishers. The Ringed Kingfisher is often conspicuous as it perches on a high branch overlooking the river, but the tiny Green Kingfisher sticks to low, concealed perches over quiet pools near the water's edge. With luck you will encounter a noisy band of Brown Jays, a recent immigrant to this country that is now spreading along the river. In the early mornings you may hear some varied mellow whistles that are similar to the sound of a person learning to whistle. By following the sound you should find the rare Audubon's Oriole, usually perched high in a tree.

At all times watch the skies above the river and the high branches over the water for the rare but always-present Red-billed Pigeon and for the less regular Common Black, Zone-tailed, and Gray Hawks. Olivaceous and Double-crested Cormorants should be festooned over dead snags that rise from the banks. At dawn and dusk the very rare Ferruginous Pygmy Owl can often be heard piping monotonously from the dense vegetation downstream from the primitive camp. When rarities are not cooperating, you will still be entertained by the myriads of more mundane Valley birds, such as Yellow-billed Cuckoo (summer), Groove-billed Ani (summer), Golden-fronted Woodpecker, Brown-crested Flycatcher, Great Kiskadee, Couch's Kingbird, Green Jay, "Black-crested" Titmouse, Long-billed Thrasher, Painted Bunting (summer), and Olive Sparrow.

All these same birds can be found at a few other points downstream near Chapena, Salineño, and at the Santa Margarita Ranch near Roma. Farther upstream, near the tiny town of San Ygnacio, White-collared Seedeaters can be found most winters, particularly in the brush and cane along the river below the cemetery.

THE GULF COAST

Few regions offer the total diversity of birdlife or the sheer numbers of birds that can be found along the Texas Gulf. Texas birders divide the coast into three regions—upper, central, and lower. For the most part the birds are the same from Port Arthur to Port Isabel, but each region has its own specialties, and all deserve coverage. Everyone's favorite time to visit is spring, when the migration spectacle has to be seen to be believed. Other seasons are also incredibly productive, and the visiting birder will never leave disappointed.

The coastline is bounded by a series of long, narrow barrier islands. Between the islands and the mainland are long, narrow stretches of shallow water called *lagunas.* The lagunas are punctuated at various spots along the coast by large bays that mark the mouths of major rivers. Coastal vegetation is typically sparse, with sandy outer beaches giving way to vast expanses of *Spartina* (salt grass) marsh. The coastal plain is mostly grassland, dotted with clumps (mottes) of live oak. Much of the area inland from the humid upper coast has been converted to rice fields. The coastal plain south of Baffin Bay is more arid, a fact reflected by the mesquite, prickly pear, and yucca that pepper the grasslands.

The upper coast extends from the Louisiana line south and west to Port O'Connor. Birders in this region are weather watchers. When a spring cold front moves in and a norther blows down, it's time to head for the coast. Trans-Gulf migrants, having struggled against the wind for hundreds of miles, drop from the sky exhausted by their labors. They "fall out" over the first clumps of vegetation available and begin to feed voraciously. If weather conditions hold, the birds begin to "stack up," and the birders are in for Texas birding at its best!

The best place for migrant fall-outs is the town of High Island, situated along the coast north of Galveston. The town sits atop a salt dome, and the small rise in elevation is enough to enable trees to grow, an exception in a flat area with a high water table. The resultant clumps of live oaks and hackberries act as magnets for weary migrants. For best results, head to Smith Woods and Boy Scout Woods, two small tracts that often harbor huge numbers of birds.

If weather conditions are right, you will have the time of your life! It is not unusual to see more than twenty-five species of warblers (including Swainson's) in a single day, often within a few hours. The first half of April is the best time for the southern-breeding species of warblers (e.g., Hooded, Kentucky, Swainson's, Worm-eating, Blue-winged), whereas the latter half of April and early May are best for the northern-breeding ones (e.g., Canada, Blackburnian, Bay-breasted). Even more impressive than the variety is the great amount of birds to be seen. Five species of thrushes cover the ground, dozens of Indigo Buntings are scattered across the lawns, and a single fruiting mulberry tree may host several dozen catbirds, orioles, tanagers, and grosbeaks.

Similar migration experiences await the birder at Galveston Island and Rockport, but because of prevailing weather conditions, the occurrence of major fall-outs is less frequent at the latter spot, which is much farther south.

The Anahuac National Wildlife Refuge, just west of High Island, is a recommended stop in any season. In winter there are thousands of ducks and geese, and harder-to-find Sedge Wrens, Sprague's Pipits, and Le Conte's Sparrows. Migration brings numerous shorebirds, and summer is the time for the colorful Purple Gallinule. Throughout the year you can find Roseate Spoonbills, Little Blue and Tricolored Herons, and King and Clapper Rails, as well as a host of other more widespread wading birds.

The biggest drawing card is the Rail buggy. During the month of April, the refuge conducts buggy rides into the marsh to search for rails. The bumpy, tractor-driven ride never fails to turn up the sought-after Yellow Rail, and on most trips you will be treated to multiple views of these elusive marsh birds as they climb up on tussocks of grass to inspect the on-coming buggy. Occasionally you will be lucky enough to find the rare Black Rail, another highly prized species.

The inland rice fields north of Anahuac (as along State Highway 61) are fabulous for migrating shorebirds, especially for such birds as Hudsonian Godwit; dowitchers; and Buff-breasted, Pectoral, Baird's and White-rumped Sandpipers.

More spectacular shore birding can be had west of Anahuac, along the narrow Bolivar Peninsula at Bolivar Flats (east of the North Jetty near the entrance to Galveston Bay). These sandy flats attract thousands of migrating shorebirds, and the diversity is as impressive as the numbers. This is the place to find American Oystercatchers; Wilson's, Piping, and Snowy Plovers; and huge concentrations of Red Knots and Sanderlings. It is also a great place to see Reddish Egret, Roseate Spoonbill, Black Skimmer, and a variety of terns, including Sandwich, Royal, Caspian, and Least. During high tides, you may find Clapper Rails forced from cover in the salt grass marshes surrounding the flats.

Galveston Island itself offers tremendous birding, particularly during migration, when shorebirds are extremely abundant and passerines fall out (much as they do at High Island). For migrant passerines, check Kempner Park and the adjacent neighborhoods. For shorebirds, try any of the grassy, well-grazed fields and pastures. These attract numbers of Lesser Golden and Black-bellied Plovers, Long-billed Curlews, Whimbrels, and Upland and Buff-breasted Sandpipers. Saltgrass marshes are great for all the expected herons, egrets, and ibis, and also for Clapper Rails.

You will probably want to stop at Galveston Island State Park, particularly during winter and migration. This park contains large expanses of salt marsh and is a particularly good spot to find Seaside (resident), Sharp-tailed (winter) and Le Conte's (winter) Sparrows; as well as Sedge Wren (winter), Gull-billed Tern (resident but more common in summer), and a variety of waders and shorebirds. Similar birds can be found at Sabine, near the Louisiana-Texas border.

Farther south, near Tivoli, is Aransas National Wildlife Refuge. The refuge is most famous as the winter home of the Whooping Crane, but there are many other attractions. This is a particularly good place to see herons, egrets, spoonbills, ibis, and waterfowl, and Anhingas are a frequent sight during winter and migration. The wooded areas are great for migrant land birds, while the nesting passerines of greatest interest are the Scissor-tailed Flycatcher, Painted Bunting, and Seaside Sparrow. The grasslands and agricultural areas

FIGURE 1.2. Gulf Coast (Laguna Atascosa National Wildlife Refuge, Texas). Artwork by Mimi Hoppe Wolf.

surrounding the refuge and Tivoli should not be ignored, for they support such rarities as the Crested Caracara, Greater Prairie Chicken, and the beautiful White-tailed Hawk.

The Whooping Cranes are best seen from the boat of the same name, which docks at the Sea-Gun Sports Inn at Rockport, and travels several times each week (October to April) to Aransas to view the cranes. In addition to guaranteed views of the whoopers, you will be thrilled by the many great views of egrets, herons, gulls, terns, and skimmers.

The tiny town of Rockport has long been a "must" stop on the spring itineraries of traveling birders. The live oak groves attract hordes of migrant passerines; the numerous ponds harbor a variety of herons, egrets, rails, and ducks; and the grassy pastures are great for migrant plovers, curlews, and sandpipers. After a couple of days here, you may not want to leave.

Mustang and Padre Islands provide numerous shorebirding opportunities, particularly for such beach species as the Snowy Plover, Whimbrel, Sanderling, and Red Knot. Gulls and terns are also common, and the beach scenery is great. Peregrine Falcons are often seen in migration. The city of Corpus Christi offers multiple opportunities for birding, and it is often possible to get repeated close studies of Tricolored Heron, Reddish Egret, Roseate Spoonbill, Clapper Rail, Black Skimmer, and Least Tern, among others.

West of Corpus Christi, U.S. Highway 77 heads south through the extensive King Ranch (more than 800,000 acres). This mesquite–grassland area is for the most part off limits to the public, but birding is worthwhile even from the car. The greatest attraction is the resident White-tailed Hawk, certainly among the most beautiful of North American raptors. Migration brings impressive numbers of Broad-winged and Swainson's Hawks that sometimes form large "kettles" in the sky. The numerous ponds attract a variety of waterfowl and sometimes harbor Least Grebes and Olivaceous Cormorants. Scissor-tailed Flycatchers are everywhere from April through October.

Farther south is Laguna Atascosa National Wildlife Refuge, one of the best birding spots on the entire coast. The refuge encompasses a variety of habitats, including dry coastal prairie, fresh-water ponds, subtropical mesquite brushland, salt-water bays, salt flats, sandy beaches, mud flats, and *Spartina* marshes. Along with the habitat diversity comes a tremendous diversity of birds. The spectacular waders (White and White-faced Ibis, Roseate Spoonbill, Reddish Egret, and Tricolored and Little Blue Herons, among others) may grab your attention, but you are likely to be distracted by the Black Skimmers, various terns, and hordes of migrating shorebirds. Two special shorebirds are the American Oystercatcher and the Wilson's Plover, both of which can be seen through the summer.

The prairie sections have nesting Botteri's Sparrows, and the wooded areas (complete with nature trails) are home to a number of South Texas specialties. Among those of interest are the Groove-billed Ani (summer), Common Pauraque, Golden-fronted Woodpecker, Green Jay, Long-billed Thrasher, Painted Bunting (summer), and Olive Sparrow. A day on the refuge is guaranteed to produce exciting birding as well as a large list, and you will find that during migration each trip around the loop produces new birds.

The southernmost point on the coast is Port Isabel and South Padre Island, which are connected by a long causeway. The area is often overrun by tourists, but good birding can still be had along isolated stretches of beach and along the laguna. The east end of the causeway is almost always abundant with terns and migrating shorebirds. After the sandy beaches of South Padre, a visit to the Brownsville Dump will prove less than esthetic. However, it is still worth the visit from November to April when you can count on finding the highly localized U.S. wintering population of tiny Mexican Crows. This is also an excellent spot to search for rare gulls.

THE GRASSLANDS

Grasslands constitute an important habitat type across much of the West and are found from the U.S.–Canadian border on the north to the U.S.–Mexican border on the south. Often considered monotonous or uninteresting by the uninitiated, the grasslands are, in fact, among the most fascinating of ecosystems. Some grasslands biomes are admittedly low in their diversity of bird species, but others are incredibly rich and should not be ignored by birders.

The grasslands that are of greatest interest to most birders are the short-grass prairies of Colorado, Wyoming, Montana, and the western Dakotas; and the mixed-grass, prairie-pothole country of the Dakotas and eastern Montana. The U.S. breeding ranges of several birds are essentially restricted to these

FIGURE 1.3. Pawnee National Grassland, Colorado.
Artwork by Mimi Hoppe Wolf.

regions, and it is here that you must travel if you are to see these specialties in their breeding dress and conducting their often spectacular courtship displays.

The Pawnee Grassland near Briggsdale, Colorado, is one of the most famous remnants of short-grass prairie. As you maneuver your car along the gravel road into the heart of the grassland, your attention is invariably drawn to the scores of Lark Buntings that adorn the fence lines and the tops of scattered saltbushes. Although it is possible to see many of the breeding specialties from your car, you can experience the true magic of the grassland only by walking out into it. Here, away from the road, the land becomes a verdant sea of buffalo grass waving in the cool morning breeze. The bubbly songs of the buntings fill the air, and on every horizon you will see the jet-black males with their white wing patches fluttering up from their perches.

Less numerous but more sought-after is the McCown's Longspur. Birds of both sexes spend much time on the ground, virtually invisible among the short grass. With patience you will be treated to the flight song of the male, an effervescent display that ends with a slow-motion, butterfly-like descent to the earth. A dry, insect-like buzz can be followed to a Grasshopper Sparrow, perched atop a small shrub or tall grass stem. At least one eye must be trained overhead, for this is raptor country. Raptors most likely to be seen are the Swainson's and Ferruginous Hawks, but Golden Eagles and Prairie Falcons are possible.

You will also want to watch the ground, for the abundant ankle-high prickly pear will leave you with a less-than-pleasant memory. Prairie rattlesnakes are also a possibility and should be watched for. All is not unpleasant at ground level, for it is here that you will find a surprising array of wildflowers, another aspect of the grasslands that is not easily appreciated from the car.

As you travel the roads of the Pawnee, pay special attention to the flat valleys where the grass is short. The Mountain Plover, a beautiful study in subtle camouflage, can be found here. Their whistled calls and their nervous distraction displays indicating the presence of young are reminders that these are indeed shorebirds, adapted to a seemingly incongruous mixture of grass and cactus.

Where lone trees stand in contrast to the landscape, you are likely to find the bulky nests of the Ferruginous and Swainson's Hawks. In the localized patches of tall grass that form the meadow zones of the few man-made reservoirs, you should search for the Chestnut-collared Longspur. Much less common here than the McCown's, it is also less given to aerial display and routinely sings from a perch. What the male Chestnut-collared lacks in behavior, it more than makes up for in plumage. It is a stunning combination of jet-black underparts, black-and-white striped head, and gorgeous chestnut nape that has to be seen to be appreciated.

You will leave the Pawnee with a list that is perhaps short on quantity but long on quality. Even when nothing new is seen, these grasslands exert a magic that transcends marks on a checklist. The life birds are merely icing on the cake.

The rolling plains of northern North Dakota share much of the atmosphere of the Pawnee but at the same time exhibit a marked contrast. There is greater zonation of different grassland types. This zonation is typically reflective of slight changes in elevation (and thus moisture and alkalinity) that are repeated from hill to hill, and valley to valley. Many of the valleys have potholes that provide ephemeral, semi-permanent, or permanent water sources, depending on their size.

It is the potholes (and the resulting zonation) that are responsible for the incredible diversity of bird life to be found here. The marshes teem with activity—Wilson's Phalaropes spinning constant circles on the surface, Black Terns cruising back and forth overhead, bitterns and rails skipping through the reeds, and ducks of several species crowding the water. Larger bodies of water host nesting colonies of Eared and Western Grebes. The bizarre courtship dances of the latter species will make a visit worthwhile.

The wet, reedy border is the refuge of the Marsh Wren, its rattling calls almost drowned out by the din of the brilliant Yellow-headed Blackbirds that are festooned over the cattails. Further back, in the wet sedges, you will find the colorful but elusive Le Conte's Sparrow, and the tiny bob-tailed Sedge Wren.

Still more specialties await in the drier mixed grasses that extend up from the valleys onto the hillsides. Once again, you will find the Chestnut-collared Longspur. In North Dakota, it is much more common and widespread than the McCown's. With it are the two biggest prizes for the lister—the Baird's Sparrow, and the Sprague's Pipit. Neither bird is very colorful, but both have very restricted ranges and are highly prized by birders. Nowhere are they more common than in this prairie-pothole country. Your first encounter with the pipit may be auditory as you become aware of a disembodied swishing sound from overhead. This is the flight song of the pipit, and it is often delivered from amazing heights.

Select rises on the landscape may be lek sites for Sharp-tailed Grouse. The dawn courtship dances of these prairie birds (imitated by the Plains Indians) are always an eye-catching sight. The fence posts along the roadsides are the province of large numbers of Western Meadowlarks and lesser numbers of Upland Sandpipers. The weird mating calls of the sandpipers constitute one of the true sounds of spring in this unique and wide-open country.

THE ALPINE TUNDRA

Sooner or later, most Western birders will make a pilgrimage to the alpine tundra that marks the above-timberline points of scattered high peaks in the northwest, Rocky Mountains (and associated ranges), and Sierras. They are drawn by the lure of a few highly specialized birds that are restricted to this limited habitat. The charm of the alpine regions is such that many birders keep coming back long after the possibilities for new birds are exhausted.

Most alpine zones south of Canada have the same half-dozen or so resident bird species. The differences lie mainly in their accessibility. To reach the tundra on many mountains requires a walk of several miles. Not so in Rocky Mountain National Park (Colorado), where you can follow paved roads right into the tundra.

Trail Ridge Road climbs from the lower elevations of the park up through the firs of the subalpine zone and then breaks onto the tundra. The vistas here are spectacular from every angle. At nearly 12,000 feet in elevation, you have an unimpeded view of massive snow-capped peaks in the distance and of dark green conifer forest below. At timberline, the trees are stunted and twisted by the cold, pounding winter winds. Above timberline, the ground seems to be covered by a plush carpet of sedges, mosses, forbs, and lichens. Early in summer the landscape is brown, but by July the tundra will be ablaze with color. The tiny flowering plants (nearly all of which are perennial) come in a dazzling variety of blues, purples, yellows, reds, and oranges, making it easy to forget about birds. The only vegetation of any height is the alpine dwarf willow, which is concentrated in scattered clumps.

A stop at Rainbow Curve is always a treat. There are usually large numbers of Clark's Nutcrackers mobbing the tourists for handouts, and you can see and photograph them to your heart's content. Occasionally they are joined by a Gray Jay, like the nutcracker, a visitor to the tundra from lower elevations. Here also are Golden-mantled Ground Squirrels, chipmunks of two species, and the chinchilla-like Pika. All can be seen darting among the rocks below the turn-out.

FIGURE 1.4. Alpine tundra (Rocky Mountain National Park, Colorado). Artwork by Mimi Hoppe Wolf.

Because the tundra is a fragile habitat, it is best to stick to established trails as much as possible. A great place for seeing tundra specialties is along the nature trail and old quarry road at Rock Cut. Three of the most common tundra birds are ones that are familiar to most birders but which will seem novel because of the very different surroundings. How strange it seems to see Horned Larks strolling about the tundra, surrounded by lichen-covered rocks and patches of snow. Even stranger are the breeding-plumaged Water Pipits, which look very different from the birds that we see in late fall and winter. White-crowned Sparrows nest in the willow thickets, but often feed along the road.

But it is not for these birds that one ventures to the mountain tops. Rather, it is for two specialties that are supremely adapted to the treeless, wind- and snow-swept slopes—the White-tailed Ptarmigan and the Brown-capped race of the Rosy Finch.

Although the ptarmigan are both large and fairly common, they can still prove elusive. Birds of both sexes are incredibly camouflaged. The female blends so well with the tundra that it is possible to be looking right at a sitting bird from several feet away and still not see it. Early in summer the males respond well to taped recordings of their calls, and can be easily lured. This is preferable to tramping all over the tundra both for ecological and practical reasons. Ptarmigan can be walked up, but it usually takes a lot of walking, since the territories are large and the birds are rarely spotted until you are practically on top of them.

Once you spot a ptarmigan, resist the urge to scramble upslope after it at any speed. Should you forget, the altitude will bring a quick halt, and it may be several minutes before you can stop gasping long enough to enjoy the bird. Besides, once spotted, these birds are easily approached. They walk away rather than fly and can often be approached to within several feet. To stand, breathing the thin mountain air, reveling in the surrounding scenery and the carpet of flowers while a beautiful pair of ptarmigan walk at your feet, is to experience the tundra at its finest.

If the ptarmigan is the most spectacular bird of the tundra, then the Rosy Finch could at least be described as the quintessential alpine bird. Almost every alpine setting in the west has its Rosy Finches, although the birds differ racially from region to region. The Colorado-breeding bird is the Brown-capped, but in behavior and habitat preference it is virtually identical to the other forms.

Your first views of these birds may be of a pair hurtling wildly downslope and disappearing in a talus field. This less-than-satisfactory experience will be quickly forgotten when you finally encounter several individuals feeding at the edge of a snowfield. Here, the finches seem surprisingly docile, and can be approached quite closely. At one moment they are serene, feeding quietly on the wind-blown insects that have been trapped and immobilized by the snow. Their subdued brown and pink colors blend subtly in a way that can only be truly appreciated from close range. In a flash, the birds spring to the air and go bouncing over the next ridge, their "chew" notes carried back by the wind. This is the real lure of the tundra.

THE CONIFER FOREST

The conifer forest is one of the most extensive of western habitats. There are many types of forest that fall under this broad heading, ranging from the arid, low-diversity pinyon-juniper forests of the southwest, to the high-diversity temperate rain forests of the northern Pacific coast. Each forest type has its own component tree species, as well as its own special birds. However, when allowances are made for some geographical replacement species (different species occupying similar niches in geographically removed areas), there remains a central core of birds that are typical of most western conifer forests.

This brief introduction to the general habitat and its birds will focus on three specific locations, each representative of different types of conifer forest:

1. The pine-fir forest of Yosemite National Park (California)
2. The coastal Redwood Forest of northern California
3. The subalpine fir forest of Olympic National Park (Washington).

YOSEMITE

The Yosemite high country is one of the premier birding areas of the West. Although the good habitat is extensive, most birders confine their efforts to the area surrounding Bridalveil Campground. Here, at an elevation of 7200 feet, is a magnificent forest of red fir and lodgepole pine, which opens at many

FIGURE 1.5. Fir forest and ambient meadow (Yosemite National Park, California). Artwork by Mimi Hoppe Wolf.

places into lush green meadows. The birding is incredible and provides chances for seeing some of the most sought-after of montane birds.

Dawn and dusk are the times to explore the nearby meadows. At these times the dense forest is dark and still, but the meadows are alive with sunlight and bird activity. The stream meanders through the meadow, and in many adjacent areas the earth is boggy and wet. Calliope Hummingbirds wage battles over the many wildflowers, Lincoln's Sparrows are everywhere in the grass, and the noisy Brewer's Blackbirds seem distinctly out of place.

There is bigger game in the meadows, however, for this is the habitat preferred by the magnificent Great Gray Owl. These rare owls of the far north breed in scattered montane forests south of Canada. Yosemite is the area where they are most frequently observed during the breeding season. Within the park a few pairs of owls occupy the forest adjacent to select meadows. These pairs often switch meadows from one year to the next, which makes finding them all the more difficult.

For most of the day these great predators remain in clumps of fir inside the forest proper. But early in the morning and again at dusk they can often be found atop a conspicuous perch overlooking the meadow. With extreme luck you may get to see the owl in action as it glides over the meadow like a huge gray moth while searching for rodent prey.

Dawn and dusk are also the times when Blue Grouse are apt to be seen strolling through the tall grass. They will often allow close approach, particularly when young are present.

As the day warms up you will want to head into the forest itself. Here there is much bird activity, and at times it is hard to focus your attention on any one bird. Western Wood-Pewees, Steller's Jays, Mountain Chickadees,

Yellow-rumped Warblers, and Dark-eyed Juncos are among the most conspicuous summer residents, but with searching you should also find Hammond's and Olive-sided Flycatchers, Red-breasted Nuthatch, Hermit Warbler, Western Tanager, Pine Grosbeak, Pine Siskin, and Cassin's Finch. Red Crossbills are somewhat more sporadic, but in some years can be seen in good numbers.

It won't take long to realize that this is woodpecker country. Along with such widespread species as the Hairy and Common Flickers are more localized ones like the Pileated, White-headed, and Williamson's and Red-breasted Sapsuckers. Most prized of all is the Black-backed Woodpecker, a few pair of which are in the vicinity every year.

THE REDWOODS

The coastal redwood forest, which stretches from northern California to southern Oregon, is one of the most amazing plant assemblages anywhere in the world. Confined to the fog belt, this is truly a temperate rain forest with some areas receiving more than 100 inches of rain per year. The birding is not spectacular, although it is unique. The forest itself is somewhat low in bird diversity, but the edges (where secondary growth exists) can be quite "birdy."

As with other deep-forest areas, it is best to start the day along the forest edge where lighting is good early in the morning. Birds are common in the thick, secondary growth, with Allen's Hummingbirds, Wilson's Warblers, Dark-eyed Juncos, and Purple Finches being among the more common species. By looking up occasionally, you may spot a Vaux's Swift. Regardless of your success, that incredible forest beckons, and you take one of the many trails that dissect Redwood National Park.

Almost at once the forest closes in, and noises from the nearby highway disappear. At first, any thoughts of birds are lost in the amazement of what surrounds you. The immensity of the trees, the giant ferns, the huge slugs creeping across the trail, and the filtered sunlight that barely penetrates the towering canopy, all combine for a surreal and almost prehistoric atmosphere.

By now you are ready for anything—even *Tyrannosaurus*—but your reverie's broken by an unearthly sound, by *the* sound of the redwoods. It is the ethereal notes of the Varied Thrush, ascending, shrill, but somehow organlike. It filters up through the canopy, like the sunlight in reverse. Enjoy the sound, for it may be some time before you can find the bird. This thrush has a way of drawing your attention, only to melt away into the woods upon your approach. Once seen, it is a fine study in orange and black, one not done justice by most illustrations.

Now that cognizance has returned, you are aware that there are birds everywhere. That bubbly, endless song must belong to the tiny Winter Wren, but it seems to be leap-frogging through the undergrowth. The Ruffed Grouse that exploded from underfoot was a good find, but it disappeared too fast for a good look. And the canopy! There seem to be Western Flycatchers, Steller's Jays, Chestnut-backed Chickadees, Golden-crowned Kinglets, and Hermit Warblers calling from every tree top, but the views are less than stunning. There's something about six-inch birds 300 feet up. . . .

As you may have guessed, birding the redwoods can be an exercise in frustration. With patience, however, you should eventually find these species and others (like the Swainson's Thrush). With real fortune, you could stumble across a snoozing Spotted Owl. No matter your eventual luck, the two most vivid memories are likely to be of the forest itself and of that unearthly sound.

SUBALPINE FOREST

The subalpine forest, from the upper Canadian Zone to the lower Alpine Zone, is a widespread feature of the higher western mountain ranges. Excellent examples of this forest type are found along Trail Ridge Road in Rocky Mountain National Park (Colorado), along Hurricane Ridge in Olympic National Park (Washington), and in the high country of Mt. Rainier National Park (Washington). Although plant and bird diversity is less than at lower elevations, there is still plenty to see.

Birds are encountered sporadically in this forest, particularly near timberline, in the stunted, twisted, Krummholz vegetation. Northern Ravens are common sights overhead, their low croaks and somber appearance being perfectly suited to the somewhat austere surroundings. Mountain Bluebirds sometimes breed in the areas where the forest gives way to the tundra, particularly if park service structures are nearby for nest placement.

Some of the more common and widespread nesting birds of this habitat include Mountain Chickadee, Red-breasted Nuthatch, Brown Creeper, Townsend's Solitaire, Hermit Thrush, Dark-eyed Junco, and Pine Siskin. Pine Gros-

FIGURE 1.6. Subalpine forest (Hurricane Ridge, Washington). Artwork by Mimi Hoppe Wolf.

beaks and Red Crossbills can often be found feeding side by side on the conifer cones.

In some areas (like Hurricane Ridge) Blue Grouse are common, and their hooting sounds resound across the hillsides. Seeing the calling birds is another matter entirely because calling is often done from high in a dense cluster of firs and because the sound is more than a little ventriloquial.

The real kings of this habitat are the Clark's Nutcrackers, whose raucous calls can be traced to birds perched high atop the trees. Between bouts of squabbling and territorial advertisement, these birds go bouncing through the air, surveying their mountain domain. Where turn-outs exist along the road, the nutcrackers will frequently mob tourists for hand-outs. Occasional Gray Jays join in, presenting an interesting comparison between two gray, black, and white denizens of the high western mountains.

THE PACIFIC COAST

Coastal birding has a charm all its own, and there is no denying either the species diversity or the numbers of birds to be seen. Although much of the Pacific Coast is heavily populated (particularly in southern California), pockets of good habitat exist (in the form of bays, river estuaries, and rock jetties) in even the most developed of areas. From San Francisco north to British Columbia, lies some of the most picturesque and fascinating coastline anywhere on the continent. There are birds to be seen in all seasons.

The most productive coastal habitats are the shallow bays, river estuaries, and tidal flats. Here can be found an incredible number of birds during migration and winter. Loons and scoters of six species are routinely found in bays and harbor areas throughout the nonbreeding season, and a few nonbreeding birds typically summer each year. Western, Eared, and Horned Grebes; Red-breasted Merganser; and a variety of diving ducks round out the list of commonly expected transients, while Brown Pelicans and Double-crested Cormorants are present throughout the year. Great Blue Herons and Black-crowned Night Herons routinely perch on the decks of docked fishing boats, and gulls and terns of several species are in constant attendance everywhere.

The river estuaries and tidal flats produce even more diversity, especially at low tide, when the recently exposed mud flats are teeming with invertebrate life. As many as twenty species of shorebirds (some in huge numbers) can be seen feeding feverishly upon the flats and along channels of water through the marsh. Among them are American Avocets; Willets; Marbled Godwits; Long-billed Curlews; both species of yellowlegs; both species of dowitchers; Ruddy Turnstone; Wilson's and Red-necked Phalarope; Black-bellied, Semipalmated, and Snowy Plovers; Sanderlings, Dunlin, and several species of peeps. To be able to observe the varied feeding habits of the different species is to understand more fully the diversity of morphological adaptations (particularly bill structures) found in the shorebirds.

The shorebirds are not the only occupants of the mud flats, for here too are Great and Snowy Egrets, puddle ducks of many species, and sometimes, flocks of Brant. In California, the Forster's and Caspian Terns are joined by Least, Elegant, and Royal Terns, and several species can often be found standing side by side on the same sandbar.

The bays, estuaries, and tidal flats are somewhat devoid of birds in early and mid summer, but by July the shorebirds are already moving back through, leaving little void in the excitement of coastal birding.

The Pacific Coast also features a habitat not found along the Texas Gulf—that of rocky shoreline complete with tide pools. Although it is not as rich in species composition or total numbers of birds as are the more estuarine habitats, the rocky coast is host to more specialized groups of birds.

It is here, among the barnacle-encrusted, wave-battered rocks that we find several species of western shorebirds which are virtually restricted (in the nonbreeding season) to this habitat. These are the Black Oystercatcher, Black Turnstone, Surfbird, Rock Sandpiper, and Wandering Tattler. Of these, only the oystercatcher nests; the rest are winter residents and/or transients. Oddly enough, the transient species are tundra inhabitants on their arctic breeding grounds.

These shorebirds (dubbed "rockpipers" by some) are the avian lifeblood of the rocky intertidal. The turnstones and surfbirds scramble about the slippery rocks with nimble agility, rarely minding the deluge of spray that comes with each wave. Only when a very large wave threatens do they take to the wing, revealing flashy patterns of black and white. They are social birds and are often found together in groups of ten to twenty. The Rock Sandpiper is an uncommon to rare winter visitor (south to the San Francisco area) that often associates with groups of turnstones and surfbirds.

FIGURE 1.7. Rocky coast (San Diego to British Columbia). Artwork by Mimi Hoppe Wolf.

Tattlers are less social and are typically found individually or in very small groups. The Black Oystercatcher is the most spectacular bird of the group, and despite its larger size, seems equally adept at climbing about the rocks. Whimbrels, Ruddy Turnstones, Willets, and Black-bellied Plovers are other common inhabitants of the rocky coast, and Sanderlings and Snowy Plovers become common given some sandy stretches between the rocks.

Gulls usually stand about the rocks, among them (depending on season and specific locale) Western, Glaucous-winged, Herring, Thayer's, Heermann's, Mew, and Ring-billed. Scoters bob in the surf, often surrounded by sea lions or some other pinnipeds. Where large, offshore rocks or islands are present, you can expect to find many Brandt's and Pelagic Cormorants, Common Murres, and Pigeon Guillemots. The cormorants frequently adorn the tops of large rocks and coastal cliffs, often in large numbers. Favored perches are marked by a conspicuous covering of white-wash. Both the cormorants and the alcids often join the scoters in the surf, and when hundreds of birds are present (as is typical near nesting rocks), the water may be literally boiling with birds.

THE DESERT

Perhaps no habitat is as misunderstood or as unappreciated as the desert. To most people (including far too many birders), it is a scorching, unforgiving, barren wasteland. "It's so monotonous" is a common complaint. In point of fact, the desert is one of the most heterogeneous of habitats. Depending on one's classification system, there may be nearly as many types of desert on this continent as there are types of forest. Extreme spatial and temporal variability combine to make deserts endlessly fascinating places to all who have come to appreciate the myriad adaptations of organisms to the harsh physical surroundings.

Of the various deserts found in the United States, the Sonoran Desert of Arizona boasts the richest avifauna. Some might argue that this is because much of the Sonoran is not true desert, but thorn forest. Regardless, the Sonoran is probably what comes to most people's minds when they conjure up images of American deserts.

Nearly everything that grows here has thorns. Cholla, prickly pear, and a multitude of less common cacti are scattered across the landscape. Mesquite, acacia, and palo-verde are among the dominant tree-shrubs, and creosote bush, Mormon tea, and ocotillo are locally common. Nothing dominates the landscape, though, as does the majestic saguaro cacti. With their grotesque arms directed skyward, the saguaros stand as ghostly giants—symbols of the American Southwest.

To really appreciate this land you must be out at sunrise and again at sunset. Once the heat sets in, your time is more profitably spent elsewhere.

FIGURE 1.8. Saguaro desert (Arizona). Artwork by Mimi Hoppe Wolf.

At dawn there is a special vitality to the land. The varied warblings of the Curve-billed Thrasher and Northern Mockingbird may be the first to greet the day, but they are soon joined by the guttural offerings of Cactus Wrens and the metallic chips of Verdins. Soon, the entire avian community is in full voice, and a group of distant coyotes may lend their voices to the chorus.

It doesn't take long to realize that there are birds here—lots of them. Greater Roadrunners and coveys of Gambel's Quail dart across the roads, while Costa's and Black-chinned Hummingbirds vie for the flowering ocotillo. Hooded and Scott's Orioles compete for the title of flashiest bird, one that is also contested by the Pyrrhuloxia and Northern Cardinal. The tinkling notes of Black-throated Sparrows come from everywhere, but the thin, harsh, "spizzz" notes of the Black-tailed Gnatcatcher are most likely to be issued from the thicker vegetation that lines the arroyos. Here too you may find Bell's Vireo, Lucy's Warbler, Varied Bunting, and the Rufous-winged Sparrow.

A number of the desert birds rely on the saguaros for their nest sites. Gila Woodpeckers and Gilded Flickers excavate cavities in the flesh of a cactus as they would in a tree. When not occupied by the woodpeckers, these cavities are used by such birds as the Elf Owl, Brown-crested and Ash-throated Flycatchers, and Purple Martins. Even the rare Ferruginous Pygmy-Owl is occasionally found in the saguaros near Tucson.

During the heat of the day most desert birds are inactive. Only the Black-throated Sparrows seem physiologically adapted to the searing heat. At dusk the desert takes on an entirely new character. The sunsets are always spectacular, and the cool air that accompanies the approaching darkness signals relief to the parched land. As darkness descends, the chuckling calls of Elf Owls are joined by the distant hoots of the Great Horned Owl, the monotonous cadence

FIGURE 1.9. Desert riparian forest (Guadalupe Canyon, Arizona/New Mexico). Artwork by Mimi Hoppe Wolf.

of the Common Poorwill, and the wild yips of the coyotes. The desert floor becomes alive with skunks, kangaroo rats, snakes, scorpions, and other equally interesting creatures.

Another feature of southwestern deserts is the presence of rivers whose floodplains, though often dry, support magnificent riparian stands of forest. Towering cottonwoods contribute the bulk of the canopy, but in some areas the Arizona sycamore is nearly as common.

These riparian woodlands support incredible densities of birds and provide a welcome respite from the desert sun. The nearly incandescent Vermilion Flycatcher is one of the more conspicuous occupants of the bottomlands. They are particularly common in the immediate vicinity of water. Black Phoebes patrol the stream banks, while Cassin's and Western Kingbirds, all three western *Myiarchus*, and Western Wood-Pewee, round out the impressive contingent of breeding flycatchers. In a few localized spots in southeastern Arizona, the Thick-billed Kingbird, Rose-throated Becard, and Northern Beardless Tyrranulet make the list even more impressive.

Yellow-breasted Chats add their comical grunts, squawks, and chatter to the bickering of the kingbirds, making the canopy a constant source of noise. Bell's Vireos sing monotonously from adjacent mesquite groves, endlessly answering their own inquisitive phrases. Both Gila and Ladder-backed Woodpeckers are present, as are Northern and Hooded Orioles. The cherry-red Summer Tanagers and the violet-blue Blue Grosbeaks add further dashes of color, a real change from the desert, where brown is the usual motif. Phainopeplas and Bridled Titmice are among the more common birds but are eclipsed in numbers by both Lucy's Warblers and Bewick's Wrens.

Two of the most spectacular birds of this habitat are also among the rarest—the Gray Hawk and the Common Black-Hawk. Both of these neotropical raptors reach the northern limit of their ranges in Arizona, and both are restricted to these riparian forests. Both also have suffered harassment from over-zealous birders whose actions have resulted in several cases of nest desertion. A more lethal problem is that of habitat destruction. Several currently proposed dams would result in the flooding of huge portions of the few remaining riparian forests in Arizona. Should conservationists lose their battles against the proposed development, it would be the end for the hawks and for some of the richest animal and plant communities in the southwest.

SOUTHWESTERN MOUNTAINS

The first-time visitor to the southwest is often astonished by the mountains. He or she comes expecting barren, rocky peaks overlooking equally barren desert floors. Indeed, many southwestern ranges are very xeric with few trees of any kind. However, there is another type of mountain range to be found here— mountains covered by forests of pine, oak, and juniper, with firs predominating at still higher elevations. Such ranges are scattered across southern Arizona, southern New Mexico, and west Texas, and with few exceptions, each range has its own special combination of flora and fauna. Two of the most attractive ranges to birders are the Chiricahua Mountains of Arizona and the Chisos Mountains of west Texas.

THE CHIRICAHUAS

The Chiricahuas are one of several mountain ranges in southeast Arizona that are on the "must visit" list of American birders. They have been called "Sky Islands," and no name could be more biologically appropriate. Forested mountains do stand as biological islands in the desert seas of the southwest. Each range exists in geographic isolation from similar habitats, and for both plant and animal species each range represents a refugium that leads to genetic isolation. For this reason, many highly specialized plants and animals are found in these mountains, and the Chiricahuas are no exception.

Because birds are so mobile, they are not subject to the same restrictions that are placed on other organisms. There are no birds in Arizona that are restricted to one mountain range. However, because of the proximity of Mexico, several west-Mexican birds that cannot be found elsewhere in this country are common in the mountainous habitats of southern Arizona.

To receive the full impact of these mountains, you should approach them from the east. The road from Rodeo, New Mexico, first passes through several miles of Chihuahuan Desert, replete with creosote-bush, snakeweed, and mesquite. There are few birds here, but you may still be interested in such southwestern specialties as Scaled Quail, Greater Roadrunner, Lesser Nighthawk, Bendire's

FIGURE 1.10. Cave Creek Canyon (Chiricahua Mountains, Arizona). Artwork by Mimi Hoppe Wolf.

Thrasher, and Black-throated Sparrow. Farther on, the mesquite and acacia grow taller and form dense stands. Gamble's Quail begin to replace the Scaled, and Lucy's Warblers become common.

Your first view of Cave Creek Canyon (beyond the tiny village of Portal) is awe-inspiring and is guaranteed to elicit the same feelings of excitement and wonder on every trip. There is history here, and you can feel it etched on the massive canyon walls. This was the land of the Apache, of Cochise and Geronimo, and it is easy to understand why they fought so hard to keep it. The slopes are covered with junipers, and the peaks and walls are sculpted masses of stone whose color seems to change and deepen with each passing hour of the day. The canyon bottom is forested with live oaks, sycamores, alligator junipers, pines, and a variety of less common trees and shrubs.

It is at this point that the parade of new birds begins. If you have timed your visit for the height of the breeding season (May through August), you may be overwhelmed by unfamiliar species. It is a common phenomenon on one's first foray into this region not to know where to look first. Noisy bands of Gray-breasted Jays are among the more conspicuous residents, both of the lower canyon and of the upper reaches. Their calls are most likely to waken you should you be camping. Bridled Titmice chatter through the sycamores, while the harlequin-faced Acorn Woodpeckers make their presence known with a steady stream of noisy dialogue.

Should you be staying at Cave Creek Ranch, it may be hard to get past the grounds. A variety of feeders attract Gamble's Quail, White-winged Doves, Acorn Woodpeckers, Gray-breasted Jays, Plain and Bridled Titmice, Black-headed Grosbeaks, Scott's Orioles, Summer Tanagers, and Bronzed Cowbirds among others. Your attention may be understandably drawn to the hummingbird feeders, where dozens of hummers wage continuing dogfights among themselves. The Black-chinned are by far the most common, but the giant Blue-throated and Magnificent Hummingbirds are also readily found.

At some point you will have to tear yourself away and penetrate deeper into the canyon. The best area is up the South Fork, particularly along the trail out of South Fork Campground. Most of the birds of the lower canyon are here as well but are joined by a new cast of characters. A mournful "peeur" from the top of a pine signals that the Dusky-capped Flycatcher has replaced the Ash-throated and Brown-crested, which occupy the lower parts of the canyon. Here also, is another new flycatcher—the Sulphur-bellied—a handsome, streaked bird with a rusty tail and an excited, squeaky call. Acorn Woodpeckers are still present, but they are now joined by the Strickland's Woodpecker, unique among U.S. Picids (with the exception of the Common Flicker) in being brown-backed. Hepatic Tanagers have replaced the Summers, and groups of Bushtits join the Bridled Titmice in their foraging.

The diversity of warblers is especially impressive. Virginia's occupy the drier slopes above the floor, whereas Black-throated Grays are common throughout. Grace's Warblers are most often heard from the tops of pines but may be hard to see. The flashiest of the bunch is the Painted Redstart. Once you have found one of these animated beauties it should be easy to get good looks. They are often seen very close to, or on, the ground and seem to be in perpetual motion. As if their coat of jet-black, scarlet-red, and snow-white colors are not enough, these birds insist on constantly posturing so as to show their colors to maximum advantage.

The most impressive bird of this canyon (and indeed, of Arizona) is the Elegant Trogon. This is one bird that must be experienced to be appreciated. You will probably hear it before seeing it. The far-reaching call is unlike that of any other U.S. bird, being something of a cross between a hen turkey and a pig! The male often delivers a "whisper song" that sounds as if it's coming from a mile away when the singer may be within thirty yards. Follow the call quietly making sure to avoid sudden movements. When you spot the bird it will probably be facing away with its back in a curious humped posture and its tail drooping downward.

Even from this angle the bird is magnificent! The wings are silver-gray, the upper surface of the tail is copper, and the remainder of the upper parts are emerald green. A red eye ring and yellow bill provide perfect accents to the face. Just as you think it can't get any better, the bird will flip around and face you head-on. A scarlet belly divided from the emerald throat by a white breast band completes an already dazzling picture. Now the bird begins to call again, his throat feathers seeming to burst outward with each gurgling effort. The sound, the bird, and the entire setting seem to be out of some distant tropical land. There is perhaps no better way to develop an incurable yearning for tropical birding than to get a good view of a calling trogon.

After the trogon nearly everything will seem anticlimactic, but there are still plenty of good birds to be seen. A drive to the high country of the Chiricahuas is a necessity for some of the remaining specialties. As you stand surrounded by towering pines and firs at Rustler Park, it is hard to believe that you vacated the mesquite desert only thirteen miles back. A hike along the Barfoot Trail will reveal the Greater Pewee, Mexican Chickadee (probably the most localized of Arizona mountain birds), the incredible Red-faced Warbler, Olive Warbler, and Yellow-eyed Junco, as well as more widespread species such as Steller's Jay, Pygmy Nuthatch, and Western Tanager.

There still remains yet another birding frontier for you to explore. No trip to Arizona and the Chiricahuas is complete without at least one night of owling. As darkness descends on the canyon you would do well to check the sycamores at Cave Creek Ranch for Elf Owls. They usually begin chattering at dusk and are easily spotlighted as they move to and from their nest holes. The bouncing-ball call of the Western Screech-Owl may be heard at the same time and place. Common Poorwills call from the dry slopes above the ranch, and the hooting calls of the Great Horned Owl carry across the desert near Portal.

Farther into the canyon (in the oaks) the Whiskered Owls seem to replace the Screech. Spotted Owls are present but seldom seen, whereas the tiny Flammulated Owl may call incessantly from a pine in South Fork without being spotlighted. Whip-poor-wills are the most persistent night singers on the canyon floor, and their vibrant songs bring a feeling of intensity to the night. Other animals are out too, among them Ring-tail and Javelina. With a little luck you may even spot a Coatimundi.

THE CHISOS

Big Bend National Park in west Texas encompasses a variety of productive birding spots. But the principal attraction is the lure of the Chisos Mountains and its two specialty birds—the Lucifer Hummingbird and the Colima Warbler. The hummingbird is a rare but regular visitor to Arizona and probably breeds there and in nearby New Mexico in small numbers, but nowhere is it more common than here. The warbler is a common summer resident in a few localized areas in the Chisos but is found nowhere else in the United States.

The focal point for an assault on the Chisos and its specialties is the Chisos Basin. The Basin is a large, natural amphitheater that sits in the shadow of the Chisos at an elevation of more than 5400 feet. The lodge and/or campgrounds here make for an excellent home base for birding the mountains, and a number of good trails lead to the better spots.

One of the most productive trails is the one that leads to the Window. As you follow the trail down from the Basin you will be traversing an elevated, brushy grassland that in some areas is reminiscent of chaparral. The drainages are lined with live oaks, while junipers dot the hillsides.

The focus of this hike is the Lucifer Hummingbird. They can be encountered anywhere in the Basin but are most common along this trail. As likely as not, you will find your first hummingbird at one of the magnificent flowering agaves (century plants). Before the agaves are in bloom, the orange-red flowers of the ocotillo are a favorite food source. You will still have to pick the Lucifer out from among the numbers of Black-chinned Hummingbirds which zealously guard every flower head.

There will be many distractions in your hummingbird search; for a variety of birds occupy this transitional habitat. There are representatives of both desert and montane avian communities here. Among them are White-winged Doves; Acorn and Ladder-backed Woodpeckers; Ash-throated Flycatchers; Gray-breasted Jays; "Black-crested" Titmice; Bushtits; Rock, Canyon, Cactus, and Bewick's Wrens; Curve-billed and Crissal Thrashers; Gray Vireos; Scott's Orioles; Blue and Black-headed Grosbeaks; Brown Towhees; and Rufous-crowned Sparrows.

Two of the most sought-after birds to be found along the trail are the Varied Bunting and Black-chinned Sparrow. The female buntings are somewhat drab and inconspicuous, but the purple and red males are always a treat. The sparrow can be located easily by its beautiful Field Sparrow-like song—a few loud, clear notes followed by a long trill which is delivered from a conspicuous perch.

The other essential trail to hike is the one that leads from the Basin to Boot Springs, home of the Colima Warbler. A dawn start is necessary in order to assure your arrival in Boot Canyon while the birds are still active and singing. The trail consists of 4.5 miles (one way) of switchbacks and is mostly uphill. An abundance of interesting birds and scenic views will ensure frequent stops to catch your breath. Most of the trail is through pinyon-juniper and oak woodlands, with attendant Gray-breasted Jays, "Black-crested" Titmice, Bushtits, Bewick's Wrens, Hutton's Vireos, Hepatic Tanagers, Black-headed Grosbeaks, and Rufous-sided Towhees. Hummingbirds, including the Lucifer, congregate at flowering agaves and mountain sage.

Farther along you will likely find Band-tailed Pigeons, although your views may be brief. These birds tend to fly overhead at fast speeds, seldom allowing good views. You would do well to give every seeming vulture a thorough once-over, because the similar Zone-tailed Hawk is often seen from this trail.

Boot Canyon is a narrow, moist canyon forested with juniper, oak, maple, Arizona cypress, and Douglas fir. The spring is ephemeral, but even in dry times there are often a few shallow pools of water in the streambed. These shaded streamside areas provide suitable habitat for Blue-throated Hummingbirds, Western Flycatchers, and Painted Redstarts. Noisy bands of Gray-breasted

FIGURE 1.11. Trail to Boot Springs, Chisos Mountains (Big Bend National Park, Texas). Artwork by Mimi Hoppe Wolf.

FIGURE 1.12. California chaparral. Artwork by Mimi Hoppe Wolf.

Jays, Acorn Woodpeckers, and "Black-crested" Titmice will readily devour any trail mix that you happen to leave.

The Colimas tend to concentrate in the shaded portions of the canyon. They are not colorful, especially by warbler standards, and when they are not singing, they can be difficult to find. With persistence you should be able to find at least one of these rare birds, and their somewhat sluggish nature makes them fairly easy to follow once sighted. Finding a Colima puts the topping on a trip that is always rewarding, and it provides another example of the birding wealth of the southwestern mountains.

THE CALIFORNIA CHAPARRAL

One of the most fascinating and unique of all western habitats is the chaparral country that stretches from Baja to Oregon. The term *chaparral* is often used somewhat loosely in reference to various types of brushlands throughout the west. True chaparral occurs in this country only in California and Oregon, where it is found in the coast ranges, the foothills of the interior mountains that lie west of the deserts, and as a successional stage in some of the higher parts of the southern California ranges.

There are different subtypes of chaparral, each with its own component plant species. In general the term refers to areas covered with a dense, dwarf forest of stiff-twigged, evergreen (but not coniferous) shrubs, with sclerophyllous leaves and interlocking branches. The canopy may vary in height from about five to fifteen feet. Some of the more common shrubs of this habitat include chamise, *Ceanothus*, manzanita, sage (several species), scrub oak, and others.

Chaparral is typically subject to winter rainy seasons and dry summers. Its existence is closely tied to the regular occurrence of fires. Frequent burning actually stimulates productivity in these communities by returning nutrients to the soil that were locked up in the ground litter. By removing litter periodically, fires also prevent the accumulation of dangerous amounts of volatile fuels that might feed a devastating, community-threatening blaze. The seeds of many chaparral plants are fire-resistant, and do not even germinate until exposed to scorching heat. Chaparral that is not burned at least every fifteen years actually becomes senescent.

The birds of this habitat are fairly uniform from one sub-type to the other. Most exceptions come from the montane areas where chaparral is a successional rather than climax habitat (occupying fire breaks, wind-throws, and other disturbance areas in the forest). A handful of birds are almost restricted to this habitat, and it is these species that lure birders from throughout the country to the California foothills.

Because the avifauna is fairly uniform, the exact spot you visit will not matter much. What is important, is that you arrive early when the birds are most vocal. The dense nature of the vegetation often makes it difficult to view birds well, and once singing has diminished for the day, you may be in for a frustrating time. As if this were not enough, many of the chaparral birds are by nature somewhat shy and given to skulking through the underbrush.

The most noteworthy song of the chaparral belongs to the characteristic and indigenous bird—the Wrentit. Its loud, marble-dropping song seems to issue from every surrounding slope. Unfortunately, you may have a difficult time seeing the bird. The Wrentit is the quintessential chaparral bird. It is dull in color and usually stays hidden in the dense shrubbery. They often respond well to "pishing" or "squeaking" but even then are likely to scold from cover, flitting restlessly from branch to branch. If you are patient and remain still, you will eventually be treated to the sight of a little, gray-brown bird with a bright golden iris and a seemingly too long tail that is held cocked or is jerked from side to side.

Once you have conquered the Wrentit, you can turn your attention to the equally shy California Thrasher. The thrasher stays mostly on the ground where it runs under the canopy and uses its sickle-like bill to probe the soil and litter for arthropods. The thrasher may be less responsive to "pishing" than the wrentit, but at least it often perches up to sing, providing you with your best chances for sustained views.

Other species are more visible, if not appreciably more colorful. Among the more common ones (depending on area) are Scrub Jay; Bewick's Wren; Orange-crowned Warbler; Green-tailed (montane), Brown, and Rufous-sided Towhee; and Sage, Fox (montane), Rufous-crowned, and Black-chinned Sparrow. A dash of color is provided by male Lazuli Buntings, undoubtedly the brightest of the breeding species. Colorful too are the Costa's and Anna's Hummingbirds which swarm about the flowering sage and other plants. The "zee-zee-zee" song of the male Anna's (one of the few temperate-zone hummers to sing) is one of the most characteristic sounds of the chaparral.

Two species of quail are found here with the Mountain replacing the California at higher elevations. Both species frequently scurry about on the ground under complete cover, but the California is much more the likely one to be seen perched in the open or along the roadside. Mountain Quail are fairly secretive and are easy to see only after their young have hatched. At these times you may encounter family groups along the roadside in the early mornings.

Although the diversity of bird life here is somewhat low, you will no doubt find the chaparral a fascinating place, both for its specialty birds and for its unique lessons in ecology.

·2·

Techniques of Birdfinding

This chapter deals with the techniques necessary for finding birds. Included are discussions of useful literature, how to plan pelagic trips, luring birds with tape recorders, using rare bird alerts, and a myriad of other practicalities for finding birds. However, good birdfinding ability involves more than these straightforward methods. It involves developing a conceptual framework that allows one to understand why a bird might be found in one place and not in another. Most people have developed such a framework on a broad scale, but recognition of the subtleties of bird distribution and habitat selection are usually lacking. For that reason, several factors that influence the distribution and movements of birds at various times of the day and year are discussed. Several examples have been included to help illustrate each concept. The list of examples is by no means comprehensive. Specific information on where and when to find western birds is given in Chapter 3.

HABITAT RECOGNITION

Any discussion of the techniques of finding birds should begin with a discussion of habitat recognition. Being adept at birdfinding goes beyond the knowledge of specific locations for desired species. Competent birders are able to extrapolate from known specific locations to areas with which they are not personally familiar. This is done through a basic understanding and recognition of bird–habitat associations. Such an ability is not contingent on being a master of plant identification, although this certainly would not hurt. Rather, it calls for a feeling for the overall physiognomy of a given habitat, along with recognition of a handful of important plant species.

Some habitats are broadly defined and easily recognized. Examples include open ocean, freshwater lake, coniferous forest, deciduous forest, desert, and grassland. Each of these habitats has its own characteristic suite of birds, and knowledge of these associations is the first step in developing good birdfinding technique. However, keep in mind that birds sometimes inhabit very different environs in separate parts of their ranges.

Other species defy pigeonholing even within a limited geographic area. Some of these, like the Great Horned Owl, are supreme generalists, able to survive and prosper across a broad range of conditions. Others may be more restricted but may still occupy two or three habitats. This is the case with many desert species that are typical of arid desert scrub, and at the same time are found in higher densities along well-forested river floodplains that dissect the southwest. Still other species may be specialists typical of ecotones, areas in which one habitat blends with another.

As most neophytes learn very rapidly not to expect albatrosses in the desert or woodpeckers on the beach, it may be less apparent that there are subtleties of habitat selection that go far beyond the broad categorizations of freshwater versus saltwater, and conifer forest versus deciduous forest.

Many species will remain elusive until you learn to recognize their respective microhabitats. Many interrelating factors of the physical and biological environment define the niche that a particular species occupies. This is true of any species. However, the degree to which the birder must be able to recognize specific environmental requirements in order to find the desired bird can vary substantially between species. Some birds are capable of occupying an incredible diversity of habitats, and finding them is only a matter of recognizing habitats on a broad scale. Others may be keyed into one specific factor or combination of factors that combine to make up the microhabitat. Finding these birds is dependent on the awareness and recognition of these minute differences in habitat. Some important considerations that may determine or influence microhabitat selection include elevation, presence of key plant species, and nest site availability, all of which may be related.

ELEVATION

Clinton H. Merriam (1855–1942) was among the first naturalists to devote considerable attention to the influence of elevation on the distribution of plants and animals. On his explorations of the West, Merriam noted elevational similarities of plant and animal life from one mountain range to the next. This led to the formulation of his life zone concept based on the belief that temperature was the most important environmental factor to the distribution of plant species. Merriam believed that discrete plant communities yielded to one another along an elevational gradient based on temperature. Thus, the Sonoran Zone gives way to the Transition Zone, which in turn is followed by the Canadian Zone, Hudsonian Zone, and Alpine Zone. Along with these elevational changes in plant life are associated changes in the species composition of animals, including birds. Many authors have in fact described various bird species and groups of species as being characteristic of one life zone or another.

As with many classification schemes, the life zone concept has proved to be too simplistic in its approach and has been generally discarded by scientists. Neither the plants nor the birds vary so rigidly and predictably across the continent with elevation, and numerous underlying environmental factors can lead to great local and interregional variation in the distribution of species. Two examples are the Band-tailed Pigeon and Steller's Jay. Both species range widely across the pine-fir forests of Northern America's western mountain ranges, usually at elevations above 6000 feet. As such, they could be considered Transition Zone or more probably Canadian Zone species. However, both species are also common residents of the oak-covered hills and lowlands of the central California coast, an entirely different habitat, at elevations that are thousands of feet lower. Still other birds may inhabit two life zones within the same geographic area. This is the case with the Northern Pygmy-Owl, which in the mountains of southeast Arizona may range from oak-wooded canyons at 5000 feet to pine-fir forests above 8500 feet.

Despite the numerous exceptions, the life zone concept still has some use to the birder as a convenient way of pigeonholing groups of species in a way that makes sense and often works. This is perhaps best demonstrated with birds of the Alpine (above tree-line) Zone, where species such as White-tailed Ptarmigan and the various rosy finches breed almost exclusively.

There are numerous instances where several species within a family replace one another (with some overlap) altitudinally. Such is the case with the three western species of nuthatches in the mountains of Arizona. The White-breasted Nuthatch is common in the oaks and sycamores of the canyon bottoms. They are replaced higher up in the ponderosa pine belt by the Pygmy Nuthatch, which in turn gives way to the Red-breasted at still higher elevations. In California, finches of the genus *Carpodacus* show a similar pattern. House Finches inhabit the lowlands, Purple Finches the wooded foothills up into the mountains, and Cassin's Finches the highest elevation conifer forests at the edge of timberline.

Elevation is often intimately linked to the distribution of particular species or groups of species. Its influence may be largely an indirect one, with birds selecting areas based on plant species, which are in turn more directly influenced by parameters of the physical environment. There are undoubtedly many instances, however, in which elevation directly determines the distributional boundaries of birds through differing temperature, moisture, and radiation regimes. This is probably at least partly responsible for the fact that many boreal forest birds have ranges extending much farther south in western North America than they do in the eastern half of the continent. The Rockies, Sierras, Cascades, and other western mountain ranges serve to pull such northern species as the Great Gray Owl, Boreal Owl, Black-backed Woodpecker, Three-toed Woodpecker, Gray Jay, and Evening and Pine Grosbeaks far south into the central United States. In the east, where such high elevation ranges are lacking, the same species typically reach their southern boundaries in Canada or the extreme northern edge of this country.

KEY PLANT SPECIES

Many birds seem intimately bound to one species, genus, or family of plant. In other cases it is the life–form (that is, sapling, mature tree, senescent tree) and not the taxa that is important. In any event, finding these specialized birds becomes much easier once you are aware of the association and are capable of recognizing the plants involved.

Examples of specific bird–plant associations are numerous. The Golden-cheeked Warbler is found only where cedar (*Juniperus*) stands exist on the Edwards Plateau region of Texas. Two southwestern warblers of conifer forests, the Grace's and Olive, are also associated with specific types of trees. The Grace's is a bird of the ponderosa pine forest, while the Olive seems to require the presence of firs. Both species can be found together where Douglas fir and/or white fir is mixed with the pines. More specific still is the Kirtland's Warbler of Michigan, which not only requires one type of tree (the jack pine), but which will only inhabit forests where that tree is of a certain height (6 to 20 feet).

Slightly more generalized are several species of woodpeckers that key into whole genera (rather than one species) of trees. Even here, however, one sees specialization directed at the age or health of the tree. Acorn Woodpeckers require large numbers of oaks (no one species) to provide the mast that is the staple of their diet. Areas with a multitude of oak species may even be preferred because it is less likely that the acorn crop of several species will fail simultaneously. Red-cockaded Woodpeckers are totally dependent on old-growth pine trees that are infected with red heart disease to use as nesting sites. Where there are several pines infected with this disease the birds form small colonies. This leads to a very patchy distribution, with concentrated groups of woodpeckers surrounded by large tracts of similar forest that have none. Similarly, Black-backed Woodpeckers often invade and loosely colonize burn areas in conifer forests while leaving unburned areas nearby unoccupied.

Hummingbirds of all species depend on the presence of tubular-shaped flowers such as penstemon or tree tobacco for nectar. Areas that have large numbers of these flowers are usually swarming with hummers, whereas identical macrohabitat that lacks these plants may have few or none.

Many prairie birds are not tied to one species of plant but to recognizable physiognomic types of grasslands. Bobolinks and Dickcissels prefer the weedy, tall-grass meadows or old-fields; Sprague's Pipits, Baird's Sparrows, and Chestnut-collared Longspurs do best in medium height, mixed-grass prairies; and Mountain Plovers, Brewer's Sparrows, and McCown's Longspurs stick to more xeric short-grass prairie. In all instances species composition seems less important than the general structure of the grassland.

NEST SITE AVAILABILITY

An additional consideration in locating some species during the breeding season is the availability of suitable nest sites. For most songbirds in most habitats nest sites are not limiting factors of distribution. For some larger birds and for colonial species the availability of nest sites may be of overriding importance.

Swifts and falcons depend on cliffs or rock faces for the placement of their nests. Areas that lack these features are usually unoccupied even though they are within the geographic ranges of the birds and provide otherwise suitable habitat. Black Swifts are even more specific, seemingly requiring cliff faces with waterfalls for their nesting areas. Where trees are lacking (as in some deserts and grasslands) such species as Red-tailed, Ferruginous, and Zone-tailed Hawks, and Great Horned and Barn Owls may be dependent on canyon walls, cliff faces, or steep sand banks for the location of their nests. Likewise, Bank Swallows and kingfishers require sand banks, Cliff Swallows and phoebes utilize bridges or building eves, and Cave Swallows need caves. The latter species has steadily expanded its range in recent years by finding a substitute for cave walls—concrete road culverts.

More generally, many species require some sort of cavity in which to place their nest, and the absence of such cavities may result in local gaps in the geographic ranges of these birds. Birds such as Elf and Screech Owls, *Myiarchus* Flycatchers, Tree and Violet-green Swallows, Purple Martins, Bridled and Plain Titmice, chickadees, House and Bewick's Wrens, and bluebirds utilize old woodpecker holes to a large extent. In parts of the Sonoran Desert of Arizona, Gila Woodpecker holes in the giant saguaro cacti provide homes for Elf and Ferruginous Pygmy-Owls, Ash-throated and Brown-crested Flycatchers, Purple Martins, and Lucy's Warblers. Although most of these cavity dwellers are found in areas where woodpeckers abound, nest sites may be limited by the presence of large numbers of Starlings which aggressively displace other species from cavities. Burrowing Owls depend largely on the burrows of prairie dogs, badgers, and the like for their nest holes. In parts of the west the distribution of these little owls is almost wholly coincident with the distribution of prairie dog towns.

Ground-nesting colonial species such as some Procellarids, gulls, and alcids require remote rocky islands for nesting. Such islands must be far enough from shore so as not to be exposed to invasion at low tides by land predators.

In parts of the Chihahuan and other deserts many species may be limited to arroyos (desert washes) because of the lack of large shrubs suitable for nest placement elsewhere. Such is the case in much of western Texas and southern New Mexico where the divides between arroyos are often vegetated by nothing but creosotebush, tarbush, snakeweed, and other shrubs of spindly or small stature. Only the Black-throated Sparrow uses these shrubs to any great extent for nesting. Because of this, large expanses of desert may host little more than Black-throats and the ground-nesting Scaled Quail and Lesser Nighthawk. The visiting birder should concentrate his search along the arroyos where sumac, desert willow, and mesquite provide nest sites for such species as Greater Roadrunner, Black-chinned Hummingbird, Ladder-backed Woodpecker, Western Kingbird, Ash-throated Flycatcher, Verdin, Black-tailed Gnatcatcher, Cactus Wren, Crissal Thrasher, and Brown Towhee.

A different case is provided by prairie grouse. Sage and Sharp-tailed Grouse, and Greater and Lesser Prairie Chickens establish leks for the purpose of mating. These leks are areas of high visibility where the males gather to display their charms through ritualized dancing and calling (often called "booming"). Females visit the lek to select males for mating. Primary requisites for lek location seem to be the availability of hilltops, rises, or flats that are devoid of tall vegetation that obscures visibility. Areas lacking such sites may harbor no birds, and away from the display grounds individuals are often widely scattered across feeding or nesting areas. Knowledge of lek locations can save much fruitless searching across otherwise suitable habitat in addition to affording the opportunity to observe the spectacular displays of these prairie grouse.

TIME OF DAY

Knowing *when* to look for particular birds is almost as important as knowing where to look. Birds exhibit cyclic patterns of daily activity that make them easy to find during some hours and difficult to find during others. This is yet another case where doing some preparatory homework on the life histories of sought-after species can save much time and frustration.

Passerines are typically most active during the early morning hours. Cooler morning temperatures allow for maximum foraging activity with minimum heat stress. Song activity usually peaks at this time as well. Many forest dwelling species can be almost impossible to locate unless they are calling, which makes an early start all the more desirable. Most desert birds shut down all activity during the heat of the day for obvious reasons. Desert thrashers are particularly difficult to find after the first few hours of daylight. They usually sing from a conspicuous perch early and then spend the remainder of the day running quietly through arroyos or sitting in the inner shade of some densely vegetated shrub. A pre-dawn start is also usually essential for seeing prairie grouse on their leks. The birds begin their booming or dancing in the dark and activity usually peaks shortly after dawn. Within an hour or two most birds will have left the lek for the day, scattering to their feeding areas where they can be very difficult to find.

Waterbirds such as herons, ducks, shorebirds, gulls, and terns are rarely affected by rising daytime temperatures and can be found in appropriate locations throughout the day. When a day's birding activities call for both landbirding and waterbirding, it is usually best to save the aquatic habitats for later in the day when songbird activity has slowed down.

There are several exceptions to this line of reasoning. While any hour may be good for shorebirds in freshwater areas, the same is not always true of coastal locations, where tidal fluctuations must be taken into account. Low tide is generally better than high tide because a greater abundance of food is available. This is particularly true of the rock inhabiting shorebirds of the Pacific Coast such as Black Turnstone, Surfbird, Black Oystercatcher, and Wandering Tattler. These become much easier to find when low tides expose mollusk-encrusted rocks and beach large masses of kelp, which harbor numerous crustaceans. The same beach which is swarming with shorebirds at low tide may be devoid of birds at high tide.

Similarly, freshwater areas such as rivers below large dams, irrigation control ponds, and fish hatchery ponds may be subjected to periodic fluctuations in water levels that will in turn influence waterbird abundance. A case in point is provided by the Green Kingfisher. This small, tropical kingfisher reaches the northern limit of its range in the southern-most United States, where it breeds regularly only in south Texas. Its distribution in Texas centers on a small stretch of the Rio Grande below Falcon Dam and several rivers and streams in the hill country farther north and west. Many of the latter areas are privately owned and inaccessible to birders. Therefore, most people rely on finding the kingfisher below Falcon Dam. The time of day is all-important however, due to the daily fluctuations in the river below the dam. The Green Kingfisher hunts from a perch and prefers small, shallow pools in which to fish. When the water below the dam is low (morning) there are numerous isolated pools of water with an abundance of trapped minnows. There are also many snags and large rocks available as perches. Consequently, a walk along the river during the low water mark offers the birder a good opportunity to see the kingfisher. In the afternoon the water level is much higher, most perches are submerged, and there are no isolated pools to concentrate the fish. At these times the kingfishers tend to retreat to sheltered spots along the river banks where they become much harder to find.

Many colonial water birds such as pelicans, storm petrels, some herons, and many alcids have feeding areas that are far removed from their nesting grounds. The birds may make continuous trips to and from the foraging areas, or they may remain on the feeding area most of the time, returning to their nests only late in the day. An example of the latter strategy is provided by many storm petrels. These birds nest in burrows on isolated, rocky islands off the Pacific Coast. They forage over the open ocean, often many miles away from the nesting colony. On the wing, petrels are master fliers, but on land they are extremely slow and awkward. This makes them vulnerable, when leaving or entering their burrows, to the predatory Western Gulls that often inhabit the same islands. Consequently, the petrels will usually remain at sea during the day, returning with food only at night when they are safe from the gulls. Birders wishing to see storm petrels should therefore concentrate their daytime searches on the open ocean and visit the nest islands (if these are accessible) only at night.

A similar activity pattern is displayed by Black Swifts, which typically forage far from their nest cliffs during the day and return just before dusk. Watching at the nesting area at any time other than late afternoon is often an exercise in futility. A knowledge of such variations in daily activity patterns can save much time and energy when searching for some of these colonial species.

Nocturnal species also exhibit marked changes in activity within the course of an evening, and these patterns may affect your chances of finding the birds.

Some owls like the Burrowing, Northern Pygmy, Ferruginous Pygmy, Snowy, and Great Gray are at least partially diurnal, and your chances of finding them may be better during the day. Many of the nocturnal species call continuously for some time after dusk, but stop for long periods in the middle of the night to hunt. They may resume calling at different points, particularly just prior to dawn. Similar patterns are often seen in some caprimulgids like the Poor-Will and Whip-poor-will. It is generally easiest to track nocturnal birds down or lure them in when they are calling, although vocal responses can still be elicited at other times.

The Buff-collared Nightjar is a Mexican caprimulgid whose U.S. range is restricted to a few canyons in southern Arizona. Its activities seem closely tied to the lunar cycle. It may not begin calling until the moon rises above the canyon walls, and is most vocal when the moon is full. Conversely, many of the small owls found in the mountains of the southwest may call only infrequently on nights during which the moon is full or nearly so. This may be a response to predation from larger owls, which can more readily locate their smaller cousins on moonlit nights.

TIME OF YEAR

As would be expected, time of year has a great influence on what birds are possible to see in an area. Every locale has its unique combination of resident, summering, wintering, and migrant species. Areas situated at high northern latitudes typically have an abundance of summering species with few winter residents. The number of permanent residents in an area usually increases with decreasing latitude, as does the number of wintering species. There is also much temporal variation in species composition within seasons, because birds often fail to define summer, fall, winter, and spring on the same calendar as we do. Precise timing on the part of the birder can make the difference in seeing or not seeing many of the more transient species.

SUMMER

Most breeding birds are easiest to find early in the nesting season when territorial and nesting activity is at its peak. Passerines typically sing most continuously at the onset of the breeding season. They sing less when feeding young and greatly restrict singing or cease altogether once the young have fledged. Many species are particularly conspicuous when feeding nestlings due to great increases in foraging activity and the number of trips to and from the nest. The Colima and Golden-cheeked Warblers are good examples of birds that should be looked for early in the breeding season. Colima Warblers are found only in the Chisos Mountains of southwest Texas. They arrive on the breeding grounds in April and are fairly easy to find until June when many of the birds stop singing.

They are drably colored, nonactive birds and can become difficult to find when they are not singing. Golden-cheeked Warblers are restricted to the Edwards Plateau region of Texas, and like the Colima, are relatively easy to find when territorial singing is at its peak (March through May). Song activity tapers off rapidly in June, and the birds become progressively harder to locate through the summer.

Post-breeding dispersal is also a fairly common occurrence that birders must deal with. Although we tend to think of breeding birds as ones that stay through the summer, many species will breed once or twice early in the season and then leave the nesting area in midsummer.

This is a common pattern with many hummingbirds. Desert populations of Costa's Hummingbirds breed especially early, arriving in Arizona and southern California in February. Breeding continues through March and many of the birds disperse by the end of April. The Allen's Hummingbird of coastal California exhibits yet another dispersal pattern. Allen's Hummingbirds are polygamous breeders—one male may mate with multiple females—as are other hummers, and the males provide no parental care. Once copulations have been made and the eggs laid, the males disperse leaving the females to raise the young. Visiting birders are therefore unlikely to see any male Allen's after midsummer. This leaves the females and immatures which are impossible to distinguish from female and immature Rufous Hummingbirds.

An opposite course is followed by Cassin's and Botteri's Sparrows in southeast Arizona. These two species are apparently stimulated by rain in their breeding cycles, responding to the midsummer rains common to the southwest. They are either mostly absent (Cassin's) or silent (Botteri's) prior to the commencement of the rainy season in July. At that time they become very conspicuous, either skylarking (Cassin's) or singing from prominent perches (both species). When the birds are not singing they are extremely difficult to find. This pattern of delaying singing and/or breeding until midsummer is admittedly rare in this country, but is common to several species in the deserts of western Mexico. Post-breeding dispersal is far from being a totally negative phenomenon for the birder. On the contrary, many Mexican or tropical species are seen in the U.S. only in late summer or early fall following a northward post-breeding dispersal from their nesting areas farther south. This accounts for the regular midsummer appearances in Arizona of White-eared, Berylline, and Violet-crowned Hummingbirds. Except for the latter species (which breeds in Guadalupe Canyon, Arizona) these rare visitors are almost impossible to find prior to July. More spectacular is the annual or semi-annual northward movement of many water birds from their nesting areas along the Gulf of California to the California coast and the Salton Sea (southern California). Included in this procession are Red-billed Tropicbirds and Least and Black Storm Petrels along the coast, and Brown Pelicans, Magnificent Frigatebirds (also coastal), Blue-footed and Brown Boobies, Wood Storks, various southern herons, and Laughing and Yellow-footed Gulls to the Salton Sea. Most of these birds cannot be found in California before July and will have vacated the state or expired by October. Although some of the species are commonly found in other parts of the country (for example, Wood Stork, Laughing Gull), others, such as Red-billed Tropicbird, Blue-footed Booby, Least Storm Petrel, and Yellow-footed Gull are almost impossible to find elsewhere or at other times of the year.

WINTER

Winter often offers a greater diversity of birds than does the summer (excepting inland areas in the northern part of the country), and the chances of finding rarities are almost always better. This is the time for the best variety of hawks and sparrows in the southwest; loons, grebes, waterfowl, gulls, and alcids on the West Coast; and northern owls and finches in the upper midwest and Rocky Mountain states. Montane species such as Band-tailed Pigeons, woodpeckers, jays, chickadees, nuthatches, creepers, kinglets, and bluebirds also periodically descend into adjacent lowlands where they may spend all or part of the winter. It is an especially good time for finding vagrant Mexican species (for example, Hook-billed Kite, Clay-colored Robin, White-collared Seedeater) in south Texas, whereas mid to late summer is the time for similar rarities in southeast Arizona.

As is the case in summer, not all wintering species should be looked for at the same time. For most locales early winter produces more species than does late winter. This is due to the presence of late migrants and semi-hardy species that can persist until very cold weather sets in. In inland areas in the north most large lakes are still open in December, providing habitat for lingering waterfowl and gulls. This is a good time to look for northern ducks (Oldsquaw, scoters, goldeneyes) and gulls (Glaucous, Thayer's, Black-legged Kittiwake), which are likely to move through later than other members of their families.

Winter is also the time when many boreal species stage major invasions into the northern tier of states. The onset and duration of these invasions vary from species to species and from year to year. Northern owls (Snowy, Hawk, Great Gray, and Boreal) are more likely to be found in late winter (following extreme cold spells in Canada and subsequent declines in rodent populations), but eruptions of Bohemian Waxwings and various finches (Evening and Pine Grosbeaks, Pine Siskins, Common and Hoary Redpolls, and Red and White-winged Crossbills) may occur as early as November. The arrival of longspurs in the southern states may also depend on the weather farther north. Lapland Longspurs, for example, reach the Texas panhandle during very cold winters or following late winter blizzards to the north. They are rarely present before January.

MIGRATION

Few things are as exciting to birders as the onset of spring or fall migration. Along with the return of birds not seen all winter or summer comes the greatly increased opportunity for finding rare birds. Birds may appear in out-of-range localities due to errors in following the migratory route, or because of weather events that literally blow the birds off course. In any case, these occurrences are most likely to take place when large numbers of birds are making transoceanic or transcontinental trips. The discovery of a rare bird is not the random event that one might imagine it to be. Just as there are particular places and times that are more productive for finding breeding and wintering species, so there are places and times that provide maximum opportunity for finding vagrants.

Spring is often the more predictable of the two migratory periods. Although spring migration in much of the West is less concentrated than it is in the East, there is still a more finite quality to the flow and duration of bird movement. In the interior, waterfowl and cranes usually move first. These are followed by raptors, blackbirds, sparrows, and shorebirds second, and lastly by a rush of insectivorous passerines such as flycatchers, thrushes, vireos, warblers, orioles, and tanagers.

The large build-ups or waves of migrant passerines common to eastern North America are not often encountered west of the Great Plains. However, it is still possible to find good concentrations of migrant songbirds in many areas along the central flyway from Canada through the Great Plains and on to the Gulf Coast of Texas. These concentrations usually coincide with weather events that bring a temporary halt to further northward flights, thereby causing birds to "stack up" at the edge of a frontal system. Nowhere is this type of phenomenon better observed than along the upper Texas coast during the month of April. When a cold front blows in from the north, trans-Gulf migrants drop out of the sky upon reaching land, often totally exhausted from hours of battling the wind. If the front brings rain, truly spectacular "fall-outs" of birds may occur, especially at High Island and Galveston. Every clump of trees may be swarming with birds, all in immaculate spring plumage. It is not uncommon on such occasions to find 20 to 25 species of warblers in a single hour. A single fruiting mulberry may host dozens of Gray Catbirds, Northern (Baltimore) Orioles, Scarlet Tanagers, and Rose-breasted Grosbeaks, and the ground may be literally covered with Indigo Buntings and thrushes of three to four species.

Even calm weather days can produce exciting birding at High Island. Wooded areas that are devoid of birds in the morning may come alive in late afternoon as migrants hit the coast in waves. If the winds are light and the sky is clear, the birds will be less exhausted and will not stack up. Instead they will be leapfrogging through the trees, feeding voraciously, but leaving as fast as they came. Turnover may be rapid, with new groups of birds appearing as rapidly as the first ones leave. On such occasions each walk around even the smallest wooded area will produce new birds, providing the observer a rare chance to actually watch migration take place.

Although a day of spring birding often produces more species and individuals than does a day of fall birding, it is generally less likely to produce rarities. This is especially true for such groups as waterfowl, shorebirds, gulls, pelagics, and almost any Asiatic species along the coast south of Alaska. The primary spring vagrant excitement is generated by the appearance of numbers of eastern passerines in the west. Although such vagrants may occur anywhere west of the Great Plains, they are most likely to be found in the southwest, particularly at small desert oases. These oases serve to concentrate birds in small areas, making them much easier to find. Heavily forested areas to the north undoubtedly get their share of rarities too, but the extensive nature of the habitat may allow such birds to go unnoticed. The first two weeks in May seem to be the most productive for eastern vagrants in west Texas and southern New Mexico, whereas the latter half of May through early June are usually best in Arizona and southern California. California birders go so far as to stage an annual rare warbler search in Death Valley each Memorial Day weekend, expressly for the purpose of finding eastern vagrants (particularly warblers).

Fall represents the most exciting time of year for many birders. There are typically many more vagrants to be found in this season. This is probably due to the large number of juveniles that are migrating for the first time. Lack of experience with the migratory route is undoubtedly the cause of many errors in migration, and indeed, a large percentage of fall vagrants are juveniles.

The duration of the migratory period is also more prolonged than in spring, and when all taxa are considered, it may stretch from early July to December. Hummingbirds and shorebirds are often the first to begin heading south. Rufous, Calliope, and Broad-tailed Hummingbirds begin appearing at lowland feeders in the southwest in early July. Adult males often predominate early, with adult females and juveniles following in subsequent months. Shorebirds also begin moving by midsummer. Some individual shorebirds forego breeding to spend the entire summer well south of the nesting grounds. These are typically birds that are sexually immature or in some way physiologically incapable of breeding. Most species breed in the Arctic, and the adults begin heading south as soon as the young have fledged. This means that most adult shorebirds will have passed through in July and August with the juveniles arriving later from August through October. Wilson's Phalaropes return to many areas as early as mid-June. This results from a more southerly breeding range, combined with a sex role reversal in which the females do nothing but lay the eggs, leaving the males to incubate the clutch and care for the young. Thus, females are free to travel much earlier than are the males.

Many passerine species are also on the move by August, and in the northern states numbers of some migrants may peak prior to September 1. For many groups, fall migration is a mirror image of spring in that the early arrivals on the way north are the last to arrive on the way south. Waterfowl; raptors; montane species of many taxa; and northern finches, juncos, and sparrows usually form the bulk of migrants from late October through December.

As noted earlier, patterns of vagrancy for many species in many areas are decidedly not random. Most rarities are found by birders who have studied the pattern of past occurrences and who plan their searches accordingly to be in the best places at the best times. The examples are too numerous to mention here, but a few deserve inclusion as points of illustration.

The post-breeding dispersal of boobies, frigatebirds, Wood Storks, and the like to the Salton Sea is a predictable pattern of vagrancy that has already been discussed. Some of the same species as well as more pelagic ones (for example, Red Phalarope, all jaegers, Sabine's Gull) regularly appear far inland following late-summer tropical storms in the Gulf of California. The storms are not a requisite for the wanderings of the phalarope, jaegers, and gulls, because all of these routinely travel the length of the coast from Alaska to Mexico. Periodic searches of large bodies of water from late August through November may reveal regular incursions of jaegers and Sabine's Gulls into many parts of the west and central United States. Likewise, Red Phalarope frequently appear at sewage lagoons or wherever other phalarope species gather everywhere from Minnesota to Texas.

There is increasing evidence that vagrant individuals may return to the exact same areas year after year. Some of the more exceptional records are as follows: Eurasian Skylark—six consecutive winters (1979–85) at Point Reyes, California; Smew—male at same pond in Foster City, California two consecutive years (1981–83); individual Black-headed and Little Gulls at the Stockton sewage ponds, Stockton, California seven consecutive years (1978–85); Rufous-necked Stint (July 12–17, 1981 and July 11–17, 1982) and Mongolian Plover (August 7–13, 1982 and July 26–August 3, 1983) at McGrath Beach, Ventura, California two consecutive years; and a female Black-backed Wagtail—two consecutive autumns (1980 and 1981) at the Watson City, California sewage ponds. These are just a handful of many such records and should provide further impetus for birders to study past records of rarities and plan their own searches accordingly.

TAPPING THE HOTLINE

Some species will remain hard to find even when one has the knowledge of their general distribution, habitat requirements, and daily and seasonal activity patterns. This is particularly true of species whose continental or regional populations are very small, and which, therefore, do not begin to saturate the available preferred habitat.

Several examples of such birds come to mind. The Great Gray Owl is a rare resident of high-elevation conifer forests that border grassy meadows in

Yosemite National Park. At first inspection this would seem like a fairly restricted niche, and that the owls would be easy to find. However, one has only to travel to the Yosemite high country once to see that there are scores of seemingly appropriate meadows. This, combined with the fact that there are relatively few pairs of owls inhabiting the park in a given year makes for a bird that is very difficult to find without prior knowledge of a specific location. Similarly, Buff-collared Nightjars and Five-striped Sparrows are found in only a few of the countless desert canyons of southeast Arizona, and Buff-breasted Flycatchers are known to inhabit only a handful of pine-forested canyons in the same state. All three species reach the northern limits of their ranges in southern Arizona, and these fringe populations are apparently not large enough or fecund enough to expand into all of the available habitat. The end result is the same for the birder: Without prior knowledge of specific locations for these birds, search may be futile.

Given all this, how does one come by the knowledge of such precise locations for the tougher species? The first course of action should be a check of the proper literature.

Two periodicals that are almost essential to avid field birders are *American Birds* and *Birding*. The former is published bimonthly by the National Audubon Society (write: *American Birds*, 950 Third Avenue, New York, N.Y. 10022) and serves as *the* journal of American bird distribution. Four issues each year are devoted to region-by-region seasonal reports of bird occurrences, reflecting the field work of thousands of observers. Records of rare birds and vagrants, and reports on population trends of all species are emphasized. Although specific directions to birding locales are seldom given, this journal provides the reader with a wealth of information on what to expect where, and when. A fifth issue is devoted to publishing results of structured breeding and winter bird surveys, which typically is of little use to most birders, but which provides important data for the scientific evaluation of many fluctuations in bird population densities. The sixth issue is a large volume containing the published results of the more than 1400 Christmas Bird Counts conducted across the country each year. These published counts allow the birder a revealing look at winter bird distribution and abundance in every state and Canadian province.

Birding is the bimonthly journal of the American Birding Association (write: American Birding Association, Inc., Box 4335, Austin, Texas 78765), an organization dedicated to the promotion of field birding as a hobby and sport. As such it features a wide variety of articles aimed primarily at bird finding and identification. Each issue contains several short bird finding "inserts" which provide explicit directions to various "hot spots" across the continent. Feature length articles on major areas, foreign countries, and/or finding particular species are also included.

In addition to these useful but wide-scope journals, there are a number of birdfinding books for particular geographic areas. The first real birdfinding guides were conceived and written by Olin Sewall Pettingill, who published *A Guide to Birdfinding East of the Mississippi* in 1951, and followed with *A Guide to Birdfinding West of the Mississippi* in 1953. Both books included separate chapters on each state in their area of coverage. The basic format centered on providing precise directions and mileages to the better birding areas in each state, as well as a list of what birds to expect in each season. Dr. Pettingill has recently revised both guides (East in 1977, West in 1981), each of which remains as the best source of birdfinding information available for the whole of eastern and western North America respectively.

Although Pettingill's guides are of wide utility, they are of necessity less than comprehensive, given the large areas covered. In the past 10 to 12 years there has been a proliferation of birdfinding guides that cover only one state or part of one state. Notable among these are the numerous guides authored by James A. Lane, which highlight such diverse locales as Churchill and southeast Arizona. The advantages of these single-area guides are many. First, they devote extensive coverage to a restricted area, thereby offering the birder more than just a skimming off the top. Secondly, an author who focuses on one region is more likely to be intimately familiar with all aspects of finding birds in his area than is one who covers half a continent. Lastly, guides to smaller areas are more readily revised, a matter of great importance considering the rapidity with which birdfinding information can become outdated. Most of the state guides are similar in general format to the Pettingill volumes. One notable difference for many is the inclusion of a number of detailed maps, a helpful feature that is lacking in the Pettingill guides.

The American Birding Association (A.B.A.) offers a number of pertinent books (including all of the finding guides) at discount prices to members. Price lists and order forms are included in each issue of *Birding*, or, if you are a non-member, write: A.B.A. Sales, Box 4335, Austin, Texas 78765.

While published material is invaluable in locating most birds, it lacks immediacy and can never present the true up-to-the-minute picture for any given area. Therefore, when traveling you will want to be able to tap the local grapevines for current news of birding possibilities. One way to do this is to obtain advance information by writing or telephoning experts who live in the area of your intended visit. The Christmas Bird Count issue of *American Birds* provides the names of all participants on each count in the country. Count compilers (who quite often are the local authorities) have both their names and mailing addresses listed. Another source of names, addresses, and phone numbers, is the A.B.A.'s membership directory, which indicates the degree of willingness on the part of each member toward providing information to others. When contacting these people use common courtesy. Write well in advance of your trip, leaving ample time for them to respond. Always include a self-addressed stamped envelope for their reply. If you are going the telephone route, remember time zone differences, and avoid early morning, late evening, and meal-time calls. Keep in mind that many of these experts are swamped with such requests for information every year, and that the more effort that you put into getting information, the less they will have to put forth in giving it.

An excellent way to stay on top of birding conditions in some areas is to use the Rare Bird Alert (RBA) hotline. RBAs typically consist of a phone number that can be called day or night which will link you to a prerecorded, taped message of bird news from the area. Some tapes are updated weekly, others more frequently or as the need arises. Most give the name and number of someone to call for more information or to report details of rare birds seen. Because many of these RBAs are maintained by local Audubon Societies, there is often news of society meetings, field trips, and so forth, included on the tape.

The main emphasis of most RBAs is the reporting of birds rare to the area. When such birds first appear there are usually explicit directions given for finding them. If your shorthand skills are rusty you may want to tape record the call because route directions are often given quite rapidly. If the rare bird hangs around for some time, later tapes are likely to skip directions and just give the locale (for example, "The Eurasian Skylark is still being seen at Pt. Reyes."). Occasionally the tapes report on sightings of birds regular to the area but of particular interest to visitors. The Los Angeles tape, for example, often reports news of recent condor sightings. Less frequently, the tapes may report on outstanding rarities currently being seen in another part of the country.

RBA phone numbers for several western cities are provided below. While many areas are without formal RBAs, there are still local Audubon Society numbers from which you may obtain information. *A Guide to North American Bird Clubs*, by Jon Rickert (Avian Publications, Elizabethtown, Kentucky), lists hundreds of Audubon societies and other bird clubs throughout North America. This publication provides mailing addresses and phone numbers for contacts from most of these organizations.

AREA	RBA NUMBER
Alaska	(907) 274-9152
Arizona—Tuscon & southeast	(602) 881-WING
British Columbia—Victoria	(604) 382-5562
Vancouver	(604) 876-9690
California—	
Los Angeles	(213) 874-1318
Monterey	(408) 899-3030
Northern	(415) 843-2211
San Diego	(619) 435-6761
Santa Barbara	(805) 964-8240
Colorado—Denver	(303) 759-1060
Iowa	(319) 622-3353

AREA	RBA NUMBER
Minnesota—	
Duluth	(218) 525-5952
Minneapolis	(612) 544-5016
Texas—	
Austin	(512) 451-3308
Lower Valley	(512) 565-6773
Texas Coast	(713) 821-2846
Washington—Seattle	(206) 624-2854

FINDING PELAGIC BIRDS

Pelagic (open ocean) birding is so different from land based birding as to merit its own section in this chapter on birdfinding. It can be at the same time the most exciting, challenging, frustrating, taxing, and rewarding kind of birding available. The excitement comes partly from the mystery of the high seas and partly from the often unpredictable nature of the birds themselves. We have only recently begun to unravel many of the complexities of pelagic bird distribution and biology. Much remains to be learned. The challenge stems from the need to identify these fast flying, subtly different birds under what are often less than ideal conditions. Frustration comes from the often poor views, unidentifiable birds, and occasional birdless stretches of ocean. Pelagic birding can be taxing depending on one's inherent equilibrium and ability or inability to tolerate a prolonged period with no firm ground underfoot. In the end, it is extremely rewarding, because by its very nature it requires a marshalling of all one's skills of spotting and identifying birds.

The first consideration is finding a boat. The best option is to obtain passage on one of the regularly scheduled boat trips run by various bird clubs or individuals. The Los Angeles Audubon Society (phone (213) 876-0202) schedules a few trips each year that depart from San Pedro, Ventura, and occasionally other ports in southern California. The Western Field Ornithologists (obtain the names of the current officers from the Los Angeles Audubon Number listed above) usually sponsor a spring and fall trip from San Diego to San Clemente Island, as well as occasional trips out of Monterey Bay. A number of birding and/or whale watching trips to a variety of areas off the central coast of California (emphasis on Monterey Bay) are offered by Debi Love Shearwater (write: Shearwater Journeys, 362 Lee Street, Santa Cruz, CA 95060, or phone: (408) 425-8111). Terry Wahl (3041 Elridge, Bellingham, WA 98225, or phone: (206) 733-8255) organizes several trips each year out of Westport, WA.

Tickets may range in price from $18 to $45 depending on the length of the trip. Most boats leave early (5:30–7:30 A.M.) and return later the same afternoon (3:00–5:00 P.M.). There are a few overnight trips to areas far offshore, and hours for these may vary considerably. All of these trips are quite popular and reservations should be made well in advance. The San Diego excursions may fill more than two months prior to the trip.

The alternative to the organized birding boat is to latch onto one of the numerous commercial fishing boats that leave most large ports daily. Tickets for these one day trips are usually sold right on the harbor on a first come, first served basis. The length of these outings is usually comparable to most of the birding trips, while the price may be somewhat less (if you don't rent tackle and purchase a fishing license). Be sure to inquire how far offshore the skipper plans to go. Trips of less than five miles out usually produce little that cannot be seen from shore.

There are advantages and disadvantages to both types of boat trips. Most of the advantages lie with the organized birding trip. Here the emphasis is on finding and observing birds. The skipper will not linger in birdless areas, but will actively chase flocks of birds. When birds are spotted resting on the water he will stop the boat for optimum viewing. Chumming—throwing bits of squid, fish entrails, suet, popcorn, bread, and so forth, into the wake of the boat to attract birds—is a common practice on organized birding trips. Another advantage is in having 25 to 50 people (many of whom are real experts) to aid in the spotting and identification of birds. The disadvantages of the organized trips stem mainly from the fact that they are relatively few in number and scheduling may be a problem. Most trips are concentrated in the fall when the quality of pelagic birding is generally at its best. If your vacation time falls in summer or over the Christmas season you may be out of luck.

The main advantage of taking a fishing boat is that you can almost always find a boat, and advance scheduling is usually not required. Another nice point for those who enjoy the thrill of discovery is the opportunity to spot and identify all of the birds yourself. This chance is rarely afforded when there are fifty other eager birders on board. The disadvantages are many. The objective of everyone on the boat but you is fish and fishing. That translates into no stopping for birds, no chasing birds, and do not get in the way of all the rods, reels, tangled lines, and fishermen. Most true pelagic birds will be seen only when the boat is going out, coming back, or otherwise moving across the ocean from one fishing spot to another. This may account for three hours of an eight-hour day. The rest of the time will be spent sitting in a couple of choice fishing spots for up to two or three hours at a time. During these periods you are likely to see little except the same gulls and cormorants that could be seen from shore. It is also at this time that you and the boat will experience the greatest amount of motion, which means bad news if you are at all prone to sea sickness.

No matter what type of boat you find yourself on, you may still have to cope with the problem of seasickness. There are few, if any, absolutes on how to avoid this unpleasant malady. Almost every veteran pelagic birder has suffered from it at least once, and some fall victim on nearly every trip. Weather conditions and indigenous underwater geographical features make every trip different in terms of motion. Monterey Bay trips are usually quite calm, as are fall excursions from San Diego. Davidson Seamount trips, which depart from Morro Bay (California) are notably rough, as are many trips that depart from the Texas coast. Size of the boat is another consideration (bigger is better). Even where you stand on the boat makes a difference, with the bow being liveliest and stern being most stable.

Traditional remedies such as Dramamine and Marazine are helpful to some people and useless to others. One possible unpleasant side effect of these nonprescription drugs is extreme drowsiness. If you do use these pills, it is best to start taking them a day or so before the trip, so that the drug has a chance to work its way through your system. A light, nongreasy breakfast eaten at least one to two hours before departing is a good idea. Snacks for the trip are also good, both to sop up the gastric juices and to renew energy levels. An empty stomach usually aggravates nausea, and contrary to what you feel at the time, eating something may be the needed cure. A few of the boats have galleys complete with short-order cooks, although the cuisine is typically overpriced and limited. Finally, if all else fails, head to the rail and get it over with. Do not use the restroom for this purpose unless you wish to be lynched by your fellow passengers.

Be sure to bring plenty of warm clothes that can be shed in layers. It is difficult to overdress for the first few hours of a pelagic trip regardless of time of year. You may also wish to bring popcorn, bread, and the like to add to the chum. Do not bother with bringing a spotting scope, since boat motion will render it useless.

Above all, this is the time to really do your homework on the finer points of identification. Most pelagic birds appear suddenly, flash by the boat, and are gone before you know it. Many have a tendency to fly low between the swells, which makes keeping them in your binocular field very difficult. Add to this light conditions that are often less than ideal (not to mention fog), boat motion that is sometimes severe, and several species that are extremely similar in appearance, and you have the makings of a very frustrating day if you are not prepared to identify the bird instantly. There is seldom time to peruse your field guides while the bird is in sight. That is something that can be saved for later when activity slows.

There is no one time or place to take a pelagic trip. Although many of the West Coast pelagics can be found anywhere from San Diego to Seattle (and beyond), there are some that are much better seen in one place than another. Likewise, different times of the year are good for different things.

Monterey Bay is usually the most consistent area for seeing several species and lots of birds. Areas farther north tend to have fewer storm petrels, whereas areas farther south are poor for alcids, skuas, and albatrosses. San Diego is almost a must for Red-billed Tropicbird and Least Storm Petrel, and Westport is best for South Polar Skua and Flesh-footed Shearwater. Trips off the Gulf Coast of Texas are often nearly birdless, but they can produce species like Cory's and Audubon's Shearwaters and Masked Booby, none of which can be found off the West Coast.

Winter is the best time for alcids, Northern Fulmar, Short-tailed Shearwater, Fork-tailed Storm Petrel, Laysan Albatross, and Black-legged Kittiwake. Fall produces the greatest variety of birds no matter the location. August through mid-September is generally best for Red-billed Tropicbird, Sabine's Gull, Long-tailed Jaeger, Arctic Tern, and Craveri's Murrelet. Late September through mid-October may produce more variety, and is the time when thousands of storm petrels raft on Monterey Bay. Spring usually offers slightly less variety, but the birds are in their best plumages. June through July is generally the dullest time, but this is the easiest time to find Black-footed Albatross out of Monterey.

Keep in mind that it takes many boat trips out of several places and at different times of the year to build a good pelagic list. You cannot expect to find all or even most of the possible species on any one trip.

CALLING BIRDS IN

Birders use a variety of sounds to lure birds out of cover. Two of the most universal are "squeaking" and "pishing." The former can be made by pursing your lips and drawing air through in either rapid or prolonged bouts. The same effect can be generated by kissing the back of your hand very loudly. More widely effective is "pishing," a hissing sort of sound that sounds like "pisssh pissssh pissssh." This is similar to the alarm calls of many passerine birds (e.g., wrens, gnatcatchers, some vireos), and by varying the cadence and volume you may produce a fair imitation of a large group of birds mobbing some would-be predator. Both of these noises are directed primarily at calling in passerines, although some hawks, owls, hummingbirds, and woodpeckers may also respond. Some species respond much better than others to these sounds, while some will show no interest at all. Chickadees, titmice, nuthatches, wrens, and gnatcatchers will almost always respond. The trick is to get these rather vocal birds agitated, and let their alarm calls attract still more species. Many mimids, vireos, warblers, and sparrows will also react strongly to your efforts. Many birds respond best early in the breeding season when territoriality is at its peak, and/or when young are in the nest.

A more specific (and often more reliable) method of calling birds is to imitate the call of the bird you are trying to attract. However, only a few bird voices are easily duplicated by people. With the advent of the compact, battery-operated cassette recorder this problem has been alleviated. One use of the tape recorder is to record the vocalizations of a singing bird and then play them back to lure the singer in. The drawback to this is that unless the bird is close and is a particularly explosive singer, the average recorder will not pick the song up, or it will be lost in background noise.

Rather than investing in parabolic reflectors and other expensive recording equipment, most birders record bird songs from records or else buy pre-recorded cassette tapes. There are numerous records and tapes of bird songs commercially available. Advertisements for these can often be found in issues of *Audubon*, *National Wildlife*, and *Birding*, or in the catalogs of any companies specializing in the sale of natural history books. Probably the most complete record/tape set is *A Field Guide to Western Bird Songs*, which corresponds by page number to Roger Tory Peterson's *Field Guide to Western Birds* (a similar record set is available to eastern North America). Although songs or calls of some (mostly rare or local) species are missing, these records/tapes include vocalizations for the majority of birds likely to be encountered in western North America.

Because so many species are included, there is only room on the Peterson records for 2 to 5 vocalizations per bird. The narrator's voice introduces each species by giving its name and the page number on which it is found in the field guide. This format becomes awkward to work around in the field because you must keep stopping and rewinding the tape. There is also the inevitable situation in which the bird you have patiently called in finally pops into the open, only to be scared away by the narrator's voice intoning "page 163. . .". To avoid this problem it is best to take a blank tape and run off long sequences (five or more minutes) of calls of the birds you are interested in. This will prove tedious at home, but you will be congratulating yourself for having done so once you use the recording in the field.

Once you have the tape and the recorder in your hands, there are definite dos and don'ts for using it. A frequent mistake is to play the tape too loudly. Most birds have pretty acute hearing, so if it sounds loud to you, it may sound even louder to them. The typical reason for birds responding to tapes of conspecific calls is that they are attempting to chase a possible usurper from their territory. If your tape is extremely loud the bird may abandon all thoughts of territorial defense and fly the other way. Another mistake is to play the tape continuously without let-up. Birds that are calling territorially to one another often pause between songs to listen for a response. Continuous, non-stop calling is unnatural. When making your tape you may wish to allow for this by leaving 15 to 30 second gaps between groups of phrases. You should also avoid standing in the open when attempting to call birds in. The bird may respond well up until it sees you standing where the song is originating from. This should also be kept in mind when "squeaking" or "pishing."

Tape recorders are particularly effective in luring in nocturnal species such as owls and rails, which would otherwise be hard to track down. A calling owl is probably best located by triangulation (assuming there are multiple observers and flashlights in your group). Keep the lights turned off until you are certain the bird is within sight. At some prearranged signal have everyone cast their light in the direction from which they hear the owl. Hopefully the bird will be caught in the crossbeams. Another advantage of multiple observers is that each person can take turns with the binoculars while the others spotlight the bird.

Another technique which is very useful in attracting many passerine birds is to play tapes of owl calls. Many of the smaller owls include birds in their diet, and the birds recognize these owls as enemies. Whenever they locate a small owl, most passerines engage in mobbing behavior—diving at the owl and making scolding calls—until the owl is driven from the area. Consequently, a tape recording of the appropriate small owl will often drive birds wild, and you may be absolutely surrounded by scolding birds. Northern Pygmy-Owl calls are almost sure-fire in any of the western mountains where these owls are found. This is probably due to the diurnal nature of this owl, which brings it into more frequent contact with small birds. Western Screech-Owl calls will also work well throughout much of the west, while Eastern Screech should be used in the midwest, eastern Great Plains, and east Texas. Ferruginous Pygmy-Owl calls may be equally as effective as Eastern Screech calls when working in the lower Rio Grande Valley of Texas. Great Horned Owl calls in the same area may produce a flock of Green or Brown Jays.

ETHICS

A discussion of ethics should probably accompany every discourse on finding birds. With ever increasing numbers of birders taking to the field, more and more instances of rude and careless behavior are causing reproductive failure for birds, and bringing about the closure of privately-owned lands to birders. Both problems stem from a lack of consideration by birders who will do anything to see "their" bird.

This attitude has led to incredible harassment of some birds (mostly rare species) by birders. The worst culprit is the portable tape recorder, that useful device described in detail above. Every time a bird responds to a tape, whether of its own call or that of an owl, it is disrupting its normal routine. During the breeding season, when young are in the nest, adult birds are on a tight time-energy budget, attempting to fulfill the energy requirements of their offspring as well as their own. Prolonged and/or repeated disruptions of their foraging schedules, along with the energy loss associated with these pseudo-bouts of territorial defense can lead to reproductive failure in the form of nestling starvation. Increased territorial or scolding behavior by the birds may also serve to draw predators to the nest.

For these reasons it is of vital importance that recorders be used most judiciously. This is especially important when working areas that host large numbers of birders (each with his or her own recorder). A perfect example is provided by Cave Creek Canyon in the Chiricahua Mountains of southeast Arizona. This canyon is inundated with birders every spring and summer. From late May to mid-June the birders often outnumber the birds along South Fork Trail. Almost everyone's primary goal is the Elegant Trogon, a tropical species whose entire U.S. range is limited to a few canyons in southeast Arizona. Trogons often respond well to tapes of their calls, and can be downright elusive if such recordings are not used. This situation resulted in hordes of birders bombarding the trogons daily with their tapes. No sooner would a trogon finish chasing down one recording than another call would issue from farther up or down the trail. This undoubtedly contributed to some known instances of nest failure or desertion, and for a period of time recorders were banned from South Fork Trail.

When dealing with rare birds like the trogon, or when birding in areas that are intensively birded by large numbers of people, tape recorder use should be curtailed greatly or stopped altogether. Even in relatively unbirded areas or with common species, discretion should be the watchword. The tape recorder is merely a birding tool, not a crutch. Many people have fallen into a lazy pattern of always calling birds in, thereby disregarding the skills necessary to track down and identify a bird on their own. Although such an approach may mean extra time and work to find a bird, the end result is almost always more satisfying.

Another place where caution should be exercised is in the vicinity of nest sites. Some species can tolerate a fair amount of disturbance near their nests, while others cannot. There are numerous known instances of birds deserting their nests because of continued disturbance from birders. This is especially critical in the case of rare species and many raptors. Most reprehensible was the incident of some years ago in Patagonia, Arizona, where a tour leader and his large group sat directly under a Black Hawk nest for an extended period of time. The adults abandoned the nest and the species has not been known to breed in the area since. The common practice of whacking trees or telephone poles that harbor nesting owls just to get the bird to emerge from the cavity should also be strictly avoided. Even when human disturbance does not precipitate actual nest desertion, the mere act of flushing the parent from the nest exposes the eggs or young to heat, cold, and possible predation. This becomes most harmful when dealing with colonial birds such as herons and terns, where one disturbance at the wrong time of day could lead to massive nest failure for the colony.

Appropriate behavior regarding the use of private property is also of concern. Many of the better birding spots across the country are located on private property. Most landowners do not object to birders entering their land so long as they are courteous and responsible in their use of the area. There have been a few instances where all birders have been barred from wonderful places due to the actions of a few inconsiderate people. Following are a few common-sense rules that should be followed.

1. Do not enter posted land without permission from the owner. Even where land is not posted it is best to acquire permission before entering unless the area is known to be open to birders.
2. Close all gates behind you.
3. Avoid contact with livestock whenever possible.
4. Keep vehicles on roads at all times.
5. Do not litter.
6. Avoid smoking, or at least use all due caution.
7. Do not harass the wildlife or trample the vegetation.
8. Always act in a way that will assure other birders of being welcome.

·3·

Finding the Western Specialties

The previous chapter concentrated on generalities and concepts of finding birds. It dealt with the importance of elevation, habitat recognition (on both micro and macro scales), time of year, time of day, knowledge of specific localities, and tapping into birding hotlines. This chapter is meant to apply that philosophical framework to the specifics of finding the specialty birds of the West.

WHAT IS A SPECIALTY BIRD?

"Specialty bird" (as I have defined the term for this chapter) has a broad, and somewhat arbitrary meaning. My first criterion was that the birds covered must be essentially western birds. Species whose ranges include large areas east of the Mississippi were left out, regardless of how common or rare they are in the West. Thus, birds such as Red-cockaded Woodpecker, Bachman's Sparrow, and Brown-headed Nuthatch (all of which are, on a regional basis, considered east Texas specialties) were left out, because on the broader scale they are essentially birds of the Southeast. A few exceptions were made in the case of some northern owls and the Three-toed Woodpeckers, all of which are so highly sought after as to warrant treatment.

Within these bounds I also eliminated western birds that were very widespread within the area covered by this book. (After all, a bird is hardly a specialty if it can be easily found in appropriate habitat over half of the continent.) This led to several judgment calls that would no doubt be treated differently by every person attempting the task. Such ubiquitous species as Swainson's Hawk, Western Kingbird, Western Wood-Pewee, Black-billed Magpie, Steller's Jay, and Black-headed Grosbeak were obvious candidates for omission. Unfortunately, several less-easily found (but nearly as widespread) species like Blue Grouse, Burrowing Owl, and Williamson's Sapsucker were also casualties of the process. Even these species occur over such wide areas, that providing specific finding information (and giving equal treatment to each state) would demand more space than is available here.

The matter of choosing which of the rare visiting species to include was also somewhat arbitrary. In general, I tried to avoid the following: (a) irruptive northern species whose movements are somewhat irregular, which invade much of the East as well as the West, and which, when present, show up almost anywhere (for example, Evening Grosbeak, Bohemian Waxwing, Hoary and Common Redpolls—but see northern owls for an exception); and (b) Asiatic species whose appearances south of Alaska are extremely rare, and unpredictable as to time and place (outside of broad generalities such as "winter on the West Coast"). Exceptions are made for Asiatic species of regular occurrence, whose movements over the years fit a somewhat predictable pattern (for example, Ruff, Sharp-tailed Sandpiper, and Curlew Sandpiper). I have included nearly all of the Mexican species that rarely cross into our country, simply because they are not likely to occur elsewhere, away from our border states.

In spite of the restrictions outlined above, more than 230 species are dealt with in this chapter. Those that are excluded should be readily found in the proper habitat and season by the traveling birder who covers any significant portion of the West.

FORMAT

Each species is covered in one paragraph of varying length. These paragraphs are designed to tell you where, when, and in what habitat you can expect to find the birds. For common and/or conspicuous species that are likely to be found just by going to representative habitats at the proper season, no further information is given. For less common or more localized species, a list of recommended locations for finding the birds is provided and is broken down by state. These lists include both very general locations (for example, Yosemite National Park) and highly specific ones (for example, Willow Lake at Santa Ana National Wildlife Refuge). It is intended that these will provide you with starting points in your searches for various birds. For precise mileages and route descriptions you will still need to consult the proper regional bird-finding guide. Such detail is beyond the scope of this book, and has been provided only in a very few instances, where a species is highly localized (for example, lekking grouse or prairie chickens).

To streamline species accounts, I have resorted to a few abbreviations that are listed below.

- National Forest (NF)
- National Park (NP)
- State Park (SP)
- National Wildlife Refuge (NWR)

No one person has the familiarity with every western state that is required to write these species accounts from scratch. My personal experience is heavy in North and South Dakota, Minnesota, Iowa, Texas, New Mexico, Colorado, Arizona, and California. I have much less experience in the other states, and so have relied on bird-finding articles and the proper regional bird-finding guides as references. My heaviest reliance in this regard was on O. S. Pettingill's *A Guide to Birdfinding West of the Mississippi* (1981), a work which all western bird–seekers should have in their libraries. In instances where I have gleaned information from an outside source, I have cited that work in the account. Full citations are provided in the bibliography at the end of this book.

Least Grebe. Uncommon and local resident of small bodies of fresh water in the lower Rio Grande Valley of south Texas, and north along the coast from Brownsville to about Corpus Christi. This grebe seems to undergo irregular population fluctuations, and during some years can be very hard to find. They inhabit wood-bordered and open-edge ponds as well as ditches and larger man-made impoundments. Areas with plenty of emergent vegetation are preferred, but not requisite. Try the small lakes at Santa Ana NWR, the freshwater ponds and ditches at Laguna Atascosa NWR, and the ponds and ditches along Highway 281 west from Brownsville.

Black-footed Albatross. Fairly common year-round visitor to the offshore waters of the West Coast. Most common from May to September, when groups of birds are often seen chasing fishing trawlers. Commonly settles on the water alongside boats and feeds on garbage and fish entrails tossed overboard. Usually seen in summer out of Monterey, California (June is best), but your best chances are from Westport, Washington, where the bird is virtually never missed between April and October.

Laysan Albatross. Very rare but regular visitor to offshore waters of the West Coast. Summers in waters around the Aleutian Islands of Alaska, from which individuals move south in fall. Appears far offshore (200+ miles) from Washington by October, and off central California by December. Most sightings near shore have come from central California, and virtually all of these have been from December through May. In recent years special boat trips have been organized out of Monterey, (CA) in March to search for this bird. Unfortunately, your chances are not good.

Flesh-footed Shearwater. Rare but regular visitor to offshore waters of the West Coast. Most birds are seen in fall (August through October), but there appears to be some spring passage in May. Sometimes seen into winter. A few individuals are regularly seen out of Monterey (CA) in fall, but your best chance is to take a pelagic trip out of Westport (WA), which regularly turns up a few birds on May trips and July through October trips.

Sooty Shearwater. Abundant summer-through-fall visitor to offshore waters of the West Coast with lesser numbers present throughout the year. Difficult to miss on any pelagic trip (except, perhaps, in winter)—more likely, you will grow tired of looking at them.

Short-tailed Shearwater. Uncommon late fall-through-winter visitor to offshore waters of the West Coast. The true status of this bird is somewhat clouded due to its extreme similarity to the abundant Sooty Shearwater. Short-taileds are seldom seen in California before November, and many individuals stay through part of the winter. Monterey (CA) trips from mid-November through February probably provide as good a chance as any for this bird.

Pink-footed Shearwater. Common spring-through-fall visitor to offshore waters of the West Coast. A sprinkling of birds is generally present from March through July (most common in May) at which time numbers begin to increase and remain farly high until late October. Aside from the Sooty, this is the most common western shearwater, and it is easily seen from boats leaving almost any western port.

Streaked Shearwater. Extremely rare fall vagrant from Asia to the offshore waters of the West Coast. Based on past records it is most likely to be seen on pelagic trips out of Monterey Bay (CA) during the first half of October.

Buller's Shearwater. Uncommon summer-through-fall visitor to offshore water of the West Coast, south to central California. Most birds are found from August to November with a peak in early October. The best chances for seeing it are from pelagic trips taken out of Westport, Washington, and Monterey (CA) from mid-September through mid-October.

Black-vented Shearwater. Fairly common August through January visitor to offshore California waters from its nesting islands off of Baja. Some individuals are seen into March. This shearwater is most common off southern California and is best seen on boats out of San Diego. It is typically found somewhat close to shore and can often be spotted from land at appropriate overlooks with the aid of a spotting scope.

Cook's Petrel. Very rare (but possibly regular) late fall migrant well off the California coast (50+ miles). Most sightings have come between October and December from boats leaving San Luis Obispo County bound for the Davidson Seamount.

Black Storm Petrel. Common spring-through-fall visitor to the offshore waters of southern and central California. Breeds on rocky islands off the extreme southern tip of California and northern Baja (notably the Los Coronados of Mexico), and in the Gulf of California. Readily seen on San Diego pelagic trips, it can also be very common over the submarine canyons out of Monterey Bay (August through November) where it rafts on the water in large diurnal roosts with hundreds to thousands of Ashy Storm-Petrels.

Ashy Storm Petrel. Fairly common spring through fall resident (uncommon to rare in winter) of offshore waters of the California coast (more common off the southern and central coast). Most of the population breeds on the Farallon Islands (CA), with lesser numbers breeding on some of the Channel Islands (CA) and on the Los Coronados Islands (Baja). These birds are most commonly seen from August through November, when huge numbers raft over submarine canyons (notably out of Monterey Bay).

Fork-tailed Storm Petrel. Fairly common the year around in the offshore waters of the Washington and Oregon coasts, rare off the coast of California, where most records come from winter pelagic trips. Nests on rocky islands from Alaska to northern California. Best seen out of Westport, Washington.

Least Storm Petrel. Uncommon-to-abundant post-breeding visitor to the off-shore waters of southern California. Yearly fluctuations in the number of birds found in U.S. waters are often pronounced. The bulk of birds are found in August and September out of San Diego.

Wedge-rumped Storm Petrel. Very rare visitor to the offshore waters of California August through January. Your best bet of seeing one is to carefully check the flocks of Black and Ashy Storm Petrels that raft over the submarine canyons off Monterey Bay in October.

Magnificent Frigatebird. Rare-but-regular post-breeding visitor (July through September) to coastal California and Texas, and to the Salton Sea (CA). Stragglers occasionally find their way into Arizona, particularly along the Colorado River. In Texas your best bet is to scope wooden pilings and buoys that dot the larger bays. Try the Texas City Dike, Galveston Bay, the Bolivar Ferry, and Corpus Christi Bay. In California your best chances are to check the Salton Sea and southern coastal RBAs (Rare Bird Alerts).

Red-billed Tropicbird. Rare but fairly regular post-breeding visitor to the off-shore waters of southern California. Has been found north to the central coast and usually well out to sea. Most records date from August to September in the vicinity of San Clemente Island. The Western Field Ornithologists typically sponsor a pelagic trip out of San Diego to San Clemente Island every September.

Brown Booby. Rare and very irregular post-breeding visitor (July through November with August and September being most likely) to the Salton Sea (CA) and the Colorado River Valley from its breeding rocks in the Gulf of California. This is the rarer of the two boobies expected to occur in California, and in most years none are present.

Blue-footed Booby. Rare and irregular post-breeding visitor (July through November with August and September being most likely) to the Salton Sea (CA), Colorado River Valley (CA, AZ), and occasionally along the southern California coast. More regular than the Brown Booby, appearing in numbers during some years. Breeds in the Gulf of California.

Masked Booby. Rare-but-regular visitor to offshore Texas waters the year around. At times (particularly summer) it can be fairly common in the Gulf. Your best bet is to latch onto a pelagic trip (irregularly scheduled, inquire with coastal Audubon Societies) or a commercial fishing boat. If you strike out there, your only recourse is to stake yourself to the end of a coastal jetty and scope every buoy and channel marker within sight.

Olivaceous Cormorant. Fairly common to uncommon resident of mostly fresh water lakes and rivers (but also found on coastal bays) from the southwest corner of Louisiana south along the Gulf Coast to Brownsville, Texas and west along the Rio Grande to about Falcon Dam. Beginning in the mid 1970s a few pairs began nesting in the vicinity of Elephant Butte Reservoir along the Rio Grande in New Mexico. Since 1982 the population seems to have increased dramatically, and it is not uncommon to see fifty or more birds in a day at such places as Bosque del Apache NWR and Elephant Butte and Caballo Reservoirs.

Brandt's and Pelagic Cormorants. These two species are common residents of rocky coastline from San Diego (CA) to Vancouver (BC) and beyond. They are easily seen perched on offshore rocks or coastal cliffs along almost any coastal overlook (often with both species side by side). Also seen on coastal jetties, pelagic trips, and fishing in bays or coastal surf.

Reddish Egret. Uncommon resident of salt marshes and beaches along the Gulf Coast from Brownsville (TX) to south Florida. In Texas it nests on offshore islands that are covered with dense, low shrubs and trees. The Reddish Egret is more restricted to salt water than any other U.S. heron or egret. Due to its preference for open habitats, it is easily seen. Look for it in appropriate habitats anywhere along the Texas coast, but especially at Bolivar Flats, Galveston Island SP, Rockport, Corpus Christi, Laguna Atascosa NWR, and along the Queen Isabella Causeway (connecting Port Isabel to South Padre Island).

Wood Stork. Uncommon post breeding visitor (July through September) to freshwater marshes, lagoons, and rice fields along the Gulf Coast (TX,LA), and to the Salton Sea in California. Often seen circling high overhead like vultures, or festooned about the upper branches of large trees (often dead ones in standing water). In Texas try Anahuac, Welder, Aransas, and Laguna Atascosa NWRs; the Sabine Marsh; and the rice fields west of Houston. Salton Sea birds are easily found around Redhill, and at Finney and Ramer Lakes.

Roseate Spoonbill. Fairly common to uncommon resident of marshes, ponds, and coastal mud flats along the Gulf Coast from Brownsville (TX) to south Florida. More common on the upper and central Texas coast than the lower.

Nests on dry coastal islands alongside other species of waders. Most individuals leave for the winter, making the bird somewhat hard to find at that season. Apparently the wintering birds are best found in the river deltas at the end of the larger bays, such as Trinity Bay near Baytown and Corpus Christi Bay (Lane 1980). At other times of the year it should be easy to find at Galveston Island SP; Sabine Marsh; Bolivar Flats; Corpus Christi; and Anahuac, Aransas, and Laguna Atascoa NWRs.

Whooping Crane. Whooping Cranes are rare and endangered. The historical population breeds in the bogs of Wood Buffalo NP (Alberta) and winters on Aransas NWR on the Gulf Coast of Texas. Individuals and small groups in route to either place during migration are occasionally chanced upon (usually at wildlife refuges in the Dakotas). The wintering birds at Aransas can often be distantly seen from the observation tower, but your best chance is to book passage on the M.V. Whooping Crane, which docks at the Sea-Gun Sports Inn (Rockport). Write to the Sea-Gun Sports Inn, Route 1, Box 85, Rockport, Texas 78382; or call (512) 729-2341 for reservations. The cranes are generally easy to see from the boat between November and April. A second population of Whoopers is being established via a management program that involves using Sandhill Cranes at Gray's Lake NWR in Idaho to incubate Whooper eggs. The Sandhills go on to raise the young Whoopers as if they were their own, and consequently, the Whoopers follow their foster parents south in fall to their wintering grounds in New Mexico. Most of the birds end up at Bosque del Apache NWR, where they are fairly easy to find between mid-November and late January.

Trumpeter Swan. Rare resident of scattered lakes and marshes in the Northwest, northern Rockies, and northern Great Plains. Once nearly extirpated, this bird is making a comeback via reintroduction programs. The isolated Alaskan population is somewhat migratory and tends to winter from southeast Alaska to the coast of Washington and Oregon (individuals occasionally show up as far south as California). Look for it at:

1. Washington (Wahl and Paulson 1977)—Turnbull NWR (nests) and Beaver Lake, Clear Lake, and DeBay Slough (0.2 mile north and 1 mile west of Clear Lake) in Skagit Cove (winter)
2. Oregon—along the Columbia River east of Astoria (winter) and at Malheur NWR
3. Montana—Red Rock Lakes NWR (the source of birds introduced to other areas)
4. Wyoming—National Elk Refuge (along Flat Creek) near Jackson and Grebe and Swan Lakes in Yellowstone NP
5. South Dakota—Lacreek NWR.

Ross' Goose. Uncommon and local winter resident of freshwater marshes and agricultural lands in the interior of California. The bulk of the world population winters in the Sacramento (try Sacramento NWR) and San Joaquin (try San Luis NWR) valleys. Ross' Goose is less common among the vast Snow Goose flocks at the Salton Sea and is also easily found in winter (November through April) at Bosque del Apache NWR in New Mexico, less commonly at Bitter Lakes NWR (NM). Small numbers winter on the TX and LA coast, where they must be picked from among the Snow Goose flocks. Try Cameron Parish, Louisiana, Anahuac NWR (TX), and the rice fields west of Houston (TX). As birders begin to scan Snow Goose flocks more closely, vagrant Ross' Geese are being found on a regular basis throughout much of the interior.

Brant. Fairly common winter resident and migrant along the length of the West Coast. It is rarely found inland, but often appears in late summer at the Salton Sea (CA). This "sea goose" favors large coastal bays, preferring to feed in shallow water and on mud flats often around river mouths. Likely spots include

1. California—the San Diego River mouth (West Mission Bay) and the Silver Strand in San Diego, Morro Bay, Dillon Beach near Point Reyes, and Humboldt Bay
2. Oregon (Pettingill 1981)—Ecola SP, Yaquina Bay near Newport, and Tillamook Bay
3. Washington (Wahl and Paulson 1977)—Dungeness NWR (near Sequim); Leadbetter Point Unit of the Willapa NWR (October-November and April-May); Draton Harbor and Birch Bay in Whatcom County, and Padilla, Samish, and Skagit Bays in Skagit Co.

Mottled Duck. Common resident of marshes, ponds, water filled ditches, and flooded rice fields along the Gulf Coast from Brownsville (TX) to Florida. In Texas it is easy to find at Sabine (the marsh near the coastguard station), Anahuac NWR, the rice fields east and west of Houston, Galveston Island SP, Aransas NWR, the King Ranch, and at Laguna Atascosa NWR, as well as at roadside ponds the length of the coast.

Eurasian Wigeon. Rare but regular winter visitor the length of the West Coast, usually with large flocks of American Wigeon. Check coastal RBAs.

Masked Duck. Very rare and irregular year-round visitor (occasionally nests) to freshwater ponds and ditches with emergent vegetation (and usually grassy borders) in the lower Rio Grande Valley of Texas and along the Gulf Coast. Santa Ana, Welder, and Anahuac NWRs have had their share of past records, but this bird is impossible to predict.

Fulvous Whistling Duck. Uncommon and decreasing summer resident (some winter) of rice fields and freshwater lakes and marshes along the Texas coast. Seen in the lower Rio Grande Valley as a migrant. Also an uncommon to rare summer visitor to California (has nested at the Salton Sea). In Texas try Anahuac (summer) and Laguna Atascosa (migration) NWRs, Welder Refuge, the Corpus Christi area, and the rice fields west of Houston.

Black-bellied Whistling Duck. Fairly common summer resident of tree-lined ponds along the lower Rio Grande Valley from Rio Grande City to Brownsville and along the Gulf Coast north to Corpus Christi (TX). This duck winters in smaller numbers in the extreme southern portion of that range, along the Rio Grande delta and is a sporadic summer visitor (sometimes nests) to southern Arizona. Look for it at Lake Corpus Christi, Welder Refuge, and Laguna Atascosa and Santa Ana NWRs. When wintering birds are located they are often in large concentrations.

Tufted Duck. Very rare but annual winter visitor (October through April) to bays and lakes along the West Coast. Most common in fall around Vancouver, British Columbia (try Lost Lagoon in Stanley Park), but also regularly found south to the Bay Area in California. Many individuals return to the same lakes for several consecutive years and remain for long periods of time. It is often found in the middle of scaup or Ring-necked Duck flocks. Your best bet is to check local RBAs.

Scoters. All three species (Surf, Black, and White-winged) occur as uncommon to very rare spring and fall visitors to larger bodies of water throughout the West. All three are regular winter residents and migratory transients along the length of the West Coast. The Surf is typically the most common coastal scoter, with the White-winged second most common (White-winged is the most widespread and expected species across the interior). Neither is hard to find in appropriate locales, and the Surf is often downright abundant. The Black is the least common and hardest to find. Scoters usually inhabit coastline (where they are seen bobbing in the surf) and saltwater bays. They are frequently viewed to best advantage inside harbors and boat marinas. During most years a few nonbreeding birds remain along the coast through the summer.

Harlequin Duck. Uncommon summer resident of fast-moving rivers and streams in the high country of Washington, Oregon, Idaho, Montana, and Wyoming. Moves to areas of rocky coast (where the winter is spent) after nesting. Here it is seen feeding in the roughest part of the surf. Winters south to central California (more common farther north). Reliable spots include:

1. Wyoming—LeHardy Cascades in Yellowstone NP
2. Montana (Pettingill 1981)—McDonald Creek in Glacier NP

3. Oregon (Pettingill 1981)—Ecola SP (post-breeding), streams in the Wallowa Mountains, and South Jetty at Newport (post-breeding)

4. Washington (Wahl and Paulson 1977)—Elwha River in Olympic NP, Rialto Beach near La Push (post-breeding), Cape Flattery (post-breeding), Birch Bay in Whatom County (post-breeding), Lanabee SP (winter), and the North Fork of the Snoqualmie River in King Co.

Barrow's Goldeneye. Uncommon to fairly common summer resident of forest lakes and ponds in the Northwest. Winters on large inland lakes, bays, rivers and along the West Coast, often considerably south of the breeding range (south to the San Francisco Bay Area in CA). Suggested spots include:

1. California—Lake Merritt in Oakland (winter)

2. Oregon (Pettingill 1981)—Lost Lake along U.S. Highway 20

3. Washington (Wahl and Paulson 1977)—Union Bay in Seattle (winter), Lake Lenore in Grant Cove (nests), and Capitol Lake near Olympia (during November large numbers arrive in the afternoon to roost for the night)

4. Montana (Pettingill 1981)—Coulson Park (Billings) along the Yellowstone River (winter), and Lake Josephine and St. Mary Lake in Glacier NP

5. Wyoming (Pettingill 1981)—Yellowstone Lake in Yellowstone NP and Grand Teton NP (at Jenny, String, Leigh, and Jackson Lakes)

6. Colorado—Lake Estes near Estes Park (winter).

Yellow Rail. Uncommon and local summer resident of fens (spring-fed swales with quaking mats of vegetation over saturated soil), grassy marshes, and wet meadows in the extreme northern Great Plains, the upper Midwest, and Canada. The Yellow Rail avoids the deep marshes with lots of standing water that are preferred by other rails. It winters in hayfields, rice fields, and fresh and saltwater marshes along the Gulf Coast from the central Texas coast to Florida and north along the lower Atlantic Coast. Occasionally this bird is seen during migration, usually by farmers mowing their hayfields or at controlled burns of tall grass fields. It is extremely secretive, so seldom seen. Recommended breeding sites include marshes in Atkin and Mahnomen (particularly near Waubun) Counties in Minnesota, J. Clark Salyer NWR (ND) and appropriate habitat in Benson County, North Dakota. A recently discovered spot in the latter county is a sedge meadow two miles north of Minnewaukon along U.S. Highway 281 (Faanes, 1984). Probably the easiest place to see this bird is on its wintering grounds at Anahuac NWR (TX). During the month of April, refuge personnel conduct daily rail-buggy tours. The buggy is pulled behind a tractor that is outfitted with balloon tires (to prevent damage to the marsh). Rails of several species flush from the path of the tractor, often giving great views. Yellow Rails are seldom missed. Contact the Anahuac National Wildlife Refuge, Box 278, Anahuac, Texas 77514 (phone (713) 267-3131) for trip information and reservations.

Black Rail. Uncommon-to-rare and local inhabitant of fresh, brackish, and saltwater marshes (CA, AZ, and Gulf and Atlantic Coasts) and wet, sedge meadows (KA). Probably much overlooked due to its extremely secretive nature. California, Arizona, and Louisiana populations are resident, upper Texas coast birds are basically winter residents, and Kansas birds are summer residents. California birds are essentially of two populations: one that inhabits pickleweed marshes at the margins of large bays on the central and southern coast (for example, Upper Newport Bay, Morro Bay, and the Baylands Marsh Preserve in San Francisco Bay in Palo Alto), and another that is found in marshes along the Colorado River near the Imperial Dam (California-Arizona border). The latter birds should be looked for at Mittry Lake (Arizona side) and around West Pond just southwest of the CA end of the dam. Hearing Black Rails at these locations is one thing (nighttime is best), seeing them is another. Coastal birds are best observed at high tide when they (like other rails) are forced out of cover by rising water. Otherwise, your best bet is to use a recording, to which this species is fairly responsive (again, night is best). Your other best chance for seeing a Black Rail is from the rail buggy at Anahuac NWR (TX), but the species is very irregular at that locale. Some years and trips produce many individuals, while others produce none.

Northern Jacana. Rare visitor to ponds in the lower Rio Grande Valley of south Texas and along the lower and central Texas coast. Up until 1977 there was a resident colony on Manor Lake (west of Freeport). This colony was apparently wiped out by a freeze, and no Jacanas have been seen there in recent years. However, it does afford ideal potential breeding habitat—a reedy border with a thick growth of water hyacinths. Recent records have been of individual birds at scattered locales. It is sure to be listed on local RBAs.

Black Oystercatcher. Fairly common resident of rocky coastline from Morro Bay, California, north. A few breed on rocky offshore islands south to the Los Coronados (Mexico) but these are rarely seen on the mainland. Not hard to find in appropriate habitat.

Wilson's Plover. Fairly common summer resident of salt flats, intertidal dunes, and mud flats along the Gulf and lower Atlantic Coasts. In our area, winters only along the lower and central Texas coast, where numbers are much reduced from summer. Some prime Texas spots include Bolivar Flats, West Galveston Island, Rockport Beach, South Padre Island at the end of the Queen Isabella Causeway, and Laguna Atascosa NWR.

Mountain Plover. Uncommon and local summer resident of high plains and xeric short-grass prairie in a narrow corridor of states from Montana to west Texas. The Mountain Plover winters (sometimes in large flocks) in plowed fields, short-grass pastures, and oil fields in south Texas and central and southern California. In summer try:

1. Colorado—the Pawnee Grassland near Briggsdale (probably the best spot), and 11 miles south of Yodera (Bartol, 1973)
2. Wyoming (Pettingill 1981)—the Laramie Plains (from Laramie—north on U.S. Highway 30 for 2 miles then west on Howell Rd.)
3. Montana (Pettingill 1981)—the Charles M. Russell NWR and west of Harlowton
4. New Mexico—east of the junction of State Highway 22 and I-25 (north of Albuquerque)
5. Nebraska—vicinity of Bushnell
6. Texas—the Rita Blanca National Grasslands in the northwestern panhandle.

In winter try:

1. Texas—appropriate habitat near San Antonio and Rockport (check with area birders)
2. California—plowed fields around the south end of the Salton Sea, near Blackwell's Corner in Kern County, the Carrizo Plain in the interior of San Luis Obispo County, and in oil fields around Santa Maria.

Wandering Tattler. Fairly common migrant along rocky coastlines the length of the West Coast. The Wandering Tattler winters in the same habitat from the central California coast south and departs its winter range by May, with first-returning fall birds reaching central California by late July. Like the other rock-inhabiting shorebirds (oystercatcher, turnstone, surfbird), this one is most likely to be seen hopping about on surf-splashed rocks along the coast, or on rock jetties and breakwaters. It is not hard to find.

Red Phalarope. Uncommon and irregular offshore migrant along the West Coast, occasionally found along coastal beaches or in coastal lagoons. This most pelagic of the three phalaropes stages periodic fall invasions, during which it is extremely common from August through October, with many individuals lingering through the winter. Spring passage typically occurs in April and May. During the peak migration periods your chances of finding it on almost any pelagic trip are fairly good. This bird is a rare but regular vagrant to inland bodies of water throughout the West.

Black Turnstone. Common-to-abundant winter resident and spring and fall transient the length of the West Coast. It is typically found on rocky coastline, along rock jetties, and breakwaters, and is sometimes seen on sandy beaches. The Black Turnstone is present in spring until early May (as far south as southern California), with the first fall birds returning by mid-July. It is almost impossible to miss thereafter.

Surfbird. Fairly common winter resident of rocky coastline the length of the West Coast. Typically less common than the Black Turnstone, it also arrives slightly later in fall and is found at the same places as the latter species. It is not hard to find.

Rock Sandpiper. Uncommon to rare winter resident (November through March) of rocky coastline from Alaska south to Bodega Bay, California (west of Santa Rosa, north of San Francisco). Rare in the latter area, more common and regular farther north. Look for it in the same places as Black Turnstones and Surfbirds. It often feeds in beached masses of kelp.

Curlew Sandpiper. Very rare but somewhat regular vagrant along the entire West Coast. Less frequent vagrant to inland areas across the continent. Most coastal records are from late July to September, with a sprinkling of April to May occurrences. Fall birds are usually juveniles; basic-plumaged individuals have never been found on the coast (Roberson, 1980). Check local RBAs.

Rufous-necked Stint. Extremely rare fall vagrant along the length of the West Coast. Most often found from late July through September. Several recent records from the Santa Clara River Estuary at Ventura, California. Check local RBAs.

Sharp-tailed Sandpiper. Very rare but regular fall migrant (September to November) along the length of the West Coast. Virtually all sightings are of juveniles. It is found most regularly around Vancouver, British Columbia, but a few typically reach California every year. Check local RBAs.

Ruff. Rare vagrant across the continent, being regular along the West Coast. In Washington and Oregon, the best time to find this bird is during fall migration (August through October). Many California birds are also found in that season, but wintering birds are nearly as likely. Found wherever shorebirds gather (for example, sewage ponds, flooded fields, marshes, and so forth). Check local RBAs.

South Polar Skua. Uncommon spring-through-fall visitor to offshore waters of both the Pacific and Atlantic Coasts. You'll have to take a pelagic trip to see this one, but even taking several won't guarantee sighting this bird. Your best chances are on the trip out of Westport, Washington, where skuas are seen on more than half of the July to September trips taken. The best time to search out of Monterey (CA) is September through October, when birds are regularly seen, but are missed more often than not. You are more likely to see skuas from Monterey than from points farther south, and you won't have to go as far off shore to do it. Skuas are also regularly seen on May and September San Diego trips, but the frequency of sightings is low.

Pomarine Jaeger. Fairly common spring and fall migrant through offshore waters the length of the West Coast. Much more common in fall (late July through late November) than in spring (March through May), with a few remaining off the California coast all winter. Generally occurs in greater numbers than the Parasitic Jaeger. At least a few are seen on most autumn pelagic trips off the Pacific Coast. Rarely seen in the Texas Gulf, and rare but regular vagrant to large inland lakes, primarily in the Southwest.

Parasitic Jaeger. Fairly common spring and fall migrant through offshore waters the length of the West Coast. Much more common in fall (late July through late November) than in spring (March through May), with a few remaining off the California coast all winter. This is the jaeger most likely to be seen close to shore. At least a few are seen on most autumn pelagic trips off the West Coast. It is rarely seen in the Texas Gulf and is a rare but regular vagrant to large inland lakes primarily in the Southwest.

Long-tailed Jaeger. Rare fall (August through September) migrant through offshore waters the length of the West Coast. This is the most pelagic of the jaegers and is very hard to find south of the breeding grounds. The optimum time for seeing it is in late August and early September (CA) or late July to early September (WA), which coincides with the peak southbound movement of Arctic Terns. Very rare vagrant to inland bodies of water throughout the West.

Heermann's Gull. Common post-breeding visitor north along the West Coast to Washington from its nesting islands off the coast of Mexico (July through April). Winters only from the central California coast south. This bird is found in large numbers over the open ocean and along the coast itself and is nearly impossible to miss for much of the year.

Mew Gull. Fairly common winter visitor (October through April) to beaches, bays, harbors, coastal mud flats, and open ocean the length of the West Coast. Decidedly more common with increasing latitude, but still readily found at San Diego, California.

Thayer's Gull. Fairly common-to-rare winter resident (October through March) the length of the West Coast. It becomes more common with increasing latitude (most coastal California Christmas Bird Counts record one to several, most coastal Washington CBCs record a few hundred). Unlike many other western gulls, this one is not restricted to the coast. It routinely shows up several miles inland, and one or two can often be found at the Salton Sea. It is also a rare but regular vagrant to inland areas throughout the West, and is becoming increasingly common on the western Great Lakes. Perhaps the easiest place to find it in California is the Santa Maria dump (San Luis Obispo County). It should present no real problem at points north of California.

Yellow-footed Gull. Uncommon but increasing post-breeding visitor to the Salton Sea (CA) from its breeding grounds in the Gulf of California. Peak numbers arrive in July and leave by September, but a few remain through the winter.

Western Gull. Common-to-abundant resident of coastal and offshore waters from San Diego (CA) to Vancouver (BC). It is impossible to miss anywhere along the immediate coastline.

Sabine's Gull. Fairly common-to-uncommon spring (April through May) and fall (July through October) migrant over offshore waters the length of the West Coast. Highly pelagic and only rarely recorded from shore. It is a rare but regular vagrant to inland lakes throughout the West (most of these birds are juveniles). This striking gull can be seen on boat trips out of any western port, but the ones from Westport, Washington are probably your best bet. It is rarely missed on May or mid-August through mid-October trips.

Arctic Tern. Uncommon spring (April through May) and fall (mid August through mid October) migrant along the entire West Coast, almost always well off shore. Your only real chance is from a boat (early fall is best), and even then success is not guaranteed.

Gull-billed Tern. Fairly common-to-uncommon and local resident (less common in winter) along the Gulf Coast from Brownsville (TX) to Florida and north along the Atlantic Coast (summer). It is an uncommon or rare summer resident at the Salton Sea, California. On the Gulf, it nests on spoil banks left over from canal dredging operations. Most often seen over salt marshes, bays, and wet coastal grasslands. Fairly easy to find at such places as the Bolivar Peninsula, Galveston Island SP, Freeport, Rockport, and Aransas and Laguna Atascosa NWRs.

Sandwich Tern. Fairly common resident along our portion of the Gulf Coast (much less common in winter). It nests mainly on sand bars and on spoil banks left over from canal dredging operations. The Sandwich Tern spends more time foraging over the Gulf itself than in sheltered bays or over coastal marshes. Look for it at Bolivar Flats, from the Bolivar Ferry, from the Whooping

Crane boat, at the end of the Queen Isabella Causeway on South Padre Island, and from the jetties at Galveston and Port Aransas.

Elegant Tern. Fairly common post-breeding visitor from Mexico to beaches, estuaries, bays, and open ocean along the West Coast north to northern California. Easy to find from July to October, when most dispersal occurs. Some birds nest in San Diego, where they can be seen locally from March on (try the South Bay Marine Biological Study Area on the Silver Strand and Imperial Marsh).

Royal Tern. Common resident (fewer in winter) along our portion of the Gulf Coast, and uncommon post-breeding (fall through early winter) visitor to the southern and central California coast. A few birds summer in the vicinity of San Clemente Island and San Diego. In Texas this species nests colonially on sand bars and spoil banks the length of the coast, particularly around major bays. Royals can be seen foraging over coastal lagoons, bays, beaches, and offshore waters. They are not hard to find.

Black Skimmer. Common but somewhat local resident (fewer in winter) along our portion of the Gulf Coast. Uncommon to rare post-breeding visitor along the southern California coast, with a few birds nesting at the Salton Sea and San Diego (where they are resident). Skimmers inhabit sand and shell beaches, bays, and estuaries. They are easily seen along the Texas coast at such places as Bolivar Flats, Galveston Island, from the Bolivar Ferry, Rockport, from the Whooping Crane Boat, Corpus Christi, and Laguna Atascosa NWR. In California try the Salton Sea, Silver Strand, Imperial Marsh, and the San Diego River Channel at West Mission Bay.

Pigeon Guillemot. Fairly common summer resident of coastal waters along the West Coast south to central California (San Luis Obispo County). Forages in bays, harbors, open surf, and around offshore rocks. After nesting the birds disperse over the open sea and are uncommonly encountered through the winter. Reliable spots in summer include:

1. California—Point Reyes, Morro Rock (Morro Bay), Montana de Oro (San Luis Obispo County), Point Lobos Reserve SP, Humboldt Bay, and the wharf at Monterey
2. Oregon (Pettingill 1981)—Coquill Point near Bandon, Haystack Rock (Cannon Beach), Cape Arago SP, Newport Wharf, and Yaquina Head (3 miles north of Newport on Highway 101)
3. Washington—straits of Juan de Fuca, San Juan Islands (reached by ferry), Point Roberts, Cape Flattery, and Port Townsend.

Marbled Murrelet. Fairly common-to-uncommon resident along the West Coast south to central California. Most often seen in coastal waters but very near shore, as from coastal overlooks or ferries along inside passages. This small alcid is unusual in that it nests on the mainland (either on the ground on talus slopes or on branches of tall conifers in coastal redwood/fir forests). Some reliable spots are:

1. California—Pigeon Point (40 miles south of San Francisco on Highway 1), the harbor in Crescent City, North Jetty from North Bay of Humboldt Bay (Pettingill 1981), and the coast immediately south of the mouth of the Russian River in Sonoma Co. (60 miles north of San Francisco) off Highway 1 (Parmeter 1974)
2. Oregon—Yaquina Head 3 miles north of Newport on U.S. Highway 101, Coquille Point in Bandon, and Ecola and Cape Arago SPs (Pettingill 1981)
3. Washington—Point Roberts and on ferry rides (particularly those to Vancouver Island and the San Juans)
4. Clover Point on Vancouver Island, British Columbia.

Xantus' Murrelet. Fairly common but local resident of rocky islands and open ocean off the coasts of southern California and Baja. The northern nesting race *scrippsi* nests on the Channel Islands (CA) and is commonly seen in southern California waters during the nesting season (March through July). After nesting, Xantus' disperses northward, commonly as far as Monterey Bay (CA) where individuals are regularly seen from August through October pelagic trips. Some birds make it as far north as Washington where they are occasionally seen from fall boat trips. After October the birds have dispersed so much that they are only occasionally encountered. They are best seen from spring boat trips out of San Diego north to Santa Barbara. After that your best bet is Monterey Bay in August through October. The southern race (*hypoleuca*) nests on islands off Baja and is occasionally seen in California waters.

Craveri's Murrelet. Rare but regular post-breeding (August through October) visitor to the offshore waters of southern and central California (north to Monterey Bay). Nests on rocky islands off the coast of Baja. Somewhat irregular in its movements, which may be dependent on the movement of warm ocean currents north from Mexican waters. Your best chances for seeing this bird are from boats out of San Diego in August through September and boats out of Monterey in October.

Ancient Murrelet. Variably fairly common to uncommon winter resident of offshore waters along the West Coast south to central California (uncommon to rare along the southern CA coast). More common farther north. This bird arrives in Monterey Bay in early October and may stay until April. Peak numbers, which vary greatly between years, occur from November on through the winter. Occasionally seen from shore (via spotting scope) at coastal overlooks like Point Pinos (CA), Pigeon Point (CA), Point Roberts (WA), and Clover Point (Victoria Island, Vancouver, BC).

Cassin's Auklet. Common offshore resident along the entire West Coast (more common from Santa Barbara, California north). Nests on rocky islands and forages on the open ocean. Typically seen in the greatest numbers from August to April, when post-breeding birds flock together.

Rhinoceros Auklet. Common offshore resident from central California north along the West Coast. Away from the vicinity of breeding islands, it is most often encountered as a winter resident (October through April) often forming huge loose flocks at such places as Monterey Bay (CA). During these times they are easily seen on pelagic trips originating from most California ports (south to San Diego). They are uncommon north of California in winter, but are easy to see between April and October from shore. Look for them along the coast wherever alcids concentrate. They are also easily seen from the ferries that navigate the various inside passages of the Washington coast. Rhinos are never missed on Westport (WA) pelagic trips taken during April through October.

Tufted Puffin. Fairly common but local summer resident of rocky islands off the West Coast from Crescent City, California (uncommon breeder on California islands south to Anacapa Island, Ventura, CA). During the breeding season it forages in the vicinity of the nesting rocks (seldom seen away from these sites). After nesting, individuals disperse far out to sea and are seldom seen in winter. Check with coastal birders from Crescent City north for the location of current nest rocks. Otherwise, try Westport (WA) pelagic trips from May to October when the species is seldom missed.

California Condor. Extremely rare and endangered resident of the Los Padres National Forest of south central California. Perhaps as few as twenty birds remain. The traditional site for viewing the condors is Mount Pinos, which also provides good all-around birding. In recent years, other sites on the edge of the forest have proven more reliable, but there seems to be some yearly (and seasonal) variation as to which place is currently best. Check with the Los Angeles Audubon Society (headquartered in Plummer Park (213) 876-0202) for current information. The best spot in recent years has been the turn-out at the Los Padres National Forest Boundary Sign south of State Highway 166 in Kern County (west of Maricopa). Although the condors are resident, your best chance by far for seeing them is from late July to August. An annual condor watch/tequila bust is held on Mt. Pinos on the first weekend of August.

By the time the tequila is finished, almost everyone is sure to have seen a condor!

Black-shouldered Kite. Fairly common resident of brushy grasslands and agricultural areas in south Texas, central and coastal California, and coastal Oregon. Seems to be expanding its range. In Texas look for it around Brownsville, on the King Ranch, along Highway 281 west from Brownsville, and at Laguna Atascosa, and Santa Ana NWRs. In California this bird is probably seen most often from the various freeways when you are not even looking for it. For specific spots try the Tijuana River Valley, U.S. Highway 101 north of Santa Barbara, the Ventura River mouth, Los Carneros Rd. in Santa Barbara, Point Mugu, the Santa Clara River mouth, the floodplain west of the Sacramento River in Sacramento, and the Sacramento-San Joaquin drainage west of Stockton. In Oregon try the William L. Finley NWR near Corvallis.

Hook-billed Kite. Rare year-round visitor and sometimes resident of subtropical forests along the lower Rio Grande Valley of south Texas. The frequency and regularity of sightings have increased in recent years. The most consistent areas are Santa Ana NWR (Chinaberry to Diclyptera Trail), Bentsen SP, and the woodlands from Falcon Dam to the Santa Margarita Ranch. Your best bet is to check the Lower Valley RBA. These kites feed on tree snails, which tend to be distributed in patches. Once a kite discovers a productive feeding area, it often establishes definite foraging patterns (to the point of flying over precise stretches of park or refuge roads at roughly the same time every day). You would do well to note exact times and places of kite sightings that are passed along by other birders. (The groundskeeper at Bentsen is often helpful in this regard.)

Gray Hawk. Rare summer resident of riparian forest (consisting of cottonwoods, sycamores, and willows) at low elevations in southeastern Arizona. Most of the U.S. population is located along the Santa Cruz River and its tributaries, but almost everyone sees his or her first one at the Sonoita Creek Sanctuary at Patagonia. At least one pair of hawks is present in this general area every year, and they are fairly easy to find from April through September. Because of the rarity of this bird, please do not go near the nest or tarry long in the vicinity of an obviously agitated pair.

White-tailed Hawk. Uncommon resident of coastal prairies and grassy mesquite-live oak savannahs in south Texas. Some of the better places to look are along U.S. Highway 77 from Kingsville to Raymondville (King Ranch), the area on and around Aransas NWR, Attwater Prairie Chicken NWR near Eagle Lake and along State Highway 35 in Aransas and Refugio Counties.

Common Black-Hawk. Uncommon-to-rare summer resident (mid March to early October) of cottonwood-willow-sycamore forests along permanently flowing streams in southeast and central Arizona, southwest New Mexico, and the Davis Mountains of Texas (casual north to southern Utah). Occasionally seen in south Texas and at Big Bend NP in migration. The current Arizona hotspot is Aravaipa Canyon (north of Tucson). In New Mexico try along the Gila (at Redrock and Cliff), San Francisco, and Mimbres Rivers. The Texas population consists of one or two pairs that breed along Limpia Creek near Fort Davis. This bird does most of its hunting from branches overlooking the water. It is also not uncommon to find one either standing on a sandbar or actually wading through water as it searches for crayfish, frogs, and so forth. These hawks are very skittish around the nest, and extreme caution should be exercised to avoid disturbing nesting birds.

Harris Hawk. Locally common but decreasing resident of mesquite brushlands in south Texas, extreme southern New Mexico (uncommon), and south-central Arizona (uncommon). This hawk is much easier to find in Texas than in New Mexico or Arizona. You should have no trouble finding them at Santa Ana NWR, the King Ranch, around Falcon Dam, along Highway 83 west of Mission to Laredo, and between San Antonio and Laredo on State Highway 16 and U.S. Highway 59. Small numbers persist in patches along the river west almost to El Paso. In New Mexico try Rattlesnake Springs (Carlsbad Caverns NP), Harroun Lake (Eddy Cove), and U.S. Highway 80 between Road Forks and Rodeo (including the San Simon Cienaga). Arizona populations are centered around Tucson and the Papago Indian Reservation to the south and west. Here they are found in saguaro desert. There are no special spots, but try State Highway 86 from Tucson to Organ Pipe National Monument and the roads from Tucson to Aravaipa Canyon.

Zone-tailed Hawk. Uncommon-to-rare summer resident (late March through early October at the extremes) of steep-walled desert canyons, pine-oak-juniper covered mountains, and lush cottonwood and sycamore forests along streams over much of Arizona, New Mexico, west Texas, and the western Edwards Plateau of Texas. This bird is often found in the same habitats as the Common Black-Hawk, but is perhaps more typical of drier, more mountainous areas. In Texas try Lost Maples SP, Campwood Road (Ranch Rd. #337) out of Leaky (Edwards Plateau), McKittrick Canyon in Guadalupe Mountains NP, almost anywhere in the Davis Mountains, and along the Boot Springs Trail (near Pinnacle Pass) in Big Bend NP. (This is the best spot.) I've also had some luck from late March to early April in finding this bird below Falcon Dam (TX). In New Mexico try the area around Los Alamos; the Gila River at Redrock and Cliff; and the Guadalupe, Burro, and Peloncillo Mountains. Arizona spots worth checking are Guadalupe Canyon, Cave Creek Canyon to the Southwest Research Station (Chiricahua Mountains), the Pinaleno Mountains, Harshaw Canyon east of Patagonia and Madera Canyon (Santa Ritas).

Crested Caracara. Uncommon resident of mesquite brush country, coastal prairies, and grassy mesquite-live oak savannahs in south Texas and along the Texas coast to about Rockport (rare farther east). Also a rare resident of Saguaro desert and mesquite country in extreme south-central Arizona (Papago Indian Reservation to about Gila Bend). In Texas it is perhaps easiest to see near Freer, along State Highways 16 and 44 and along U.S. Highway 59. Try also along Highway 83 from San Ygnacio to Mission, around Falcon Dam, along Highway 77 through the King Ranch, and at Laguna Atascosa and Aransas NWRs.

Spruce Grouse. Uncommon-to-rare resident of montane spruce-fir forests in the Northwest (mainly Washington, Idaho, Montana) and of spruce bogs and jack-pine forests in northern Minnesota. Even in areas where this bird is fairly common it can be hard to find due to its protective coloring and quiet nature. Once found, you can often view these usually tame birds at leisure. They are most often seen along gravel roads at dawn or dusk, but may be glimpsed crossing trails or perched in trees. Some suggested spots include:

1. Washington (Wahl and Paulson 1977)—Methow Wildlife Recreation Area east of Winthrop, Sherman Pass on State Highway 20 in Ferry County, the Little Pend Oreille Wildlife Recreation Area (Stevens County), and Sullivan Lake and Calispell Peak (Pend Oreille Co.)
2. Idaho (Pettingill 1981)—St. Joe National Forest (check at National Forest Service Center in St. Maries for directions to the best spots)
3. Montana (Pettingill 1981)—Glacier NP (best along the trail to Avalancho Lake west of Logan Pass) and the forest around MacDonald Pass along U.S. Highway 12 west of Helena
4. Minnesota (Pettingill 1981)—Red Lake Wildlife Management Area (near Roosevelt), Itasca SP and the Superior National Forest (especially on National Forest Road #369 north from near Isabella).

White-tailed Ptarmigan. Fairly common but local resident of alpine tundra on high peaks throughout much of the Rockies, Cascades, and adjacent ranges. Even in areas where this bird is common it can be hard to find due to its protective coloring. They often respond well to tapes. Once found, they can often be approached to within a few feet. Most birders see their first one in Colorado, along Trail Ridge Road in Rocky Mountain N.P. (June is best, when males are most responsive to tapes). Other places include Mount Evans (west of Denver) above Summit Lake, Loveland Pass at the Summit of Highway 6 (near Dillon Reservoir), and Guanella Pass (out of Georgetown) around the summit parking lot. The latter location is the place to try in winter when other areas are closed. Outside of Colorado, try:

1. New Mexico—above timberline in the Sangre de Cristo Mts.
2. Wyoming (Pettingill 1981)—the Snowy Range of the Medicine Bow Mountains (west from Laramie on State Highway 130 then north to Brooklyn Lake and take the trail to Brooklyn Ridge—also Medicine Bow Peak).
3. Montana—Logan Pass in Glacier N.P.
4. Washington—Mount Rainier NP at the Chinook Pass Summit of State Highway 410 (east side) and Burroughs Mountain (reached from Sunrise), Slate Peak Lookout off Hart's Pass (State Highway 20), and on Mount Baker (west of Bellingham).

Greater Prairie Chicken. Rare and local resident of tall grass prairies in a narrow corridor of midwestern and Great Plains states from Minnesota to Texas. Best found on the display grounds in spring (March through June in the North, February through April in the South) when courtship activity is at its peak. Afterwards the birds disperse and are difficult to find. Booming activity typically begins shortly before dawn and continues for only a few hours. While at the display grounds you should *always* remain in your car to avoid disrupting the birds. Some of the better known areas are:

1. North Dakota—Sheyenne National Grasslands around McLeod
2. Minnesota—Rothsay Wildlife Management Area near Rothsay
3. Colorado—tall grass prairie in Yuma County
4. Missouri—Taberville Prairie Refuge and Schell Osage Wildlife Area near El Dorado Springs
5. Nebraska— (Pettingill 1981)—Valentine NWR and near Burwell (go north on State Highway 11 for 18.5 miles, then 0.5 mile west
6. Kansas (Pettingill 1981)—Flint Hills NWR and the Konza Prairie Research Natural Area near Manhatten (make prior arrangements through the Division of Biology office in Ackert Hall at Kansas State University in Manhatten)
7. Texas—Attwater Prairie Chicken NWR 6 miles northeast of Eagle Lake on Farm Road 3013 (write or call the refuge manager for information— Box 518, Eagle Lake, Texas 77434 or (713) 234-3021).

Lesser Prairie Chicken. Local, uncommon to rare resident of short grass prairie and sand-sage prairie with shinnery oak in the panhandle country of Texas and Oklahoma, eastern New Mexico, extreme southeastern Colorado, and southwestern Kansas. Best found on the display grounds March through May (April is usually best) when courtship activity is at its peak. The birds disperse for the rest of the year and are often hard to find. Even at the display grounds the birds are only found for an hour or two after dawn. When viewing dancing chickens you should always remain in your car to avoid scaring them from the lek. Some reliable areas include:

1. Oklahoma—Arnett (drive east—at dawn—on U.S. Highway 60 for one mile, then south on U.S. Highway 283 for several miles, taking any side roads and listening for chickens along the way)
2. Kansas—Cimmaron National Grasslands (pick up map and directions to observation blinds at the U.S. Forest Service HQ in Elkhart)
3. New Mexico—Caprock (40 miles east of Roswell on Highway 380 to a roadside rest stop on the right, then 1 to 5 miles north on the gravel road directly across from the rest stop), Milnesand area and around Elida (check with the state game and fish office in Roswell for directions at the latter two locales)
4. Colorado (Lane and Holt 1979)—Comanche National Grassland (8 miles east of Campo then 2 miles south, 4 miles east, and 1.3 miles south).

Sharp-tailed Grouse. Fairly common resident of grasslands, sagebrush prairies, and brushy forest edges over much of the northern Great Plains east into northern Minnesota. Best observed on leks from April to mid-June. Try:

1. Minnesota—Rice Lake and Agassiz NWRs
2. Nebraska (Pettingill 1981)—Fort Robinson SP, the Bessey Division of the Nebraska National Forest, and Crescent Lake and Valentine NWRs
3. North Dakota—the Badlands in and around both units of Theodore Roosevelt NP and on Chase Lake/Arrowwood, Long Lake, J. Clark Salyer, Lostwood, and Des Lacs NWRs
4. Wyoming (Pettingill 1981)—near Fort Phil Kearney
5. Montana—Medicine Lake and Bowdoin NWRs
6. Utah (Pettingill 1981)—the Cache Valley east of Wellsville.

Sage Grouse. Fairly common resident of sage brush-covered hills and flats over much of the western interior. Unlike other prairie grouse, this species is relatively easy to find away from the leks. The following spots are just a few of the reliable areas:

1. Wyoming (Pettingill 1981)—National Elk Refuge and near Eden and Farson on U.S. Highway 187 (36 and 40 miles north of Rock Springs)
2. Colorado—Arapaho NWR
3. California—Clear Lake NWR
4. Idaho (Pettingill 1981)—area surrounding Macon Lake (north of Shoshone)
5. Oregon—Malheur NWR and the road from Fort Rock to Fort Rock SP (Pettingill 1981)

6. North Dakota—U.S. Highway 12 west from Bowman (especially north and south of Marmarth)
7. Nevada—Ruby Lake NWR;
8. Montana—south of Miles City on U.S. Highway 312 (Pettingill 1981) and Bowdoin and Red Rock Lakes NWRs.

Montezuma Quail. Uncommon resident of grassy hill country forested with pines, oaks, and junipers. Found in west Texas, southern Arizona, and southern New Mexico. This bird is not easy to find. In fact, your first one will probably find you. The best technique is to drive very slowly along roads through appropriate habitat, keeping watch for quail on the shoulders. These birds do not flush unless nearly stepped on, and even then they tend to run swiftly into cover at the first opportunity. Some reliable areas include:

1. Texas—the campgrounds at Davis Mountain State Park, the scenic loop through the Davis Mountains (Highway 17 to 18 to 166), and the road to the McDonald Observatory
2. New Mexico—the Geronimo Trail through the Peloncillo Mountains
3. Arizona—the area around the Southwest Research Station and the road to Paradise (Chiricahua Mountains), lower Miller and Garden Canyons (Huachuca Mountains), Highway 82 between Patagonia and Nogales, the area around Pena Blanca Lake, and in the vicinity of the Appleton-Whidell Research Ranch at Elgin (call the manager at (605) 455-5522 for permission to visit).

Scaled Quail. Fairly common resident of arid hill country, shrub desert, desert grasslands, and grassy mesquite savannahs in west Texas, New Mexico, southeast Arizona, eastern Colorado, the Oklahoma panhandle, and southwest Kansas. It is not hard to find and is most often seen along roadsides in the early morning and late afternoon.

Gambel's Quail. Common resident of saguaro and shrub deserts and ambient irrigated agricultural brushlands and riparian thickets of mesquite, saltbush, and tamarisk. Found in southern and central Arizona, New Mexico, and Utah; extreme west Texas (Rio Grande Valley from Presidio to El Paso); the Mojave and Colorado Deserts of California; western Colorado; and extreme southern Nevada. This quail is more closely tied to water sources than is the Scaled Quail. It is normally seen along roadsides or desert arroyos in the early mornings and late afternoons. Not hard to find.

California Quail. Common resident of brushlands, riparian forests, foothills, chaparral, and even residential areas throughout California, Oregon, and Washington. Also found in portions of Nevada, Utah, and Idaho, where many populations are the result of stocking programs. Easy to find.

Mountain Quail. Fairly common but secretive resident of montane chaparral, dense brushy edges of montane coniferous forest, and mountain meadows bordered by conifer forest. Found in coastal ranges from BC to southern California, and in interior ranges (for example, Sierra Nevada) of California and western Nevada. Introduced in eastern Washington and Oregon, and in western Idaho. Although resident, birds tend to migrate locally to lower elevations. This bird is much shyer than other U.S. quail, so seeing them can be a problem. Males call from open perches (usually rocks), but the call is somewhat ventriloqual and therefore, hard to pin down. The best time to see them is in mid to late summer when they have young. At these times whole coveys can often be seen along mountain roads. Some of the better spots include:

1. California—the road to Mount Pinos; Palomar Mountain; Hurkey Creek Campground and the forest around Big Bear Lake in the San Bernadino Mountains; Placerita Canyon SP; Switzer Picnic Area; Charleton Flats, and Chilao Recreation Areas in the San Gabriel Mountains; brushy slopes above Yosemite Valley in Yosemite NP; Cuyamaca Rancho SP (near San Diego); La Cumbre Peak off San Marcos Pass (north of Santa Barbara); and the high country of Kings Canyon and Sequoia NPs
2. Nevada (Pettingill 1981)—Incline Village at the north end of Lake Tahoe
3. Oregon—William L. Finley NWR
4. Washington (Wahl and Paulson 1977)—between Lyle and Centerville (Klickitat County), and the W. T. Wooten Wildlife Recreation Area in the Blue Mountains of Columbia County.

Black Francolin. Introduced and locally common resident of farmlands in Cameron and Calcasieu Parishes in southwestern Louisiana. This bird is usually seen along roadsides perched on fence posts or low trees (like a Bobwhite). They are best located by driving appropriate backroads and listening for the distinctive raspy, mechanical calls of the males. Try any roads south of I-10 in the two parishes, but especially State Highway 108 (south of Vinton) towards Gum Cove Ferry.

Plain Chachalaca. Common but local permanent resident of subtropical woodlands in extreme south Texas. Easiest to find at Santa Ana NWR and Bentsen SP, where they are protected. Also common along the Rio Grande below Falcon Dam, but these birds are more wary, perhaps because of poaching. Their raucous dawn choruses are an unforgettable facet of any trip to "The Valley."

Red-billed Pigeon. Rare, year-round visitor to the lower Rio Grande Valley of south Texas. Easiest to find along the Rio Grande from San Ygnacio southeast to below Falcon Dam. Also seen occasionally at Santa Ana NWR and Bentsen SP. This bird will be seen either perched high in a tree top or flying overhead at fast speeds. For this reason it is preferable to search along the river banks where visibility is high. When birding through dense patches of forest growth your only likely views will be of a large dark bird flashing by overhead. From time to time south Texas birders locate large roosts where the birds can be seen at dawn and dusk. These are usually reported on the RBAs.

White-winged Dove. Locally common resident of deserts, residential areas, agricultural lands, and riparian forests in southern California, Arizona, New Mexico, and Texas. The White-winged Dove deserts lower Rio Grande Valley in winter, but is resident in the western portion of its range. Listen for its distinctive call, which resembles the "who-cooks-for-you" call of the Barred Owl. Easy to find at such places as Big Bend NP (TX), the lower Rio Grande Valley (TX–NM), and all of southern Arizona.

Spotted Dove. Introduced species now established and locally common in city parks, residential areas, agricultural lands, and eucalyptus groves in southern California. This bird is easy to find in these habitats throughout the San Diego, Los Angeles, Ventura, and Santa Barbara areas.

Common Ground-Dove. Locally common to rare resident of brushy thickets, woodlands, and agricultural areas of southern California, Arizona, New Mexico (rare), and Texas. Usually seen on the ground in thickets or at edges of clearings. The stubby tail gives it a sawed-off look in flight. Look for it along the Rio Grande Valley of TX (most common from Big Bend NP to Brownsville); Laguna Atascosa NWR (TX); the Sonoita Creek Sanctuary at Patagonia, Arizona, and the Imperial and Colorado River Valleys of southern California.

Inca Dove. Locally common resident of city parks, residential areas, agricultural lands, and other areas of human habitation in southern Arizona, southern New Mexico, and central and southern Texas (also found in California at a few spots along the Colorado River). It is also seen on lawns, at feeders, or roosting in small groups in trees in such cities as Tucson (AZ), Phoenix (AZ), Las Cruces (NM), El Paso (TX), San Antonio (TX), and Brownsville (TX).

White-tipped Dove. Locally common resident of the subtropical woodlands of the lower Rio Grande Valley of south Texas. Typically found in dense growth, where its ghostly call (much like the sound produced by blowing across the top of a bottle) is often heard, but the bird is seldom seen. When alarmed it usually drops to the ground and walks rapidly away. Easiest to see at Santa Ana NWR (particularly from the photo blind) and Bentsen SP, but present throughout the valley.

Elegant Trogon. Rare summer resident (some individuals occasionally winter) of low to middle elevation forests in the mountains of southeastern Arizona.

This bird probably also nests in the Animas Mountains of southwestern New Mexico, which are closed to public entry. Rare vagrant elsewhere in southern New Mexico and Texas. It seems to prefer dry, oak-covered hillsides and more mesic canyons with madrones, sycamores, and pines. Despite its bright colors, this bird can be difficult to find if it is not calling. The call is far-reaching, but often deceptively ventriloqual, and sounds like a cross between an oinking pig and a hen turkey. Most easily found in Cave Creek Canyon (Chiricahua Mountains), Ramsey Canyon (Huachuca Mountains), Madera Canyon (Santa Rita Mountains) and Sycamore Canyon.

Eared Trogon. Extremely rare summer to fall visitor to mountains of southeastern Arizona. In its native Mexico this species is a resident of pine-oak forests. Most U.S. records are from the middle and upper parts of the South Fork Trail in Cave Creek Canyon (Chiricahua Mountains). Check the Arizona RBA.

Groove-billed Ani. Locally common summer resident of subtropical forest and brushland in the lower Rio Grande Valley of south Texas. Some individuals winter as far up the Gulf Coast as Louisiana, but the species is typically difficult to find anywhere prior to April. Frequent vagrant outside of breeding range. Look for it at Santa Ana and Laguna Atascosa NWRs, Bentsen SP, and down-river from Falcon Dam. These birds are cooperative breeders and as such are often encountered in small groups.

Great Gray Owl. Rare and very local resident of boreal forest/spruce bogs along the United States–Canada border (mainly northern Minnesota) and of high-elevation fir forests in select western mountain ranges. It is more common in forests of northern Canada and Arkansas. The Great Gray Owl is seen most often by birders during irregular winter invasions into the northern-most tier of states. At these times individuals are often conspicuous and easy to find (check Minnesota RBAs particularly). During the breeding season it is most often found in fir forests bordering grassy meadows in Yosemite NP (check Tuolumne Meadows and around Bridalveil Creek Campground). This bird is also found around Fort Klamath (OR), particularly at dusk near the dump and cemetery along State Highway 62 (Ramsey 1978).

Spotted Owl. Uncommon-to-rare resident of montane (mostly) forests in the West, primarily in Arizona, New Mexico, California, Oregon, and Washington. In Oregon, Washington, and northern California it mostly occupies humid, old-growth conifer forests of fir, cedar, hemlock, and redwoods. In southern California and the Southwest it is more often found in steep, moist canyons bordered by drier live-oak and pine forests. Some of the better spots include:

1. California—the Switzer Picnic Area (San Gabriel Mountains), Yosemite Valley (Yosemite NP), Palomar Mountain (near San Diego), Redwood

NP, Nojoqui Falls County Park near Solvang, and along the trail to Alice Eastwood Camp in Muir Woods National Monument (near San Francisco)

2. Oregon (Ramsey 1978)—in suitable habitat in the coast ranges (especially southwest of Eugene near Alma) and on the west slopes of the Cascades

3. Washington (Wahl and Paulson 1977)—in Mount Rainier NP, along State Highway 20 near Rainy Pass, along trails from the Hoh Ranger Station (29 miles north of Kalaloch in Jefferson County), and along the Kulshan Cabin Trail (Mount Baker Area in Whatcom County—inquire at the Glacier Creek Ranger Station)

4. New Mexico—Pinos Altos Mountains (particularly Cherry Creek Canyon and around Lake Roberts) and the Guadalupe Mountains.

5. Texas—in Guadalupe Mountains, NP.

Most birders probably get their first Spotted Owl in Arizona, where suitable habitat is more limited and the canopies less closed. The easiest spot in recent years has been along the trail up Scheelite Canyon in the Huachucas. Try also in Cave Creek Canyon (Chiricahuas) and Madera Canyon (Santa Ritas).

Snowy Owl. Breeds in high arctic tundra of Canada and Alaska. Enters the area covered here mostly during irregular winters when it stages invasions that may bring individuals deep into the interior of the West. Some individuals reach Minnesota and the northern Great Plains every winter. When present, they are highly visible in open country as they perch on telephone poles, road signs, and in plowed fields during the day. Consistently found in winter around the harbor at Duluth, Minnesota.

Whiskered Screech-Owl. Locally common resident of oak and pine-oak woodlands from 3500 to 7000 feet in the mountains of southeastern Arizona. Typically found at higher elevations than sympatric populations of Western Screech-Owls. The Whiskered Screech Owl is strictly nocturnal. It readily responds to tape recordings of its calls, which may consist of a monotone series of hoots (similar to that of Western Screech but without the acceleration at the end) or a duet call similar in cadence to Morse code. Easiest to find in upper Cave Creek Canyon and along the road to the Southwest Research Station (Chiricahua Mountains), and in upper Madera Canyon (Santa Rita Mountains).

Flammulated Owl. Uncommon-to-common summer resident of pine and pine-oak forests of middle to high elevations in the Northwest, Southwest, southern Rockies, and Pacific Coast. Despite its abundance in some areas, it is still difficult to find due to its small size, nocturnal habits, and retiring nature.

Elf Owl. Locally common summer resident of saguaro deserts, subtropical forest-brushlands (south Texas), riparian cottonwood or sycamore forests, and low to middle elevation oak woodlands in southern Arizona, New Mexico, and Texas.

It barely reaches deserts of southeastern California. The Elf Owl nests in old woodpecker holes in saguaro cacti, trees, and telephone poles. Strictly crepuscular or nocturnal, it is best found by waiting at nest holes at dusk. Locations of these birds are often passed through local birding grapevines in southern Arizona and Texas. They are also easily located by their calls, which are reminiscent of the chattering laugh of a robin. Good locations are:

1. Arizona—Saguaro National Monument, lower Madera (Santa Ritas) and Cave Creek (Chiricahuas) Canyons, the village of Portal, and Guadalupe Canyon
2. New Mexico—the Peloncillo Mountains and along the Gila River, especially around Redrock
3. Texas—Rio Grande Village at Big Bend NP, and Bentsen SP.

Ferruginous Pygmy-Owl. Rare resident of (and visitor to) saguaro deserts in southern Arizona, and subtropical scrub woodlands in the lower Rio Grande Valley of south Texas. This bird is chiefly diurnal (but most active at dawn and dusk), and responds well to tape recordings or whistled imitations of its call (a rapid "toot-toot-toot . . ." repeated incessantly). Most birders find it as the result of a stake-out advertised on local RBAs. Fairly regular (but often very hard to find) at Organ Pipe National Monument (AZ), Tucson, and along the river immediately below Falcon Dam (TX).

Northern Pygmy-Owl. Uncommon but widespread resident of montane conifer and oak woodlands west of the Great Plains. Like the Ferruginous Pygmy-Owl, this species is chiefly diurnal and most active at dawn and dusk. It too responds well to tapes or imitations of its call (a series of paired toots, not as high nor as rapidly delivered as the call of the Ferruginous). It is often mobbed by smaller birds that will occasionally lead you to the owl.

Northern Hawk-Owl. Uncommon resident of boreal forests in Canada and Alaska. In the western United States they are found (with few exceptions) only in the spruce-bog country of northern Minnesota in winter, and even then, are absent some years. When present they are often easy to find because of their diurnal nature and habit of perching high atop conifers. Minnesota RBAs usually carry information concerning their whereabouts.

Boreal Owl. Rare and seldom seen resident of boreal forests, chiefly in Canada and Alaska. Isolated small populations have recently been found nesting at high elevations in Montana and Colorado, and in the Superior National Forest in Minnesota. It is normally found in the western United States only during winter invasions (which seemingly involve far fewer birds than the similar irruptions of Great Gray and Snowy Owls), when some individuals reach the northern tier of states (mainly Minnesota). Minnesota RBAs usually carry information concerning the whereabouts of any Boreals that are present.

Buff-collared Nightjar. Rare-and-local summer resident of desert canyons in southern Arizona. This bird tends not to call until the moon has risen above the canyon walls, at which time it may call continuously. Calling is also most frequent when the moon is full. This bird responds to tapes of its insect-like call. Most recent sightings have been from Arivaipa Canyon, but look also in Guadalupe and Chino Canyons.

Common Pauraque. Locally common resident in subtropical scrub forest and brushy thickets of agricultural areas in the lower Rio Grande Valley of south Texas, and along the lower Texas coast. It is strictly nocturnal or crepuscular, but can often be flushed from the ground during the day by walking through dense cover. Easily located by its call, an unmistakable "go-wheer" or "go-go-go wheer." Best seen by driving back roads at night and looking for the ghostly reflection of their eyes as they sit on or alongside the road. Easiest to find at Bentsen SP, but look also at Falcon Dam SP, below Falcon Dam, and at Santa Ana and Laguna Atascosa NWRs.

Lesser Nighthawk. Common summer resident of arid scrublands and deserts of the southwest from south Texas west to California. Easily seen along roadsides and over stockponds at dusk and around lights and on back roads at night. Where its range overlaps with that of the Common Nighthawk, this species occupies lower, more xeric habitats.

Black Swift. Uncommon-and-local summer resident of mountain areas at scattered localities across the West. The easiest way to find one is to stake out a colony nesting site (on cliff faces, usually behind waterfalls or overlooking the ocean) at dawn or dusk to catch the birds as they leave or return to their nests. In between, these birds scatter to often-distant foraging areas, where seeing them is much less certain. During the bouts of cool rainy weather that seem to persist in summer across much of the Northwest, Black Swifts can often be seen low over the ground in valley areas. Some of the better places include:

1. Colorado—Black Canyon in Gunnison National Monument (nests), Loch Vale in Rocky Mountains NP (nests), and the town of Ouray (common over the town in the early evening)
2. Montana—McDonald Valley in Glacier N.P.
3. California—Santa Anita Canyon in the San Gabriels (nests), Mill's Canyon in the San Bernardinos (nests), Bridalveil Falls in Yosemite NP (nests), and at falls in King's Canyon and Sequoia NPs

4. Washington (Wahl and Paulson 1977)—Hurricane Ridge in Olympic NP, Cape Flattery, the Skagit Valley, the area around Newhalem (common over town in early evening), Lake Wenatchee (Chelan County), and over Puget Sound.

Vaux's Swift. Fairly common resident of conifer and mixed forests near lakes and rivers in the Northwest. Unlike the Black Swift, it is frequently seen south of its nesting range during migration. Some good areas include:

1. California—Redwood NP
2. Montana (Pettingill 1981)—McDonald Valley in Glacier NP
3. Idaho (Pettingill 1981)—St. Joe National Forest (upper division at Avery)
4. Oregon (Pettingill 1981)—Fort Stevens and Saddle Mountain SPs
5. Washington (Wahl and Paulson 1981)—Hurricane Ridge Road and Deer Park in Olympic NP, Cape Flattery, Lake Hancock Road out of Snoqualmie, State Highway 20 between Rockport and Marblemount, Mount Rainier NP, Lake Wenatchee, and the Little Pond Oreille Wildlife Recreation Area (Stevens County).

Green Violet-ear. Extremely rare but semiannual summer visitor to feeders in the Austin, Texas area. Try the RBAs for Austin and the lower Rio Grande Valley.

Buff-bellied Hummingbird. Fairly common-to-uncommon resident of south Texas. Easiest to find at feeders in Brownsville and at flower gardens surrounding the headquarters at Santa Ana NWR, but look also at patches of tubular flowers (particularly tree tobacco) anywhere in the valley, and at live-oak mottes on the King Ranch.

Berylline Hummingbird. Very rare but semiannual visitor to southeastern Arizona. Most records are from the feeders at the Mile Hi Ranch in Ramsey Canyon (mid-to-late summer), but the species has bred near the Southwestern Research Station in the Chiricahua Mountains.

Lucifer Hummingbird. Uncommon summer resident of the Chisos Mountains in Big Bend NP (TX). Most often found after the beginning of June when agaves are blooming at the higher and middle elevations. Usually found along washes and canyons above the desert floor, which is left to the Black-chinned Hummingbird (Black-chins are also found in all areas occupied by Lucifers). Also a rare but regular summer visitor to southeastern Arizona (try feeders in Ramsey and Cave Creek Canyons) where it is typically listed on RBAs when present. May be a rare summer resident in the Chiricahua Mountains (AZ) and the Peloncillo Mountains (NM).

Broad-billed Hummingbird. Fairly common summer resident of oak woodlands, desert canyons, and low-elevation riparian forests in southeastern Arizona. Easy to find in Guadalupe Canyon, along the road through the Sonoita Creek Sanctuary, in lower Madera Canyon, and at the feeders in Ramsey Canyon. Not often seen in the Chiricahua Mountains. Occasional vagrant to Big Bend NP (TX) and the California coast.

White-eared Hummingbird. Rare summer visitor to the mountains of southeastern Arizona (and more rarely to the Chisos Mountains of Texas). Most often seen at feeders in Ramsey Canyon, but may occur more frequently in higher elevation pine forests where both feeders and observers are less common. Check the Arizona RBA.

Violet-crowned Hummingbird. Rare summer resident of desert-riparian forests and oak woodlands in southeastern Arizona and southwestern New Mexico. This bird is particularly keyed into sycamores. Most regular as a breeder in Guadalupe Canyon, where it is more common in the Arizona portion of the canyon. Usually not present until late May or early June. Also occurs as an annual mid-to-late summer vagrant to feeders throughout southeastern Arizona (particularly in Ramsey Canyon).

Blue-throated Hummingbird. Fairly common summer resident of forested canyons (usually along streams) in the Guadalupe and Chisos Mountains of west Texas and in several mountain ranges in southeast Arizona. This hummingbird is rare in southern New Mexico but easy to find in Cave Creek (Chiricahuas), Ramsey (Huachucas), and Madera (Santa Ritas) Canyons in Arizona, and at Boot Springs in Big Bend NP (TX). Males call loudly and repeatedly ("seep") from perches within tree canopies.

Magnificent Hummingbird. Uncommon to fairly common summer resident of forested mountain canyons in southeast Arizona, southern New Mexico, and the Guadalupe Mountains of west Texas. Easiest to see at feeders in Cave Creek (Chiricahuas), Ramsey (Huachucas), and Madera (Santa Ritas) Canyons in Arizona.

Plain-capped Starthroat. Very rare (less than annual) summer visitor to southeastern Arizona. It is certain to be reported on the Arizona RBA if present.

Costa's Hummingbird. Fairly common breeding bird of desert arroyos and coastal and low-mountain chaparral in southern California and Arizona. Nesting may commence as early as February and end by April in some areas (notably the eastern interior populations). Males often become hard to find later in spring and summer due to post-breeding dispersal. Annual but uncommon winter resident of extreme southern California coast and Colorado Desert region. Try:

1. Arizona (February to May is best)—the Arizona–Sonora Desert Museum outside Tucson, Organ Pipe National Monument, between Tucson and Gila Bend, and along the Colorado River
2. California—Balboa Park in San Diego, Palm Springs, Joshua Tree National Monument, the San Bernardino Mountains, the Tucker Wildlife Sanctuary in the Santa Ana Mountains, Los Angeles State and County Arboretum, Griffith Park (Los Angeles), and Placerita Canyon SP.

Anna's Hummingbird. Common resident of coastal lowlands from San Diego through Washington. There is some post-breeding dispersal into the mountains. This species has been steadily expanding its winter range in recent years and is now a regular winter visitor to feeders in Phoenix (AZ), Tucson (AZ), and El Paso (TX).

Rufous Hummingbird. Common summer resident of forests and meadows at all elevations in the Northwest. Migrates north along the coast in spring but returns south through central mountain ranges in midsummer through fall. At this time it becomes common in the Southwest where it is rarely seen in spring. The colorful males are the first to leave the breeding areas.

Allen's Hummingbird. Locally common summer resident of forests, brushlands, and residential areas of coastal California (barely into Oregon). A small population on the Palos Verdes Peninsula and nearby offshore islands in nonmigratory. Adult males (the only ones that can be safely identified) of migratory populations migrate south by midsummer. Try:

1. Averill Park, the South Coast Botanic Garden, and Point Fermin Park on the Palos Verdes Peninsula
2. Tucker Wildlife Sanctuary in the Santa Ana Mountains southeast of Los Angeles (write Star Route, Box 858, Orange, CA 92667), and Rocky Nook Park (Mission Canyon) in Santa Barbara
3. Folsom Lake State Recreation Area
4. Golden Gate Park in San Francisco
5. Charles Lee Tilden Regional Park (Berkeley), and Redwood NP.

Ringed Kingfisher. Uncommon but increasing resident along the Rio Grande and around associated resacas (isolated oxbows of the river) and ponds, from just north of San Ygnacio (TX) south to Brownsville. Easiest to find along the river immediately below Falcon Dam.

Green Kingfisher. Uncommon and local resident of banks along the Rio Grande from Del Rio, Texas south to Brownsville, and rare resident along streams and rivers from the Edwards Plateau country (TX) west to the Pecos River. The Green Kingfisher is easiest to find along the stretch of river immediately below Falcon Dam. There, it is best to look for it in the morning when low water levels expose numerous potential perches. This bird can be very secretive as it sits concealed along some shady bank.

Golden-fronted Woodpecker. Common resident of agricultural areas, mesquite brushlands, riparian forest, and subtropical scrubforest from southern Oklahoma through central Texas to the lower Rio Grande Valley. Frequently seen from the highways perched on telephone poles or palm trees. Nearly impossible to miss on a trip to south Texas, especially at such places as Bentsen SP, Santa Ana NWR, and below Falcon Dam.

Gila Woodpecker. Common resident of saguaro deserts and lowland riparian forests in the arid country of southeastern California, southern Arizona, and southwestern New Mexico. Easy to find in the Tucson vicinity (particularly around the Saguaro National Monument) at the Sonoita Creek Sanctuary (Patagonia), and in Guadalupe Canyon in Arizona; and along the Gila River near the towns of Cliff, Gila, and the settlement of Redrock in New Mexico. Harder to find in California, where it is restricted to the Colorado River Valley and a few spots around the Salton Sea.

Acorn Woodpecker. Locally common to abundant resident of oak and pine-oak woodlands and adjacent canyons in the mountain ranges of southwest Texas, southern New Mexico and Arizona, and throughout coastal California north into Oregon. This bird lives in social groups that are noisy and conspicuous in their behaviors. It is particularly easy to find in the oak woodlands of coastal central California, in any of the mountain ranges of southeastern Arizona or southwestern New Mexico, and in the vicinity of Boot Springs in Big Bend NP (TX).

White-headed Woodpecker. Fairly common-to-uncommon resident of pine and pine-fir forests (above 4000 feet) of California, western Nevada, Oregon, and Washington. Try:

1. California—Cuyamaca Rancho SP and Palomar Mount near San Diego; Hemet Lake near Palm Springs (Lane 1976); Hurkey Creek Campground (along Highway 74) and Humber park in the San Jacinto Mountains (Lane 1976); Grout Bay Campground near Big Bear Lake in the San Bernardinos (Lane 1976); McGill Campground (along the road to Mount Pinos) and the condor observation area of Mount Pinos; Charlton Flats and Chilao Campground in the San Gabriels; and Sequoia, Kings Canyon, Yosemite, and Lasser Volcanic NPs
2. Nevada—Incline Village at the north end of Lake Tahoe

3. Oregon (Pettingill 1981)—Cold Spring Campground off State Highway 242 and Indian Ford Campground off U.S. Highway 20 (both northwest of Bend), near Fort Klamath and Crater lake, and in the Ochoco National Forest

4. Washington (Wahl and Paulson 1977)—Lake Wenatchee, Entiat Valley 16 miles north of Wenatchee off U.S. Highway 2197, Chelan Butte Lookout near Chelan (off U.S. Highway 97), Brender Canyon (west from Cashmere in Chelan County), and the Methow River Valley near Twisp along State Highway 20 (Pettingill 1981).

Red-breasted Sapsucker. Fairly common resident of conifer and mixed woodlands of coastal and interior California, Oregon, and Washington. Often found in winter south of the normal breeding areas, or at least at lower elevations (most often in deciduous woodlands or orchards). Try:

1. California—McGill Campground on Mount Pinos; Chilao Recreation Area and Buckhorn Campground in the San Gabriels; and Yosemite, Kings Canyon, Sequoia, and Redwood NPs

2. Oregon (Pettingill 1981)—McDonald Forest northwest of Corvallis, Fort Klamath to Klamath Agency area, and the Gray Creek Swamp Loop on William L. Finley NWR south of Corvallis (Ramsey 1978)

3. Washington—the Kulshan Cabin Trail (Mount Baker) 7.5 miles past the ranger station on Glacier Creek Road.

Three-toed Woodpecker. Uncommon-to-rare resident of pine-fir forests in the Northwest, Rocky Mountains, and various ranges over most of the central and northern mountain states. Rare resident of and winter visitor to spruce bogs in northern Minnesota. This species is frequently found in loose colonies around burned-over areas of conifer forest. They are not particularly vocal, but may often be located by a stream of bark flakes fluttering down from the top of a tree. The Rocky Mountains subspecies lacks barring across the white of the back, and females may be easily passed off as Hairy Woodpeckers. Try:

1. Minnesota—Superior National Forest

2. South Dakota—Harney Peak and burn areas anywhere in the Black Hills

3. Wyoming (Pettingill 1981)—the Big Horn Mountains (Tic Flume and Dead Swede Campgrounds along U.S. Highway 14), Canyon Creek Rd. off U.S. Highway 16 (Big Horns), and the Medicine Bow Mountains

4. Montana (Pettingill 1981)—MacDonald Pass (west of Helena on U.S. Highway 12)

5. Idaho (Pettingill 1981)—upper division of St. Joe NF (east of St. Maries)

6. Utah—Mirror Lake

7. Colorado—Brainard Lake, Echo Lake Park, Grand Mesa, Rocky Mountain NP, along Michigan Creek near Jefferson (Lane and Holt 1979), and Deadman Lookout west of Fort Collins (Lane and Holt 1979)

8. New Mexico—Sandia Crest (above Albuquerque), Silver Creek Divide (Mogollon Mountains), and from Sandy Point to Hummingbird Saddle (Mogollon Mountains)

9. Oregon (Pettingill 1981)—Lost Lake Campgrounds (Santiam Pass) off U.S. Highway 20 and the Wallowa Mountains west and south of Enterprise

10. Washington (Wahl and Paulson 1977)—the Paysayten Wilderness (east side of the Cascades), the forest above Mill Creek Canyon in the Blue Mountains, and Chinook Pass Summit (east side of Mount Rainier NP).

Black-backed Woodpecker. Uncommon to rare resident of conifer forests in the northwest and Pacific Coast states. Rare resident of spruce bogs in northern Minnesota, where it is more common than the Three-toed. Often prefers burn areas in forests. Try:

1. Minnesota—Red Lake Wildlife Management Area, and the Superior National Forest (especially near Ely)

2. South Dakota—Spearfish Canyon, Jewel Cave National Monument, and burn areas anywhere in the Black Hills

3. Montana (Pettingill 1981)—trail to Avalanche Lake in Glacier NP, MacDonald Pass (U.S. Highway 12 west from Helena), and the University of Montana Biological Station at Yellow Bay on the east shore of Flathead Lake (east and north of Polson on State Highway 35)

4. Idaho (Pettingill 1981)—Upper Division of St. Joe National Forest

5. Nevada—Lehman Caves National Monument and Incline Village (north end of Lake Tahoe)

6. Oregon (Pettingill 1981)—vicinity of Lost Lake Campground on U.S. Highway 20 (near Santiam Pass), the Wallowa Mts. (west and south of Enterprise), the trail to Mount Scott (off Rim Drive) in Crater Lake NP, and Lodgepole pine forests around Davis Lake (Ramsey 1978)

7. California—Bridalveil Creek Campground in Yosemite NP

8. Washington (Wahl and Paulson 1977)—the Paysayten Wilderness Area and Trout Lake (Klickitat County).

Ledder-backed Woodpecker. Common resident of deserts, brushlands, lowland riparian woodlands, and low elevation oak forests in the southwest. It is easy to find from south Texas west to California (east of the Sierras).

Nuttall's Woodpecker. Fairly common resident of low to middle-elevation forests and chaparral covered slopes in western California. Most common in rolling, oak-covered hills. It often announces its presence with a loud, mechanical whinny that starts out as if the bird is cranking up an old engine. This sound is very different from anything uttered by the morphologically similar Ledder-backed Woodpecker. Try Old Mission Dam near San Diego; Griffith Park in Los Angeles; Big Sycamore Canyon in Point Mugu SP; Placerita Canyon SP,

Switzer Picnic Area and Charlton Flats in the San Gabriels; Tucker Wildlife Sanctuary and Irvine Park (both near Orange in the Santa Ana Mountains); Pfeiffer Big Sur SP; the Diablo Mountains south of Livermore along Mines Road; and Mount Diablo SP near Berkeley.

Strickland's Woodpecker. Fairly common resident of oak and pine-oak forests at low to middle elevations in southeastern Arizona and the Peloncillo Mountains of New Mexico. Calls include a sharp "peek" and a chatter, both of which are similar (but recognizably different with experience) to the similar calls issued by the more widespread Ladder-backed. Easy to find in Cave Creek Canyon (particularly around South Fork Campground) in the Chiricahua Mountains; Madera Canyon in the Santa Rita Mountains; and Ramsey, Miller, and Garden Canyons in the Huachuca Mountains.

Thick-billed Kingbird. Locally common summer resident of riparian sycamore forests in southeastern Arizona. Easily found in Guadalupe Canyon and along Sonoita Creek at Patagonia, but rare elsewhere.

Tropical Kingbird. Rare and local summer resident of lowland riparian areas in southeast Arizona. Most often found in the vicinity of Nogales and around small ponds between Nogales and Tucson. Also a regular fall vagrant along the West Coast (check local RBAs).

Couch's Kingbird. Fairly common summer resident (rare in winter) of the lower Rio Grande Valley of south Texas. This bird is easy to find below Falcon Dam, at Santa Ana NWR, at Bentsen SP, and in agricultural areas in between.

Scissor-tailed Flycatcher. Common summer resident of open and semi-open country in Texas, Oklahoma, Kansas, southern Nebraska, and western Arkansas and Louisiana. Nearly impossible to miss when driving cross-country for any distance through these areas.

Sulphur-bellied Flycatcher. Fairly common summer resident of sycamore and oak woodlands in the mountain canyons of southeast Arizona. Easy to find in Cave Creek Canyon (Chiricahua Mountains), Madera Canyon (Santa Rita Mountains), and Ramsey Canyon (Huachuca Mountains), among others. Their squeaky calls are often heard when the birds are concealed and motionless in the upper reaches of the canopy.

Great Kiskadee. Common resident of subtropical woodlands/brush near water in the Rio Grande Valley of south Texas (Laredo to Brownsville). This bird generally forages from branches overlooking the river or small ponds. It is easy to find around the various small lakes at Santa Ana NWR, along the river at

Bentsen SP, at almost any resaca (isolated oxbow of the river) in Brownsville, and along the river from Falcon Dam to Santa Margarita Ranch. Particularly common at San Ygnacio, both along the river and around town (especially at the small city park).

Brown-crested Flycatcher. Fairly common but local summer resident of riparian cottonwood-sycamore (and oak-sycamore) woodlands and saguaro deserts in southern Arizona and southwest New Mexico, and of subtropical mesquite wood-lands in south Texas. Less common along the Colorado River and in Morongo Valley (California). This *Myiarchus* is more restricted to areas with large trees (or at least tall cactus) than is the Ash-throated. Easy to find at the Saguaro National Monument/Desert Museum, and in Guadalupe, Cave Creek, and lower Madera Canyons in Arizona; and at Santa Ana NWR, Bentsen SP, and below Falcon Dam in Texas. In New Mexico look along the Gila and San Francisco Rivers (particularly at Redrock), but this species is less common there than in Arizona or Texas.

Dusky capped Flycatcher. Common summer resident of live-oak mountain woodlands (as well as pine-oak woodlands and streamside oak-sycamore associa-tions) in southeast Arizona and extreme southwest New Mexico. Generally occurs in higher elevation, drier forests than the Brown-crested and Ash-throated, but it is found in a few lowland riparian forests. Listen for its mournful, whistled "peeur" at such Arizona spots as Cave Creek, Ramsey, Madera, Garden, Miller, and Guadalupe Canyons; and along Sonoita Creek at Patagonia. In New Mexico it is found only in Guadalupe Canyon, the Peloncillo Mountains, and the Animas Mountains.

Greater Pewee. Uncommon summer resident of pine and pine-oak forests at higher elevations in central and southeast Arizona (irregular in New Mexico). Best located by listening for its unique whistled "ho-say-ma-ria" song. The easiest places to find it are in Rustler Park along the Barfoot Trail (Chiricahuas) and in Sawmill Canyon (Huachucas). Try also along the upper reaches of Miller Canyon; Mount Lemmon; and the Bog Springs, Mount Wrightson, and Jose-phine Saddle trails in Madera Canyon.

Vermilion Flycatcher. Fairly common but local summer resident of desert and other arid-lands watercourses in southwestern Utah, southeastern California, Arizona, New Mexico, and west and central Texas south to the lower Gulf Coast. It winters in the southern portion of its U.S. range, and there is even a certain amount of northward dispersal in winter. The Vermilion Flycatcher prefers willow or mesquite-lined ponds and cottonwood-willow-sycamore riparian forest. It is easy to find in Arizona along Sonoita Creek at Patagonia, along the Santa Cruz River, in Sabino Canyon (Santa Catalinas) and in Guadalupe

Canyon. In New Mexico try the Gila River at Redrock and Rattlesnake Springs near Carlsbad Caverns. In Texas it is easiest at Rio Grande Village in Big Bend NP, but try also along the Guadalupe River and the Rio Frio of the hill country.

Buff-breasted Flycatcher. Rare and local summer resident of pine-oak forests in the Huachuca and Chiricahua (irregularly) Mountains of Arizona, and the Animas Mountains of New Mexico. By far the best place to see them is in Sawmill Canyon (at the end of the Garden Canyon road in Fort Huachuca) in the Huachuca Mountains. This spot is both accessible and dependable. Scotia and upper Carr Canyons (Huachucas) often have Buff-breasteds but are much harder to get to. Occasionally found in oaks near the Southwest Research Station, or in the pines at Rustler Park (Chiricahuas).

Northern Beardless Tyrannulet. Uncommon and local summer resident of mesquite, willow, and cottonwood-lined watercourses in southeast Arizona and of subtropical mesquite woodlands along the Rio Grande of extreme southern Texas. Some Arizona birds winter (perhaps more than is known due to the inconspicuous appearance and nature of the bird). This nondescript bird is often overlooked, and is best found by listening for its loud, descending "ee-ee-ee . . ." song. Easier to find in Arizona, where it should be looked for along the Santa Cruz and San Pedro Rivers and in Guadalupe Canyon.

Rose-throated Becard. A locally uncommon to rare summer resident of riparian woodlands in southeast Arizona. These birds seem to prefer areas with large cottonwoods and/or sycamores, from which they suspend their football-sized nests. The most consistent spot has been along Sonoita Creek from the Circle Z Guest Ranch to the Sonoita Creek Sanctuary. In some years this species is fairly common in Sycamore Canyon (west of Nogales). Occasionally found in the lower Rio Grande Valley of south Texas, where it has nested in past years.

Eurasian Skylark. An introduced resident of Vancouver Island and the San Juan Islands, where it is locally common in open fields. The airport on Vancouver Island has been a traditional location, but you would do best to check with local birders for current spots. An individual of the Asian subspecies has shown up at Point Reyes, California for several consecutive winters (check the Bay Area RBA).

Cave Swallow. Common but local summer resident of south, central, and west Texas, and of Carlsbad Caverns (NM). Once restricted to caves and sink-holes in the Edwards Plateau region, this bird has in recent years made major range expansions in nearly every direction by nesting in highway culverts. It is now common near Uvalde and Fort Stockton, and is being seen regularly west to El Paso. It returns much earlier (by early March) in spring than does the Cliff Swallow.

Gray-breasted Jay. Common and conspicuous resident of pine-oak woodlands (and often adjacent riparian growth) in the mountains of the Southwest. Travels in noisy groups the year around. Easy to find in the Santa Rita, Huachuca, and Chiricahua ranges of Arizona; the Pinos Altos and Burro Ranges of New Mexico; and the Chisos Mountains of Big Bend NP, Texas.

Brown Jay. Uncommon and local resident of subtropical mesquite woodlands in the lower Rio Grande Valley of south Texas. At present they are basically restricted to a several mile stretch below Falcon Dam. They are often best located by their calls, which sound similar to the screams of a Red-shouldered Hawk. They can also be lured in by a tape of a Great Horned Owl.

Green Jay. Common resident of subtropical woodlands in the lower Rio Grande Valley of south Texas. Conspicuous and easy to see at Santa Ana NWR, Bentsen SP, the area below Falcon Dam, and along the river west to San Ygnacio. Easiest to see well from the photo blind at Santa Ana.

Yellow-billed Magpie. Locally common resident of rolling foothills and valleys in central California. Usually found in oaks or riparian vegetation, but also commonly seen in agricultural areas. Particularly easy to find around the town of Solvang (north of Santa Barbara).

Mexican Crow. Common, but highly localized winter resident around Brownsville, Texas. The Mexican Crow is easiest to find at the Brownsville Dump where large numbers are present from November through March.

Northwestern Crow. The taxonomic status of this bird is in doubt. Many people consider it to be a subspecies of the American Crow. At present "pure" birds seem to be common coastal residents from Vancouver, British Columbia, north. Intergrades are more common to the south, and in Washington, only birds within the immediate vicinity of the coast are likely to be Northwesterns.

Chihuahuan Raven. Common resident of southwestern deserts and grasslands (migratory in northern portion of its range). In many areas (for example, southern New Mexico) it replaces the more montane Northern Raven in most low elevation habitats (often sharing agricultural river valleys with American Crows). In other areas (for example, southeast Arizona, Trans-Pecos Texas), both ravens are found at low elevations, but the Chihuahuan is more typical of desert-grasslands, while the Northern occupies purer shrub deserts.

Wrentit. Common resident of chaparral-covered slopes from southern California into Oregon. Less common in streamside thickets and brushy openings in conifer forests. Its rattly, accelerating song is often heard in appropriate habitat, but the bird itself can be maddeningly hard to see well. Often responds well to "pishing." Try:

1. California—Palomar Mountain (near San Diego); Border Field SP (Tiajuana River Valley) in San Diego; Torrey Pines SP (La Jolla); Silverwood Sanctuary (Wildcat Canyon northeast of San Diego); Big Sycamore Canyon in Point Mugu SP; Griffith Park (Los Angeles); Placerita Canyon SP, Switzer Picnic Area, and Chilao Campgrounds in the San Gabriels; Mission Canyon in Santa Barbara; Folsom Lake State Recreation Area; Castle Rock SP (Santa Cruz Cove); and Charles Lee Tilder Regional Park (Berkeley)
2. Oregon (Pettingill 1981)—Fort Stevens SP (near Astoria), Harris Beach SP (2 miles north of Brookings on U.S. Highway 101), and Yaquina Bay SP (Newport).

Bridled Titmouse. Common resident of oak-juniper montane woodlands, and sycamore-cottonwood riparian forests in southeast Arizona and southwest New Mexico. This bird is easy to find at lower and middle elevations in the canyons of the Chiricahuas, Santa Ritas, Santa Catalinas, and Huachucas (AZ). It is also found along Sonoita Creek at Patagonia, and in New Mexico along the Gila River and in adjacent foothills.

Mexican Chickadee. Uncommon and local resident of pine-oak and pine-fir forest at high elevations in the Chiricahua Mountains of Arizona and the inaccessible Animas Mountains of New Mexico. The best areas in the Chiricahuas are just above and below Onion Saddle and at Rustler Park along the Barfoot Trail. After breeding, many individuals wander to lower elevations (for example, South Fork of Cave Creek Canyon). Occasionally found in the Peloncillo Mountains (AZ/NM) in winter. Often responds well to Northern Pygmy-Owl tapes.

Chestnut-backed Chickadee. Common resident of northwestern old-growth conifer forests from San Luis Obispo (CA) north to Alaska. Typically found closer to the coast and at lower elevations than the Mountain Chickadee. It is also found in streamside willow thickets and eucalyptus groves. *The* chickadee of the coastal redwood forests.

Verdin. Common resident of southwestern shrub deserts and ambient riparian stands of mesquite and tamarisk. In Chihuahuan Desert of New Mexico and Texas it is best searched for in arroyos, where the larger shrubs/trees provide more potential nest sites. It is easily located by its calls, a rapid series of sharp chips, and a whistled "tee-tee-tee."

Black-capped Gnatcatcher. Extremely rare and localized summer resident of southeast Arizona, and occasional visitor there. Virtually all recent records have come from Chino Canyon in the Santa Ritas where a pair has produced multiple broods yearly since 1981.

Black-tailed Gnatcatcher. Uncommon resident of desert scrub and ambient riparian groves of saltbush, mesquite, and tamarisk in the extreme Southwest. It is also found in coastal chaparral of southern California and can be easily found in desert washes and at Rio Grande Village at Big Bend NP (TX), at Chino Canyon and Florida Wash (Santa Ritas) in Arizona, and in the dense saltbush/tamarisk stands bordering the Salton Sea (CA).

Varied Thrush. Common (but often hard-to-see) resident of northwestern conifer forest from northern California north. Winters in irregular numbers well south of breeding range in California, and individuals are frequent winter vagrants east to the Great Lakes. Most common in old-growth, coastal rain forest (particularly common in coastal redwoods), but also found at higher elevations in subalpine fir forest.

Rufous-backed Robin. Extremely rare and irregular winter visitor to lowlands and residential areas in southern Arizona and California. Somewhat cyclic in its movements, it is absent from the U.S. most years. Stake-outs are always reported on local RBAs.

Clay-colored Robin. Very rare winter visitor to the lower Rio Grande Valley of south Texas, where individuals have occurred at all of the major birding locations. A pair nested in Brownsville in 1983. Like other robins, it is most likely to be found around fruit-bearing shrubs or trees. This species is often extremely shy and may be best located by its call—a mellow whistle similar in nature to that of a Phainopepla. Your best chance is to check local RBAs.

Aztec Thrush. Extremely rare post-breeding visitor from western Mexico to southeast Arizona and Big Bend NP (TX). Typically found in forested mountain canyons (existing records from Madera and Huachuca Canyons in Arizona, and Boot Canyon in Big Bend) between June and August. Within its normal range it is often found gleaning bagworms from madrone trees. It is sure to be mentioned on RBAs.

Long-billed Thrasher. Common resident of subtropical forest and mesquite brushlands in the lower Rio Grande Valley of south Texas. This bird is easy to find from San Ygnacio to Brownsville (including at Falcon Dam, Bentsen SP, and Santa Ana NWR) and locally up the coast (for example, Laguna Atascosa NWR) for several miles.

Curve-billed Thrasher. Common but irregularly-distributed resident of deserts, grasslands, foothills, and agricultural brushlands in the Southwest. Common in the mesquite grasslands of south Texas, but farther west it is intimately tied to cholla cactus in which it often nests. Where such cactus is abundant (as in the Sonoran Desert of Arizona, the mesa grasslands of central NM, and the desert-grasslands surrounding the Guadalupe Mountains of west TX/ southern NM) this thrasher is a conspicuous resident. Adjacent arid lands that lack cholla (for example, much of the Chihuahuan Desert of west Texas and southern New Mexico) typically host Curve-billeds in winter, but lack breeding birds. Easiest to see around Tucson, Arizona.

Bendire's Thrasher. Fairly common to uncommon summer resident of open deserts and agricultural brushlands in the Southwest. Its center of abundance is Arizona, where it tends to inhabit somewhat sparser shrub desert than does the Curve-billed. In the Mojave Desert of California it is often found in Joshua Tree forest. This species is highly migratory (a small population in south-central Arizona is resident), with birds arriving in Arizona by February. They are easiest to find from February through April, when song activity is at its peak. Most breeding areas are deserted from September through January. Check appropriate habitat between Tucson and Phoenix and around Rodeo, New Mexico.

Crissal Thrasher. Fairly common resident of desert washes, riparian stands of saltbush, mesquite, and tamarisk; and low mountain chaparral in Arizona, New Mexico, west Texas, southeast California, and extreme southern Nevada and Utah. Widespread but secretive, and often hard to find. Look for it in Big Bend NP (TX), the Colorado River Valley (CA, AZ), and in the Santa Cruz River Valley (AZ). It is probably most easily found along the Rio Grande (and in adjacent shrub deserts and desert-grasslands) from El Paso, Texas to Socorro, New Mexico. This species begins nesting very early (January through February) and may exhibit somewhat of a bimodal reproductive pattern, with a first nesting completed by late March, followed by a break until the midsummer rainy season when they nest again. In between they are typically unresponsive to taped calls.

Le Conte's Thrasher. Uncommon and local resident of the sparse shrub deserts of southeast California, southwest Arizona, southern Nevada, and the San Joaquin Valley (CA). In the latter locale it inhabits open saltbush desert. Elsewhere it can be found either in open stands of saltbush or creosote. Like other desert thrashers, this one begins singing very early in spring and is easiest to find prior to April. It is extremely shy and is given to running along sandy washes with its tail cocked high. Oddly enough, most people find their first one among the disjunct San Joaquin Valley population around the tiny town of Maricopa (Kern County).

California Thrasher. Common resident of chaparral-covered hills and streamside thickets along the southern three-quarters of coastal California. Often hard to see well because of its shy nature, but not hard to find in appropriate habitat near such population centers as San Diego, Los Angeles, and Santa Barbara. This bird can be found at all of the California locations listed for Wrentit and may also be seen rather easily at the campgrounds in Leo Carillo SP.

Sprague's Pipit. Fairly common but somewhat local summer resident of mixed-grass prairies in North Dakota, Montana, northwest South Dakota, and the prairie provinces of Canada. Found both in typical mixed-species, medium-height grassland, and in the grassy meadows bordering alkaline lakes. The latter areas often harbor very high densities of pipits. Some better known sites are Des Lacs, J. Clark Salyer, and Arrowwood/Chase Lake NWRs in North Dakota; and Bowdoin and Medicine Lake NWRs in Montana. The species winters locally in the grasslands of extreme southern Arizona (for example, San Rafael Valley) and New Mexico (Animas Valley); in grassy pastures, meadows, fallow fields, and alfalfa fields from central Texas to Arizona and Louisiana; and in coastal grassland from Louisiana south to Laguna Atascosa NWR (TX).

Red-throated Pipit. Very rare fall vagrant along the West Coast. Most records are from California, and are concentrated in late October and early November. However, it is not recorded every year. If present, it is certain to be mentioned in RBAs.

Phainopepla. Fairly common resident of riparian forests/mesquite groves, and oak-juniper foothill forests in the desert Southwest and coastal southern California. This species is very unusual in that birds from some desert populations have been shown to nest early in spring and then migrate west toward the coast for a second nesting. Likewise, many individuals move altitudinally (up-slope) after their first nesting. This species is strongly tied to mistletoe, which in Texas and New Mexico is most commonly found as a parasite of oaks and cottonwoods, and which in Arizona commonly parasitizes palo verde and mesquite. Especially easy to find in the Sonoran Desert and ambient riparian woodlands of southeast Arizona (for example, Aravaipa and Guadalupe Canyons, Patagonia area).

Crested Myna. Locally common introduced resident of Vancouver, British Columbia, where it is best seen by cruising residential areas and fast-food restaurant parking lots.

Black-capped Vireo. Uncommon and local summer resident of scrub-oak and juniper forests in the plateau country of central Texas and Oklahoma. This bird is very elusive, and although it is often quite vocal, it can be extremely difficult to see well in the dense oak thickets. Popular areas for finding it in Texas include Lake City Park in Austin, Neal's Lodge near Concan, Johnson Canyon (12 miles south of Kerville on Highway 16), Perdenales Falls State Park, and the Lost Maples State Natural Area. This bird arrives in late March to early April, three to four weeks later than its fellow "hill country" specialty— the Golden-cheeked Warbler.

Gray Vireo. Uncommon summer resident of arid hillsides and canyons from Colorado and Utah south. This bird is found in a variety of dry, open or semi-open wooded habitats, ranging from live-oak forests to xeric, mesquite and juniper-spotted hills and mesas. However, it is probably most closely associated with pinyon-juniper forest. Some favored locales include Zion National Park (UT), the Window Trail in Big Bend NP (TX), and the Guadalupe Mountains (particularly near the entrance to McKittrick Canyon) of TX–NM.

Virginia's Warbler. Common summer resident of brushy slopes (primarily transition zone to 8000 to 9000 feet) from the Great Basin southward. This bird is most common in areas where deciduous oak thickets (such as Gambel's) grow among live-oak and pinyon-juniper and pine.

Colima Warbler. Locally common summer resident of oak woodlands in a small portion of the Chisos Mountains of Big Bend NP (TX). This bird is found nowhere else in the United States. The bulk of the population is found in Boot Canyon and along its drainages, where Arizona cypress and maples interface with junipers and live oaks. To be assured of finding this bird, you must hike the 5.5-mile one-way trail to Boot Springs which takes off from the parking lot in the Chisos Basin. The birds are easiest to find in April and May when singing is at its peak, but with patience they can still be found through August. After nesting they are nonvocal, but can still be located by their sharp chip notes (similar to those of Virginia's Warbler).

Lucy's Warbler. Common summer resident of southwestern riparian forests and ambient mesquite and/or tamarisk thickets. Also found in the densely vegetated Sonoran Desert of southeast Arizona, particularly along arroyos. This bird is nearly impossible to miss at such locales as Guadalupe Canyon (AZ–NM), the lower Gila River (NM), the San Simon Cienega (NM–AZ), and the Sonoita Creek Sanctuary (AZ).

Tropical Parula. Very rare resident of subtropical forest and live-oak mottes in the lower Rio Grande Valley of south Texas. For several years in the 1970s scattered pairs were found in the groves of live oaks adjacent to roadside rest stops along Highway 77 on the King Ranch (most consistently at the first rest stop south of Sarita). More recently sightings have come from scattered locales in the valley, particularly from Santa Ana NWR.

Townsend's Warbler. Fairly common summer resident of conifer forests from Oregon to Alaska. Breeds in much the same type of forest as does the Hermit Warbler (whose range it extensively overlaps and with which it often hybridizes), but also shows a tolerance for drier conifer forests that are generally avoided by that species. Townsend's also breeds farther east (well into Montana) and is a generally more common and widespread migrant across most of the west than is the Hermit. Migrants are commonly seen at low elevations (even in the deserts), and good numbers winter along the California coast.

Hermit Warbler. Fairly common summer resident of moist, old-growth conifer forests along the coasts of Oregon, Washington, and northern California. The Hermit Warbler also breeds in some drier interior mountain ranges such as the Sierras in California. It migrates south very early in fall and can actually be common in the Arizona mountains in early August. Migrants also appear in the lowlands, and individuals winter along the southern two-thirds of California coastline.

Golden-cheeked Warbler. Fairly common but local summer resident of juniper woodlands and the hilly Edwards Plateau region of central Texas (which harbors the entire world's breeding population). Returns early in spring (first week of March) and is fairly easy to find until mid-June, by which time song activity has dropped off tremendously. Even singing birds can be difficult to see well, given the low fairly-closed canopy of the juniper-covered hillsides. The buzzy song is reminiscent of that of the Black-throated Green Warbler. Favored locales include Lake City Park (Austin); Friedrich Park (San Antonio); Perdenales Falls, Garner, and Lost Maples SPs; and in Johnson Canyon south of Kerrville. Check with Austin or San Antonio birders for directions to current Golden-cheek hot spots.

Grace's Warbler. Fairly common summer resident of conifer forests from southern Colorado and Utah south through Arizona and New Mexico. Also breeds in the Guadalupe Mountains of west Texas. This bird is closely tied to ponderosa pines. In the lower mountain ranges where live oaks predominate, Grace's Warblers are found only where pockets of ponderosa pines exist. In pure stands of pine forest in Arizona and New Mexico, Grace's is often the most common breeding bird. They are also found at high elevations where firs interdigitate with the pines. Easily found in such places as McKittrick Canyon (Guadalupe Mountains, Texas), Rustler Park (Chiricahua Mountains, Arizona), Sawmill Canyon (Huachuca Mountains, Arizona), and Cherry Creek Canyon (Pinos Altos Mountains, New Mexico).

Painted Redstart. Fairly common summer resident of pine-oak forests in the mountains of southern Arizona and New Mexico. A few usually nest in Boot Canyon in the Chisos Mountains of Big Bend NP (TX) as well. It seems to be particularly partial to canyons with streams. Easy to find in Cave Creek, Madera, Ramsey, Miller, and Garden Canyons in Arizona; in Cherry Creek Canyon in New Mexico; and in most years, at Boot Springs in Big Bend NP (TX).

Red-faced Warbler. Fairly common summer resident of conifer and mixed forests in the mountain ranges of central and southern Arizona and southwestern New Mexico. Seldom found in pure stands of pine, it is more common at higher elevations where fir and/or spruce are also present. However, it is often found lower, in areas dominated by live oaks. When searching the high country, pay special attention to the draws, where fingers of Gambel's oak (a deciduous species) run through otherwise pure conifer forest. These are often the best places for Red-faced Warblers. Reliable spots include Cherry Creek Canyon (Pinos Altos Mountains, New Mexico); Iron Creek Campground (Black Range, New Mexico); Rustler Park (Barfoot Trail), Onion Saddle, and Pinery Canyon (Chiricahua Mountains, Arizona); Mount Wrightson Trail in Madera Canyon (Santa Rita Mountains, Arizona); and upper Miller and Sawmill Canyons (Huachuca Mountains, Arizona).

Olive Warbler. Uncommon and local summer resident of high mountain (7000+ feet) conifer forests in southeastern Arizona and southwestern New Mexico. Often seen at lower elevations in late fall and even winter. This bird shuns the pure stands of ponderosa pine for higher elevations where Douglas Fir, White Fir, and even Blue Spruce occur with the pines. It typically forages somewhat high in the trees. Males sing a loud "wheeta wheeta wheeta," whereas individuals of both sexes and all ages utter mellow, short whistles that are reminiscent of bluebird contact notes. Responds well to tapes of Northern Pygmy-Owl. The best place to find it is along the Barfoot Trail in Rustler Park (Chiricahua Mountains, Arizona). Other locations include Mount Lemmon (Santa Catalina Mountains, Arizona), the Mount Wrightson Trail in Madera Canyon (Santa Rita Mountains, Arizona), Emory Pass (Black Range, NM), and the road to Signal Peak (Pinos Altos Mountains, NM).

Pyrrhuloxia. Fairly common resident of thorn-scrub deserts and adjacent riparian and agricultural lands in southeastern Arizona, southern New Mexico, and southern and western Texas. Within its range the species has a somewhat spotty breeding distribution. There are areas in southwestern New Mexico, extreme west Texas, and extreme southeastern Arizona where this bird is abundant in winter but only a rare breeder. In winter it occurs in groups (often numbering ten to twenty birds). Within its range it is easy to find almost anywhere where either mesquite or acacia is found.

Varied Bunting. Uncommon and local summer resident of thorn-scrub desert in southern Arizona and New Mexico, and along the Rio Grande Valley of Texas. This bird is often found near water and is almost always found in either canyons or arroyos. Family groups often congregate in weedy patches or in fruit-bearing desert hackberry trees. Easiest to locate when the males are singing early in the morning. Reliable locations include Chino Canyon and Florida Wash (Santa Rita Mountains, Arizona), Guadalupe Canyon (NM–AZ), hills above the roadside rest stop near Patagonia (AZ), and the Window Trail and the Old Ranch at Big Bend NP (TX).

Olive Sparrow. Common resident of subtropical forest and thornscrub in the lower Rio Grande Valley of south Texas (Del Rio to Brownsville) and northeast along the lower Texas coast. Its loud song (a series of sharp chips, starting slowly then accelerating as if a marble had been dropped on a hard floor) is easily heard, but the bird is difficult to see as it scoots along the ground through the dense brush. Often responds well to a tape of its song. Look for it at San Ygnacio, below Falcon Dam, the Santa Margarita Ranch, at Bentsen SP, at Santa Ana NWR, and at Laguna Atascosa NWR (along the wooded nature trails). One of the best places is the photo blind at Santa Ana, where the sparrows come into the open to feed on seeds.

Abert's Towhee. Locally common resident of desert riparian habitat with dense cover in Arizona, southwestern New Mexico, southeastern California, southwestern Utah, and extreme southern Nevada. This species is perhaps most commonly found in cottonwood/willow/mesquite associations along the major river systems of the Southwest. It is also found in riparian habitat dominated by tamarisk and saltbush and in such places as Phoenix it is even found in agricultural and residential areas. This bird is often shy and given to hiding in streamside thickets, but it is still easily found in appropriate habitat along the Gila, San Pedro, Santa Cruz, and Colorado Rivers in Arizona; along the Gila River near Redrock in New Mexico; and around the Salton Sea in California.

Brown Towhee. Common resident of desert canyons and mountains in the Southwest; and of chaparral, oak-woodlands, and residential areas along the coast of California and southern Oregon. The coastal and interior populations are racially distinct. Coastal birds are easily found in chaparral, but are perhaps most easily found in wooded residential areas along the California coast. Interior birds tend to occupy elevations intermediate between the lowland desert-riparian areas favored by Abert's Towhees, and the higher, more wooded conifer forests preferred by the Rufous-sided. Arid canyons, arroyos, and hillsides, as well as brushy, middle elevation slopes dominated by live oak, juniper, and/or pine are all acceptable habitat.

Baird's Sparrow. Uncommon and somewhat local summer resident of mixed-grass prairies and weedy fields in the Dakotas, Montana and the prairie provinces of Canada. Uncommon to rare winter resident of grasslands in southeast Arizona (particularly around Sonoita and Patagonia-Nogales) and Big Bend N.P., Texas (road to Castolon). This bird arrives rather late on the breeding grounds (late May—migrants are still coming through southern Arizona in mid-April), and is best seen during June and early July when song activity is still high. Look for it at Fox Lake and Bowdoin, Benton Lake, and Medicine Lake NWRs in Montana; Des Lacs, Lostwood, Long Lake, and J. Clark Salyer NWRs in ND; and at the S. H. Ordway Prairie (Nature Conservancy land near Leola) in South Dakota.

Le Conte's Sparrow. Fairly common but local summer resident of wet meadows, fens, grassy bogs, and lake/pond edges in the extreme upper Midwest (Minnesota, Michigan, Wisconsin), northern Great Plains (North Dakota, Montana), and Canada. Winters in similar habitats, as well as in coastal marshes and grasslands and a variety of weedy fields throughout much of the south-central U.S. This bird is very secretive and is given to skulking or running through mats of reeds or grass. When flushed, it typically flies only a short distance before dropping to the ground at which time it quickly vacates the area on foot. Population levels on the breeding grounds are somewhat cyclic with more birds present in wet years. Look for it at Des Lacs NWR, J. Clark Salyer NWR, and around Kelly's Slough (near Grand Forks) in North Dakota; and at marshes in Aitkin, Marshall, and Mahnomen (particularly near Waubun) Counties in Minnesota. Fairly easy to find in east Texas and along the Gulf Coast from mid-October through mid-April. Check especially at Galveston Island SP and at the Yellow Rail Prairie at Anahuac NWR.

Sharp-tailed Sparrow. Uncommon and local summer resident of wet meadows and lake/pond edges in North Dakota, northwestern Minnesota, and the prairie provinces of Canada. Birds breeding in these areas are of the subspecies *nelsoni*, a much brighter form than is found on the Atlantic Coast. Winters in salt and brackish marshes along the Gulf Coast. Like the Le Conte's Sparrow (with which it shares many breeding areas), this species undergoes population fluctuations in tune with weather cycles. Unlike Le Conte's, Sharp-tailed is typically more common in drought years when low water levels expose more emergent vegetation for nesting. Sharp-taileds tend to breed in wetter habitats than Le-Conte's, frequently exploiting the marsh zones with standing water. Away from the actual water's edge, they are more often found in areas with coarser grass such as cattails and bulrushes. Also like the Le Conte's, this species is typically shy and elusive, although it more frequently perches in plain view. Look for it at Des Lacs and J. Clark Salyer NWR in North Dakota, and in the marshes near Waubun (Mahnomen Cove) Minnesota. In winter try Anahuac and Aransas NWRs, the marshes at Sabine and Bolivar Flats, and Galveston Island SP in Texas.

Seaside Sparrow. Fairly common resident of salt and brackish marshes along the Gulf and Atlantic Coasts. In our area it breeds commonly along the Texas coast from about Corpus Christi north (winters south to Brownsville). In spring, males sing from the tops of vegetation. At other times these birds stick to cover, where they run about on the mud bars and banks at the edge of channels in the marsh. They are best seen by sitting quietly at the edge of a channel and waiting for a bird to run into the open. They also respond well to pishing. Try the marshes at Sabine, Sea Rim and Galveston Island SPs, Bolivar Flats, and Anahuac and Aransas NWR's.

Five-striped Sparrow. Rare and highly localized summer resident (a few may winter) of arid slopes and ravines in southeast Arizona. This species has rather strict habitat requirements, being found on dry, rocky hillsides (and in draws) that at the same time support a thick growth of ocotillo and shrubs. The very small U.S. population is subject to some fluctuation, and not all sites are occupied every year. The best locations are Chino Canyon (Santa Rita Mountains) and California Gulch (near Sycamore Canyon).

Botteri's Sparrow. Uncommon and local summer resident of grasslands in southeast Arizona and the lower Texas coast. In the former area Botteri's inhabits open grassland with scattered mesquite and other desert shrubs. It sings from the ground or from an elevated perch and responds well to tapes. The Texas population is found in mesquite/huisache-peppered savannahs, as well as in bunch grass and prickly pear-covered flats along the coast. Texas birds are present from April to August. Arizona birds are more of a mystery and may be rain stimulated in their breeding efforts like their close relatives, the Cassin's Sparrows. At any rate, Arizona birds are probably present from late May on, but are most easily found during their peak singing period, which coincides with the midsummer rainy season. In Arizona try the Nogales airport, the experimental range grasslands below Madera Canyon (Santa Ritas), the research ranch at Elgin, and the first several miles along the road to Gardner Canyon (Santa Ritas). In Texas try the Gunnery Range Tour at Laguna Atascosa NWR.

Cassin's Sparrow. Common summer resident of arid grasslands and mesquite-grass savannahs from eastern Colorado and western Kansas south through Oklahoma, New Mexico, Texas, and Arizona. In Texas, where the species is common from the lush grasslands of the panhandle to the bunch-grass-dotted coastline of the Gulf (and is found across an elevational gradient of 5000 feet) birds are present and nesting as early as March. Populations in Oklahoma, Kansas, and Colorado also follow a traditional pattern of spring through summer nesting. Western populations in west Texas, west New Mexico, and Arizona are usually not in evidence until the onset of summer rains, which usually begin in July. Breeding males are conspicuous because of their aerial flight displays (they also sing from perches). This species winters throughout much of its southern range, but due to its drabness and retiring habits during the nonbreeding season it is seldom seen.

Rufous-winged Sparrow. Uncommon and local resident of southeast Arizona, principally around Tucson, the Papago Indian Reservation, and the base of the Santa Rita Mountains. Seems to favor washes or flat desert with a lush growth of tall shrubs or trees (for example, mesquite and palo verde) and good amounts of grass for ground cover. Like other *Aimophila*, may be at least partly rain stimulated in its breeding efforts. Not all sites are occupied every year, and your best bet may be to check with Tucson birders for current locations. Some fairly reliable spots include Florida Wash (below Madera Canyon) and Gardner Canyon in the Santa Ritas, and along Speedway Blvd. 5+ miles east of its junction with Wilmot Road in Tucson.

Rufous-crowned Sparrow. Common resident of rocky slopes over much of the Southwest and California. Also found on grassy hillsides with scattered oaks, junipers, and rock outcroppings. Found in much the same habitats as Rock Wrens and Brown Towhees. Easy to find over most of its range, it is amazingly abundant in many of the sparsely vegetated desert mountain ranges.

Black-chinned Sparrow. Uncommon bird of chaparral-covered slopes in California, extreme southern Nevada and Utah, southern Arizona and New Mexico, and extreme west Texas. Birds in Texas, New Mexico, and the eastern part of Arizona are resident; those in California, Nevada, and Utah are summer residents only; and those in southwest Arizona represent a wintering population only. In California this bird occupies true chaparral; elsewhere it occupies slopes with similar physiognomic plant associations (including scrub-oak thickets, manzanita, juniper, mountain mahogany and Apache plume). Even in areas where the species is resident there is a pronounced downward altitudinal migration in winter. The best time to find these birds is from April to June when their loud, Field Sparrow-like songs are delivered from prominent perches. In California try Mount Palomar and the old Mission Dam near San Diego, the Switzer Picnic Area in the San Gabriel Mountains, Big Sycamore Canyon in Point Mugu SP, La Cumbre Peak off San Marcos Pass (Highway 154) north of Santa Barbara, and Mount Diablo SP near Berkeley. In New Mexico try Aguirre Springs in the Organ Mountains (east of Las Cruces), the Burro Mountains,

Carlsbad Caverns NP, and the Guadalupe Mountains. The best Texas locations are the Chisos Basin in Big Bend NP and McKittrick Canyon in the Guadalupe Mountains.

Yellow-eyed Junco. Common resident of pine-fir and pine-oak forests in the mountains of southeast Arizona and the Animas Mountains of southwest New Mexico. Often moves to lower elevations in winter. Easy to find at Rustler Park and Onion Saddle in the Chiricahuas, Mount Lemmon in the Santa Catalinas, along the Mount Wrightson Trail in Madera Canyon (Santa Ritas), and along the higher trails in the various canyons of the Huachucas.

Golden-crowned Sparrow. Common winter resident of woodlands and brushy thickets along the entire West Coast. Shuns the open areas that are favored by White-crowned Sparrows. Easy to find in appropriate habitat from November through March.

Chestnut-collared Longspur. Fairly common to common summer resident of mixed-grass prairies, meadow zones around lake edges, hayfields, and pastures throughout most of the northern Great Plains. This species tends to breed in more lush, tall grass areas than does the McCown's. It winters across much of the southern Great Plains (southern Colorado and Kansas through central Texas) and west through the desert grasslands of New Mexico and Arizona to California. In winter it is more often found coming to stock tanks in true grassland areas and is less likely to be found in plowed fields than is the McCown's. In summer try Bowman-Haley Dam, Des Lacs, Lostwood, Long Lake, Arrowwood, Chase Lake, and J. Clark Salyer NWRs in North Dakota; U.S. Highway 85 north of Belle Fourche in South Dakota; Medicine Lake, Bowdoin, and Benton Lake (near Great Falls) NWRs in Montana; and the Pawnee National Grassland (local) in Colorado. In winter try the Cimarron National Grassland (Morton County) in Kansas; Wichita Mountains NWR in Oklahoma; the areas surrounding Amarillo and Valentine (west TX) in Texas; the Jornada Experimental Range (near Las Cruces) and State Highway 26 from Deming to Hatch (especially near Nutt) in New Mexico; and the Sonoita Plains (around Sonoita), San Rafael Valley (near Patagonia), and the Sulphur Springs Valley (near Willcox) in Arizona.

McCown's Longspur. Uncommon to common but local summer resident of short-grass prairies, and stubble and fallow fields from the southern prairie provinces of Canada south through Montana, western North Dakota, Wyoming and northern Colorado. This species occupies grazed areas and more xeric, shortgrass prairie (often with prickly pear) than does the Chestnut-collared. Various types of retired croplands are commonly used in some areas. Look for it from April through September near Marmarth, Bowman-Haley Dam

NWR, and the south unit of Theodore Roosevelt NP in North Dakota; at Benton Lake NWR (near Great Falls), Fox Lake (near Sydney), and along U.S. Highway 191 north from Harlowton in Montana; and on the plains west of Laramie along Highway 130 in Wyoming. Perhaps the easiest place to see breeding birds is the Pawnee National Grassland near Briggsdale, Colorado. In winter this bird is commonly found in plowed fields with Horned Larks. The center of winter abundance is in Oklahoma and Texas, while the species is uncommon to rare in New Mexico and Arizona. McCown's is the common wintering longspur in the Texas panhandle where huge flocks can be found in the plowed fields surrounding Amarillo.

Smith's Longspur. Uncommon to rare and local winter resident of grasslands, pastures, and airport fields over much of the southern Great Plains (southern Nebraska south into Texas). Occasionally seen in migration at points farther north, sometimes in small flocks. Your best bet is to check with birders in Oklahoma City for current hot spots. The Taberville Prairie Refuge near Clinton, Missouri is also a possibility.

White-collared Seedeater. Very rare winter (December through March) visitor to the lower Rio Grande Valley of south Texas. Virtually all recent records have been from the tiny town of San Ygnacio, located on the Rio Grande west of Falcon Dam. Three consistent spots have been the weedy field near the old cemetery, the patch of cane along the river past the cemetery, and the brush near the river at the end of Washington St. However, the birds are often seen right in town. White-collared Seedeaters are not present every year, but when they are present they are sure to be listed on the valley RBA.

Tricolored Blackbird. Locally common summer resident of freshwater tule and cattail marshes along the coast and central valley of California and marginally into southern Oregon. Often breeds in dense colonies. After nesting they can be very hard to find because of their tendency to wander, especially to agricultural areas. Try:

1. California—the Tijuana River Valley from San Diego (winter); Upper Newport Bay; Lake Sherwood (near Thousand Oaks); marshes on Point Mugu; Goleta Slough in Santa Barbara; Mojave Narrows Regional Park (San Bernardino County); Neary's Lagoon Native Area in Santa Cruz; fields on Point Reyes (huge flocks gather in winter); and San Luis, Lower Klamath, Clear Lake, and Tule Lake NWRs
2. Oregon (Ramsey 1978)—Agency Lake and Lynn Newbry Park (near Medford).

nzed Cowbird. Abundant summer resident throughout south Texas (west Bend NP), uncommon and more restricted to the southern tip in winter.

Fairly common but local summer resident in southeast Arizona and extreme southwest New Mexico, uncommon along the Colorado River Valley of Arizona-California. Some birds winter in the Santa Cruz River Valley of Arizona. Seems to be expanding its range in west Texas and southern New Mexico. Hard to miss in open areas anywhere in the lower Rio Grande Valley of south Texas. Farther west try Rio Grande Village at Big Bend NP (TX); Redrock (Gila River) and Guadalupe Canyon in New Mexico; and Cave Creek and Madera Canyons, Sonoita Creek Sanctuary, the Tucson Sewage Ponds, and feed pens anywhere in the Santa Cruz Valley in Arizona.

Audubon's Oriole. Rare and local resident of subtropical forest/brushland along the Rio Grande in south Texas. Look for it along the river at San Ygnacio, below Falcon Dam, at the Santa Margarita Ranch, and at Santa Ana NWR. Of these areas, below Falcon Dam (boat landing at the settlement of Salineno, and the stretch of river immediately below the dam) is the best. This oriole is best located by following its song—an almost humanlike variable whistle—to the bird, which is most often perched high in a tree near the river's edge.

Streak-backed Oriole. Extremely rare fall and winter visitor to hummingbird feeders in southeast Arizona and coastal southern California. Many of the records from recent years have proven to be of Hooded Orioles in basic plumage. Your best bet is the Arizona RBA.

Altamira Oriole. Fairly common but local resident of subtropical forest/brush in extreme south Texas, from San Ygnacio to Brownsville. It can be readily seen below Falcon Dam, at the Santa Margarita Ranch, Bentsen SP, and Santa Ana NWR. At Bentsen it frequently nests around the campgrounds and feeds at hummingbird feeders put up by the campers. Best seen from the photo blinds at Santa Ana, where they also come into sugar-water feeders.

Hooded Oriole. Fairly common summer resident along the Rio Grande Valley of Texas, in southwestern New Mexico, southern Arizona, and north along coastal California. In Texas this bird seems to be declining in numbers, while in California it is expanding its range northward. This oriole is found in a variety of habitats. In Texas it is found primarily in subtropical woodlands along the Rio Grande to Big Bend NP where it occupies the large riparian stands of cottonwoods. In Arizona it is often found in riparian woodlands as well as in saguaro desert. Throughout its range it is commonly found in city parks and residential areas, concentrating in areas with palm trees, which are used for nesting.

Hepatic Tanager. Fairly common to uncommon summer resident of pine-oak woodlands in the mountains of west Texas, New Mexico, and Arizona. Easy to find at:

1. Texas—McKittrick Canyon and The Bowl (Guadalupe Mountains NP), the Chisos Basin and trails above it (Big Bend NP), and the Madera Canyon Picnic Grounds (Highway 118 in the Davis Mountains)
2. New Mexico—Little Walnut Picnic Area (Silver City), the Guadalupe Mountains, the Burro Mountains, and Aguirre Springs Recreation Area (Organ Mountains)
3. Arizona—appropriate habitat in the Santa Catalinas, Chiricahuas, Huachucas, and Santa Ritas.

Lawrence's Goldfinch. Uncommon and local (and somewhat erratic) resident of dry pine-oak forest and montane chaparral over most of southern and central California. After breeding the birds tend to become very nomadic, often concentrating in weedy fields in lowland areas. Regularly winters in southern Arizona (mostly along the Santa Cruz River and its tributaries), but abundance varies considerably between years. Probably the best time to find it in California is the month of April. Try the Diablo Mountains south of Livermore along Mines Road (Remsen 1972), Mount Pinos (bare area near the summit), Placerita Canyon SP and the Switzer Picnic Areas in the San Gabriels, and Folsom Lake State Recreation Area.

"Brown-capped" Rosy Finch. Fairly common resident of alpine tundra of scattered mountain ranges in Colorado, Wyoming, and New Mexico. Sometimes moves to lower elevations in winter, where they can be seen along roadsides in foothills. The center of abundance is Colorado, where the following locations should be searched: Summit Lake on Mount Evans, Trail Ridge Rd. in Rocky Mountain NP, Pass Lake on Loveland Pass, Squaw Mountain (comes to feeders in winter—try October and November while the road is still driveable), and Red Rocks Park (uncommon to rare in winter). In winter they are best seen around Gunnison. In New Mexico try the high peaks of the Sangre de Cristo Mountains in summer, and the area at the top of the ski lift in the Sandia Mountains (Albuquerque) in winter. In Wyoming look for them on Medicine Bow Peak and Brooklyn Ridge off State Highway 130 (Snowy Range Pass) in the Snowy Range of the Medicine Bow Mountains (Pettingill 1981).

"Black" Rosy Finch. Uncommon resident of alpine tundra on scattered high peaks in the northern Rockies, Northwest, and Great Basin. Generally breeds farther north and west than the Brown-capped form. This is generally the hardest Rosy Finch to find. Like the other subspecies, this one feeds at the edges of snowfields (on windblown insects that are immobilized by the cold of the snow) and is often found in the vicinity of talus slopes and rock outcroppings. Also like the others, these birds often descend to lower elevations in winter. Good areas include:

1. Colorado—Squaw Mountain (October through November), Red Rocks Park (uncommon-rare in winter), and the Gunnison area (winter)

2. Wyoming (Pettingill 1981)—the summit of Mount Washburn in Yellowstone NP, the Jackson Hole Aerial Tram out of Teton Village to the summit of Rendezvous Mountain, Bear Tooth Pass 45 miles east of Tower Junction (Starks 1981), and high country in the Grand Tetons and Big Horn Mountains in general

3. Utah (Pettingill 1981)—above Mirror Lake (Bald Mountain) 33 miles east of Kamas on State Highway 150

4. Idaho (Pettingill 1981)—U.S. Highway 93 from Haily to Samon

5. Oregon (Pettingill 1981)—Steens Mountain (reached via Steens Mountain Loop Road east from Frenchglen) and the area between Enterprise and Zumwalt (winter roadside flocks).

"Gray-crowned" Rosy Finch. Fairly common resident of alpine tundra on scattered high mountains of the West and Northwest. This is the most widespread of the Rosy Finches (breeding as far north as Alaska) and perhaps the one most likely to be seen in huge flocks roaming the lowlands in winter. Try:

1. California (Pettingill 1981)—Tioga Pass in Yosemite NP (especially along the margins of Saddlebag Lake); the Mammoth Pass area (reached from Casa Diablo Hot Springs on U.S. Highway 395, 42 miles northwest of Bishop); the trail up Mount Whitney (from the road up Lone Pine Canyon—off U.S. Highway 395, 59 miles south of Bishop); and at Lower Klamath, Tule Lake, and Clear Lake NWRs in winter

2. Colorado—Squaw Mountain (October through November), and Red Rocks Park (winter)

3. Montana (Pettingill 1981)—Logan Pass and the Hidden Lake Trail off of the pass in Glacier N.P.

4. Oregon (Pettingill 1981)—the Crater Lake area (Rim Village, the trail to Garfield Peak from the Crater Lake Lodge, Mount Scott, and the east face of Applegate Peak), above timberline in the Big Horn and Walowa Mts., Mt. Hood, Steens Mountain (via Steens Mountain Loop Rd. east from Frenchglen), and between Enterprise and Zumwalt (roadside flocks in winter)

5. Washington—Mount Baker, and trails leading up from Paradise and Sunrise in Mount Rainier NP.

·4·

Techniques of
Identifying Birds

Field identification of North American birds is reasonably simple compared to the problems encountered in many other parts of the world. A multiplicity of factors contribute to this situation, among them:

1. a relatively sparse avifauna when compared to much of the tropics
2. our development of a very stable taxonomic classification with solid knowledge of sexual, age, and geographic variation
3. availability of a number of good field guides to help speed the identification process. In many regions of the world both field guides and extensive knowledge of avian systematics, geographic variation, and distribution are lacking.

The innovation of the field guide has changed the shape of bird identification in this country into a skill that can be acquired with some proficiency by anyone in a relatively short period of time. Unfortunately, field guides by their very nature have several shortcomings when used as a sole reference point and have even created new problems in the identification of birds.

Because of publishing considerations of cost and space, and because of the need to simplify the identification process from the incredibly lengthy plumage descriptions of earlier works, field guides have traditionally focused attention on one or two key field marks per species. Indeed, this approach has great use and is probably adequate for the identification of most species. However, the goal of efficiency has exacted a price, and that price is one of oversimplification. Many species have been written off as unidentifiable in the field or unidentifiable except by voice because then-current knowledge and/or publishing considerations did not allow the publication of workable techniques. Worse yet, the separation of many species complexes has been made to appear much easier than it is, thus causing and perpetuating a multitude of identification errors (many of which have found their way into print). In the process, much information that is useful and often necessary for identification (such as geographic and polymorphic variation, molt sequences, and subtle structural and behavioral differences) has been ignored.

This chapter and the next will attempt to fill in the gaps left by most field guides and supplement what is already there. This chapter is largely conceptual in nature, and is intended to point out vital considerations in the identification of birds. Hopefully it will provide you with a philosophical framework with which to build identification skills. Numerous specific examples of the various points are included.

FORM AND STRUCTURE

Taxonomists have arranged birds (as well as other organisms) in a hierarchy of categories based on degree of relatedness. For categories above the species level, such relatedness is inferred from the sharing of certain evolutionarily derived characters, implying a common ancestry. There are seven major levels in this hierarchy:

- Kingdom
- Phylum
- Class
- Order
- Family
- Genus
- Species

As we move down the scale from kingdom to species, we find that each category is less inclusive, so that the higher levels contain many organisms that are often distantly related, while the lower levels have fewer but more closely related members. By way of example, an American Crow is:

1. an animal (kingdom Animalia)
2. a chordate (phylum Chordata)
3. a vertebrate (sub-phylum Vertebrata)
4. a bird (class Aves)
5. a perching bird (order Passeriformes)
6. a corvid (family Corvidae)
7. a crow/raven type bird (genus *Corvus*) and
8. an American Crow (species *Corvus brachyrhynchos*).

Usually, the more closely related are two species, the more they will resemble one another in overall appearance.

For identification purposes it is often easier to place an unknown bird in a higher category first, before attempting to key it out to species. Ordinal characters are often so broad as to include many highly dissimilar birds within one order and are therefore of little use in the recognition process. However, family characters are usually consistent for most members of the group, and are often distinctive enough to make visual separation of families relatively easy. A correct family identification will serve to narrow down your choices of species considerably and saves you from having to page laboriously through a field guide (for example, identify a bird first as a hummingbird, then narrow it down to Broad-tailed).

Color and other plumage characters are often used by untrained observers as the primary or only clues to bird identification. However, on many occasions it is impossible to accurately determine the color or plumage patterns of a bird due to distance, light conditions, and so forth, *or* color may not be diagnostic for the particular species under observation. Color is, in fact, a poor separator of families, since color differences within families are usually as great as differences between families (for example, such unrelated birds as storm petrels, cormorants, some ducks, some hawks, crows, blackbirds, and some finches may be mostly or entirely black).

Much more reliable in placing a bird in the correct family is overall form and structure. This includes size, bill shape, leg and foot structure, size of head and bill versus body size, wing spread and shape, and length of tail relative to body length.

TROPHIC STRUCTURES

Trophic structures—those used in gathering food—are often the best indicators of family status, and may vary dramatically between groups. Avian bill morphology is adapted to a variety of feeding modes and diets. Bills may be stout and conical for crushing seeds, hooked for tearing meat, chisel-like for drilling through bark, long and needle-like for nectar feeding, and so forth. Leg and foot structure may also be related (at least indirectly) to food procurement, and indicative of family status. Examples include long stilt-like legs for wading, strong and heavily clawed feet for snaring vertebrate prey, and zygodactylous toe arrangement (two toes forward and two back) for clinging to tree trunks.

Such structural variation can also be important in separating species within a family. Examples are provided by loons, cormorants, ducks, shorebirds (Figure 4.1), gulls, terns, alcids, corvids, and mimids, where trophic structures (particularly bills) are often as important as plumage in separating similar species.

WING/TAIL SHAPE AND FLIGHT CHARACTERISTICS

Equally or more important to the identification of some families and to species within families, is the overall shape of the bird, particularly of the wings and tail. Wing shape and associated flight characteristics are among the best ways to immediately recognize such groups as shearwaters, albatrosses, storm petrels, raptors, terns, hummingbirds, swifts, and swallows. They are also extremely important clues to separating species within groups.

An appreciation for differences in flight characteristics is especially invaluable in the identification of species within such groups as shearwaters, storm petrels, jaegers, gulls, terns, and hawks. For example, the combination of wing/tail structure and flight habits are of primary importance in narrowing the identification of an unknown raptor to one or a few species. Consequently, the following discussion will focus on the use of wing and tail structure and flight characteristics in the identification of raptors and pelagic birds. These

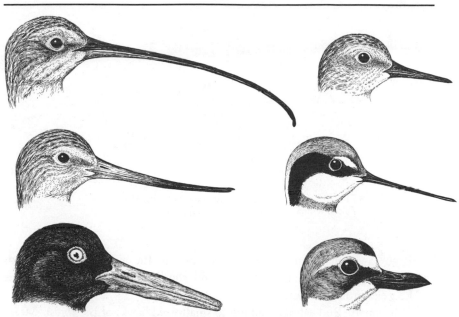

FIGURE 4.1. Shorebird bill diversity (left column, top to bottom: Long-billed Curlew, Marbled Godwit, Black Oystercatcher; right column, top to bottom: Least Sandpiper, Wilson's Phalarope, Wilson's Plover). Artwork by Mimi Hoppe Wolf.

groups provide the best examples of the importance of learning wing/tail structures and flight characteristics.

Raptors. When dealing with raptors, the first step is to place an unknown bird into one of five major structural groups. Excluding owls and vultures, these groups are:

1. eagles
2. soaring hawks
3. Accipiters
4. falcons
5. kites

The kites and eagles contain multiple genera, but the other groups are for the most part monogeneric. Descriptions of wing/tail shapes and flight habits for each group follow (see also Figure 4.2).

Eagles. These are huge soaring raptors with broad wings that are also very long. The primaries form distinct "fingers" at the ends of the wings. Tails are broad and of short to medium length (two species in continental U.S., both in the west).

Soaring hawks. Comprised mostly of members of the genus *Buteo*. These

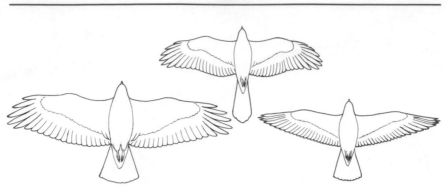

FIGURE 4.2. Left to right: Buteo outline, Accipiter outline, Falcon outline. Artwork by Mimi Hoppe Wolf.

are large hawks that soar or glide lazily, high in the air. They have broad, rounded wings (not as long as eagles), and short, broad tails (twelve species in U.S., eleven in the west).

Accipiters. Bird-eating, medium to small-sized hawks of the forest. Members of the genus *Accipiter* have short, rounded wings, with proportionately long tails. They are typically sit-and-wait predators, remaining perched and chasing passing prey in short, rapid bursts. They also occasionally soar. Typical flight pattern (except when in direct chase or when riding a thermal) consists of two to four flaps followed by a glide, usually at low to medium heights above ground. Wing shape and manner of flight are most helpful in separating these hawks from falcons (three species in U.S., all in the west).

Falcons. Members of the genus *Falco* are mostly small to medium-sized hawks with long, pointed wings, and long, squared tails (may appear rounded when fanned). Straight away flight is rapid and powerful, with continuous choppy strokes. When hunting they typically soar high until prey (usually birds) is spotted, and then fold their wings and dive (stoop) on their quarry from above, striking it on the wing. When doing so they achieve tremendous speeds. Kestrels hunt by hovering and then dropping to the ground (six U.S. species, all are found in the west).

Kites. This is a polygeneric group of medium-sized raptors that shows extreme variation in wing/tail structure and flight characteristics. Some species are falcon-like in appearance, with long tails and long, pointed wings. These are typically white and black or gray and black in plumage, and are more buoyant and graceful fliers than falcons, banking and sailing frequently, while ruddering with their tails. Other kites are more *Buteo*-like in appearance, with broad, rounded wings. Their proportionately long tails will help separate them from the Buteos (five species in the United States, only three are likely to be seen in the west).

Three species of diurnal raptors do not fall easily into any of the above categories, and each is the sole representative of its genus in the United States.

Northern Harriers have long tails and long, slender wings that are somewhat intermediate between Buteos and falcons. They typically fly low over the terrain with wings held in a dihedral, and frequently tilt back and forth. Ospreys are very large and somewhat eagle-like, but with a distinctive crook to the wings (flexed backwards at carpals) that gives them a gull-like appearance in flight. The Crested Caracara has a wingspan equivalent to that of the larger Buteos, but its wings are narrower and the tail is longer. All three of the above species are so distinctively plumaged as to make misidentification unlikely.

Once you have properly placed an unknown raptor into the correct group, identification as to species can often be made on the basis of plumage characters. However, wing/tail structure and flight habits should not be ignored because they can still provide important clues, particularly when dealing with immature or aberrantly plumaged birds or when viewing conditions do not allow ready color differentiation.

Structural points to note are the width of the wings relative to their length, and the length and width of the tail relative to wing shape. For example, Common Black-hawks and White-tailed Hawks have wings that are very broad with tails that are somewhat short, giving both species a diagnostic wide-winged look in flight. This is more pronounced in the Common Black-Hawk, since its wings are shorter and more rounded at the tips. On the other hand, Swainson's Hawks have long, very slender wings with pointed tips, giving them a look that is quite unlike other Buteos. Likewise, Rough-legged Hawks have long, somewhat slender wings, whereas their close relatives, the Ferruginous Hawks, have long broad wings that may still appear narrow due to their longer tails.

Once again, such terms as slender or broad are relative and require some comparative experience to assess. Careful and repeated study of the structure of a common species (such as the Red-tailed Hawk) is the best way to develop a feel for structural differences in the group as a whole.

Additional flight characteristics to note include:

1. Does the bird frequently hover while hunting (Ferruginous and Rough-legged Hawks, American Kestrel, Black-shouldered Kite)?
2. Does it tip or teeter back and forth while soaring or cruising (Turkey Vulture, Zone-tailed Hawk, Northern Harrier)?
3. What is its flight attitude when soaring (that is, flat-winged, or wings raised in a dihedral)?

Be aware that flight habits can vary tremendously depending on wind conditions, so that a bird that normally soars with a flat-winged attitude may have a pronounced dihedral at any given time. Also, many raptors will hover on occasion, although the four mentioned do it habitually.

Pelagic Birds. For many pelagic birds, flight characteristics take on added importance due to the often poor viewing conditions and brevity and distance of observations, which do not allow for the discrimination of plumage characters.

Different characters of flight are important for the different groups of pelagic birds. Accordingly, the important points to note for each group are listed separately. The following flight characteristics are in some cases obvious, and in other cases subtle. They require much practice and experience to master, but once you have done so your success on pelagic trips will increase many-fold. Take every opportunity to study the flight of even the most common pelagic species, and use their flight patterns as a yardstick with which to measure less familiar species.

Albatrosses. The master fliers of the ocean, albatrosses glide on long bowed wings above the water, seemingly without effort. Flaps are usually few and far between. Flight characteristics are fairly inconsequential in the separation of the few albatrosses seen in our waters.

Shearwaters. This is a group of amazing fliers, all of which have a very characteristic alternation of rapid wing beats with stiff-winged glides over the water. Their glides are similar to those of albatrosses, but they flap more frequently. There are numerous subtle differences within this diagnostic style of flight that can aid in nailing down the specific identification of a distant bird. Ask yourself the following questions:

- Are the glides long or short?
- How rapid are the beats between glides?
- Does the bird rise and fall in height above the surface?
- Does the bird arc or wheel above the water, and if so, how high and how frequently?
- Does the bird bank frequently, alternately showing upper and lower surfaces?

Storm Petrels. This is a group with many extremely similar species, where plumage is of little help. Consequently, flight habits are of vital importance in separating members of the group. Storm Petrels are highly variable in their manner of flying, but nearly all are fast, low fliers which occasionally glide. Flight is often bounding or somewhat erratic. When feeding they usually skip or patter across the surface. Points to note include:

- Depth of wingbeat (are the wings brought above the horizontal plane of the body, and if so, how far?)
- Timing and constancy of beats
- Flight path—direct or zigzag, and level or up-and-down.

Jaegers. Because these birds are frequent kleptoparasites (steal food from other birds, frequently by chasing them until they disgorge), much can be told from the birds they chase and how well they keep up. The large and heavy Pomarine is a strong flier that chases larger, not overly maneuverable gulls. At the other end of the spectrum is the Long-tailed Jaeger, which is small enough and maneuverable enough to chase such aerobatic fliers as terns. The Parasitic Jaeger is intermediate in size and bulk and usually confines its chases to terns or small to medium-sized gulls. If other birds are not present for comparison, note the degree of power or buoyancy to the flight.

Note: As with raptors, the flight habits of pelagic birds can vary tremendously with wind conditions and should not be used as the sole basis for an identification.

Tail structure is probably more important in helping to separate species within groups than it is in differentiating one family from another. However, it is still an important aid in the recognition of such groups as frigatebirds, adult jaegers and tropicbirds, terns, some wrens and mimids, and gnatcatchers.

Within groups tail structure can be extremely important in the separation of species, especially among the gulls, jaegers (length of tail points as well as their shape), kites, hummingbirds, swallows, some corvids, some sparrows, and some icterids. Occasionally, birds within other families have tails that are so long or unusually shaped as to make them instantly recognizable on the basis of tail structure alone (for example, Scissor-tailed Flycatcher).

BODY PROPORTIONS

General body proportions should also be taken into account when identifying birds. Especially important is the relative size of the head, bill, and tail compared to the body. Relatively large heads when combined with short tails give many species a top-heavy, sawed-off look. A large bill will accentuate such an impression. Alternatively, a bird's head may be counterbalanced in its extent of protrusion by the tail, lending a symmetrically sound look to the bird as a whole. These contrasting impressions of relative proportions are especially important clues to the identification of *Sterna* terns and *Empidonax* flycatchers.

The combination of a relatively small head with a somewhat plump body gives many groups such as grouses, quails, doves, and thrushes, a rotund look that is instantly recognizable. Likewise, Buff-breasted and Upland Sandpipers are noticeably different in form from other shorebirds because of their small-headed, full-breasted look. This appearance is heightened by their slender necks.

Head shape is just as critical as head size to the identification of many species. It is particularly helpful in the separation of grebes (Horned versus Eared), scaup, goldeneyes, eiders, scoters, swans, and diving ducks in general. Many of these species and others (for example, Canvasback, Ring-necked Duck, Tufted Duck) can be distinguished in poor light on the basis of head/bill profile alone. Special structures such as crests or prominent head plumes should always be noted.

Neck structure (particularly relative thickness) too should not be over-looked as an aid to identification, particularly when dealing with loons, grebes, cormorants, and waders.

COLOR AND PLUMAGE PATTERNS

Despite the importance of the various structural features noted in the previous section, plumage patterns and color remain as primary characters of identification for most species. As noted previously, structure is more important in the recognition of families or orders, whereas plumage becomes most useful in the area of specific discrimination.

Plumage goes beyond color, to the presence or absence of such features as eye rings, eye stripes, eye lines, malar stripes, spectacles, median stripes, wing bars, rump patches, and tail spots. Also important to note is the presence, boldness, and extent of patterns of barring, streaking, spotting, or scalloping to the breast, belly, flanks, back, and upper and under surfaces of the wings. Bright patches of color on the crown, back, shoulders, crissum, and axillaries are important in the identification of many species, as is the presence of contrastingly-colored caps, hoods, breast and belly bands, bibs, collars, and outer tail feathers, and others. Because of the diversity and complexity of bird plumages, it is important to become familiar with bird feather anatomy. A thorough review of the bird topography illustrated in Figures 4.3 through 4.7 should provide you with the necessary background information. Specialized terminology is also explained in the glossary. Note that different feather groups are more prominently displayed in some groups of birds than in others (for example, tertials and scapulars on the dowitcher versus the secondaries and primaries on the flycatcher).

PLUMAGE VARIATION

Recognizing birds by their plumages is complicated by the fact that those plumages are seldom constant for all individuals of a species at all times. One of the most common types of variation is geographic or racial variation. A race (or subspecies) is an aggregate of local populations of a species that occupies some subdivision of the range of that species and which are morphologically or vocally different from other populations of that species. Such racial variation is maintained by reduced gene flow between populations and by at least slightly different selection pressures between different geographic areas. The list of species that vary geographically is long, and the nature and extent of that variation is different from one species to the next. Some species show more or less continuous variation from one extreme to another (that is, light to dark), which usually coincides with some environmental gradient such as latitude.

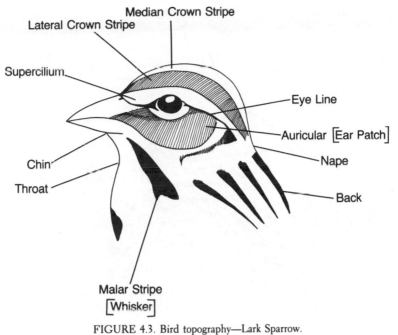

FIGURE 4.3. Bird topography—Lark Sparrow.
Artwork by Janet Rucci.

FIGURE 4.4. Bird topography—Western Gull.
Artwork by Janet Rucci.

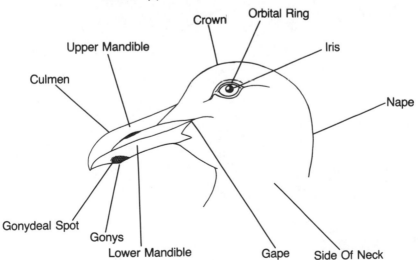

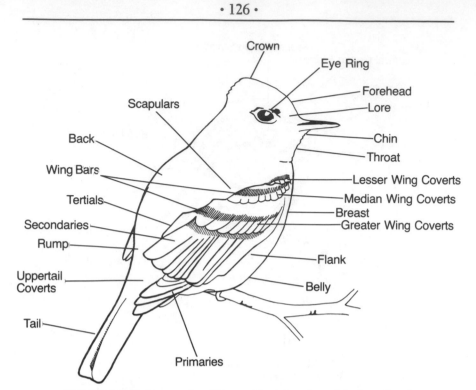

FIGURE 4.5. Bird topography—Western Flycatcher. Artwork by Janet Rucci.

FIGURE 4.6. Bird topography—Dowitcher. Artwork by Janet Rucci.

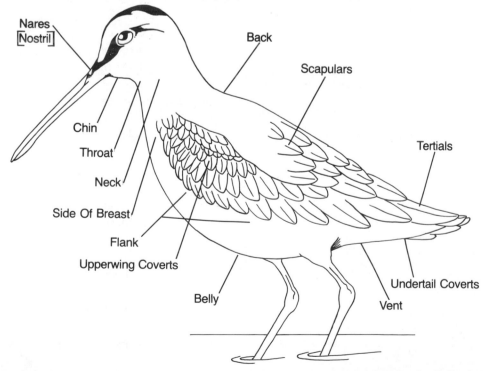

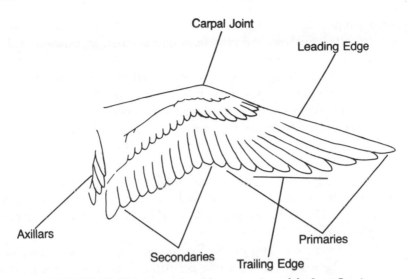

FIGURE 4.7. Bird topography—falcon wing. Artwork by Janet Rucci.

Others have discretely different races that may differ greatly or slightly but with no intermediate types.

Some of the species that exhibit marked geographic variation include Leach's Storm Petrel; Red-tailed Hawk; Merlin; Peregrine Falcon; Gyrfalcon; Bar-tailed Godwit; Lesser Golden-Plover; Short-billed Dowitcher; Clapper Rail; Western Gull; Northern Flicker; Gray Jay; Cliff Swallow; Tufted Titmouse; thrushes of the genus *Catharus*; Solitary Vireo; Yellow-rumped Warbler; Savannah, Song, Grasshopper, and Fox Sparrows; Dark-eyed Junco; and Northern Oriole. This list is not comprehensive, but it does demonstrate the existence of geographic variation in most families of birds. In the case of the storm petrel, hawk, dowitcher, gull, thrush, and vireo, your knowledge of geographic variations in plumage could be the vital factor in correctly identifying the bird.

Plumage variation can also occur within a single population. A species that has two distinct plumage types (morphs) within a population is said to be dimorphic. If more than two morphs occur in a population the species is polymorphic. The most common types of dimorphism result from plumage differences between males and females and between young and adults. Sexual dimorphism is extremely common (particularly among passerines) but is most pronounced in groups such as ducks, gallinaceous fowl, hummingbirds, warblers, finches, icterids, and tanagers. In many cases the differences between male and female plumages in a species are greater than they are between species. Age dimorphism is also common, and in such groups as sulids, waders, hawks, jaegers, and gulls, immature birds may possess plumages that are radically different from their adult counterparts.

Still another type of dimorphism involves the existence of two genetically inherited morphs that are not correlated with age or sex. Such morphs (or phases) are often markedly different from one another, as demonstrated by the white versus blue morphs of Snow and Ross' Geese, the white versus dark morphs of the Reddish Egret, the light versus dark morphs of many Buteos, and the red versus gray morphs of the Eastern Screech-Owl.

The term polymorphism is usually reserved for cases where more than two discretely different variants that are not the result of age and/or sexual differences exist within a population. This situation is most closely approached among North American species by the Ruff, a rare but regular vagrant from Europe and Asia that also breeds in Alaska. Male Ruffs in breeding plumage possess a ruff of feathers around the head and neck that is erected during courtship. The ruff may be orange, black, or white in color. Females (Reeves) are not polymorphic.

More frequent are cases in which a species may show a continuum of color variation between individuals in a population. This is not true polymorphism, because there is a gradation of plumage types, without discretely different morphs. Such is the case with Northern Fulmars, jaegers, and some Buteos, where there exist all manner of intermediate forms between dark-phase and light-phase birds.

MOLT AND PLUMAGE SEQUENCE

Still another cause of plumage variation is seasonal/age variation resulting from molt, feather wear, and the unique plumage of each species.

Molt is a periodic shedding and replacement of old feathers with new ones. Feathers are subject to extreme abrasion, and because of their vital role in flight, insulation, and protection, it is important that they should be constantly renewed and maintained. Molt is very expensive from an energetic stand point and must be timed so as not to compete with other energetically expensive activities such as nesting or migration. Consequently, most species have a yearly complete molt (all, or the vast majority of feathers replaced) immediately following the breeding season, just prior to or after their southbound migration.

Feather loss during molt usually follows an orderly and bilaterally symmetrical pattern. Particularly important is the molt of primary and secondary feathers of the wings (the so-called flight feathers) and the tail feathers, all of which are so important for maintenance of flight. There are numerous patterns of wing/tail molt, but only a couple need to be mentioned here. Most common is a sequential feather replacement from the first primary (innermost) outward, and the first secondary (outermost) inward, while the tail feathers are molted from the central pair outward in both directions. Many waterbirds (notably waterfowl, loons, grebes, and alcids) undergo a synchronous molt in which all primaries are lost simultaneously. Because most of these birds would be rendered nearly flightless by the loss of even one or two primaries (due to high weight loading per wing surface area), it is best that they compress the molt into a short period and get it over with all at once. During this time they are incapable of flying and must utilize their swimming and diving abilities to escape predation. Alternatively, some large birds such as eagles may require more than one year to completely recycle their plumage.

In addition to the yearly complete molt, many species also undergo a partial molt of head and body feathers just prior to the breeding season. This accounts in many species for the bright breeding dress of the males. Most species have acquired essentially adult plumage by their first or second winter. This is not true of many larger species such as sulids, albatrosses, raptors, and gulls, which may take three to eight years to attain full adult plumage. Identification of these groups is greatly complicated by their lengthy and often complex plumage sequences.

Progressive birders must gain some understanding of patterns of molt and plumage sequence if they are to attain full competence in the field identification of birds. This is no easy task, for there is extreme variation in molt sequence from one family or species to the next. However, there are some common threads that run across taxonomic lines, and if these are understood thoroughly it becomes much easier to pick up the nuances of specific groups. For that reason, a "typical" plumage sequence is outlined below. There are two popular systems of molt terminology, and when these differ in terms, one set is included parenthetically.

Typical Plumage Sequence

1. Young bird starts out wearing natal down.
2. Natal down is replaced by a complete molt into juvenal plumage by time of fledging.
3. This is followed by a partial or complete post-juvenile (prebasic) molt in fall into first winter (first basic) plumage.
4. First nuptial (first alternate) plumage is acquired in spring either through feather wear or by a partial pre-nuptial (pre-alternate) molt.
5. This plumage is lost by a complete post-nuptial (post-alternate) molt following the breeding season, at which time the second winter (second basic) plumage is acquired. In many species this is equivalent to adult winter (basic) plumage.
6. This cycle is then repeated through the life of the bird, with complete molts into winter plumage following breeding, and either feather wear or partial molts in spring producing the nuptial plumage.

As can be seen above, birds acquire their nuptial or alternate plumage through feather wear or by way of a pre-nuptial molt. Feather wear involves the gradual wearing away of the usually dull-colored tips of winter feathers to reveal what are usually much brighter colors below. This phenomenon is found in hawks and most passerines, including parids, mimids, thrushes, vireos, some warblers, many finches, orioles, blackbirds, grackles, and Summer and Hepatic Tanagers. Birds that molt into nuptial plumage usually do so by a partial molt of head and body feathers. Included in this group are such birds as gulls, shorebirds, most flycatchers, some warblers, and most sparrows. A few birds (terns, Lesser Goldfinch) undergo a complete pre-nuptial molt, whereas in others (Marsh and Sedge Wrens) this molt is nearly complete.

As noted earlier, there are numerous variations on the so-called "typical" molt sequence, and often, closely-related species may show different patterns of molt. One striking variation on the common theme is found in ducks, which undergo a partial post-nuptial molt each fall. This molt produces a very dull "eclipse plumage" on the normally striking males. It is no coincidence that males acquire this dull plumage at a time when they are rendered very vulnerable to predation by the simultaneous loss of their flight feathers. This plumage is retained for about two months at which time the ducks undergo a complete molt into winter plumage, which is then retained through the following summer.

An ability to correctly determine a bird's age is a prerequisite for identification in many difficult groups such as sulids, shorebirds, and gulls. Such an ability is dependent on a knowledge of molt timing and plumage sequence in the birds being studied. Without this knowledge accurate identification will be greatly hampered, and in some cases made nearly impossible. For still other birds it is important to realize that post-nuptial molts often produce plumages that are much brighter than the worn breeding dress, thereby dramatically changing the color of familiar species in fall. This realization, combined with a knowledge of the timing of molt in particular species, is especially important when attempting to identify flycatchers of the genera *Empidonax* and *Myiarchus* during late summer and fall.

Where patterns of molt and plumage sequence are critical points in the identification of a difficult group, they are treated in detail under appropriate sections in the next chapter.

VOCALIZATIONS

Understandably most beginning birders rely heavily or entirely on visual clues to a bird's identity. The lesson that auditory discrimination is often as easy or easier comes with experience. Experienced birders may identify 75 percent or more of the birds encountered in a day's work by voice alone. This is particularly true in forests, where the nature of the vegetation can make it difficult to obtain more than a fleeting glance of a bird.

Vocalizations are generally most important in the identification of passerines but are also important when identifying rails, shorebirds, doves, cuckoos, owls, caprimulgids, hummingbirds, and woodpeckers, and are of supplementary use in almost every group of birds.

Some species complexes cannot be safely identified in the field solely on the basis of visual characters. Others can be identified, but only by experienced birders and under good viewing conditions. Often these same species can be instantly separated by their songs or calls. Examples include basic-plumaged dowitchers, Western Screech Owl versus Whiskered Owl, Common Nighthawk versus Lesser Nighthawk, female hummingbirds of several species (especially Black-chinned versus Costa's), Couch's Kingbird versus Tropical Kingbird, Eastern Wood-Pewee versus Western Wood-Pewee, Willow Flycatcher versus Alder Flycatcher (as well as almost any pair of *Empidonax* species), Northwestern Crow versus American Crow, Cassin's Sparrow versus Botteri's Sparrow, and Eastern Meadowlark versus Western Meadowlark.

As with visual identification skills, auditory skills are best acquired and perfected by spending many hours in the field. An excellent way to speed your progress in this area is to purchase some of the many records or cassette tapes of bird songs and calls that are commercially available. These can be played repeatedly until the vocalizations are firmly entrenched in your mind. Be aware, however, that widespread species may have regional populations that sing dialects quite different from those recorded on the records or tapes.

Another technique that is especially helpful for remembering songs heard in the field, is the verbalization of a song or call into words or distinct phonetic syllables. The vocalizations of many species will defy your best efforts in this regard, but others will lend themselves well to such a memory device. Examples include the "fitz-bew" of the Willow Flycatcher, the "ho-say ma-ree-ah" of the Greater Pewee, the "witchety witchety witchety" of the Common Yellow-throat, the "what-cheer" of the Northern Cardinal, the "drink your tea" of the Rufous-sided Towhee, and the calls of the Plain Chachalaca, Whip-poor-will, Common Poorwill, Chuck-will's-widow, Eastern Wood-Pewee, Great Kiskadee, and chickadees, all of which say their names.

When learning songs and calls in this way, be sure to note which syllable is accented and whether the cadence is varied or constant for the duration of the vocalization. Are the notes delivered explosively or in a lazy, slow manner? Are they combined in a trill or warble or is each note distinct? Is the sound sharp, metallic, nasal, harsh, lispy, or gutteral? These are just a few of the questions that you should ask yourself when committing a vocalization to memory.

By all means do not confine your work to songs or to distinctly different call notes. Even such seemingly similar calls as the "chip" notes common to warblers and sparrows can be separated with much practice. Such an ability can be of great value in keying into one rare bird from among a rapidly moving flock of more common species.

BEHAVIOR

The behavior exhibited by a bird is often among the most useful of clues as to which family it belongs and in narrowing the choices even further.

As noted earlier, trophic structures are useful clues to a bird's identity. As might be expected, unique structural adaptations usually coincide with characteristic behavioral adaptations, allowing birds to maximize their foraging efficiency. Because most birds spend a great deal of their time foraging, it follows that foraging behavior is an easily seen character that may greatly facilitate identification. When watching birds forage, try asking yourself some of the following questions:

- Does it feed in large flocks, small groups, or by itself?

- Does it swim? If so, does it periodically dive under water disappearing from view for periods of time (e.g., loons, grebes, diving ducks), or does it tip forward leaving its tail up (dabbling ducks)? Does it spin in circles (phalaropes)? Does it swim with only its head and neck above water (cormorants and anhingas)?

- If it dives into the water from the air, does it hover over the surface first and come up immediately (e.g., terns and kingfishers), or does it dive from great heights without hovering and stay under longer (e.g., pelicans, tropicbirds, sulids)?

- If it is a large wader (heron, crane, ibis, stork-type bird) does it wade in deep water or close to the shore? Does it remain motionless (or wade very slowly) most of the time, only to dart its bill out after passing prey (many herons and egrets), or does it dash back and forth, stirring up prey as it goes (e.g., Tricolored Heron)? If the latter strategy is adopted, does the bird also hold its wings out to the side to shade the water below ("canopy feeding") as does the Reddish Egret? Instead of stabbing at prey does the bird swish its bill back and forth in the water (e.g., spoonbills)?

- If you are dealing with a shorebird (sandpiper/plover/curlew/godwit-type bird), does it feed in the water, and if so, how far out does it go? In feeding does the bird pick (most sandpipers), probe deeply into the substrate (godwits, dowitchers), skim the water (avocets and stilts), or turn rocks over (turnstones)?

- If you are dealing with a terrestrial species, is it: (1) aerial—doing most or all of its foraging on the wing, (2) arboreal—feeding above ground in the trees and shrubs, or (3) cursorial—running about on the ground?

- If it is an aerial forager, is it constantly flying in the manner of a nighthawk, swift, or swallow; or does it spend most of its time perched, flying out only to nab passing prey (e.g., most flycatchers)?

- If arboreal, does the bird hitch up and down tree trunks and limbs while probing the bark? If so, does it remain upright (creepers and woodpeckers), or does it often move upside down (nuthatches)? Does it pick insects from leaf and twig surfaces (foliage gleaning), often hanging from under leaves to do so? What part of the canopy does it utilize, and at what height (i.e., central, middle, outer, and high, medium, low)?

- If the bird is cursorial, does it run, walk, or hop? Does it feed in the open or under heavy cover? Does it scratch back and forth vigorously in the litter (towhees, some sparrows), or pick quietly with its bill?
- Regardless of the foraging substrate used, what is the general foraging strategy (sit-and-wait, or active searcher)? If it is an active forager (as most birds are), does it forage at a slow, deliberate pace (vireos) or more rapidly (warblers, kinglets, titmice, and chickadees)? Does it flick its wings or tail while moving (e.g., kinglets, some warblers)? Does it keep its tail cocked like a wren or gnatcatcher?

While foraging behaviors are usually the ones most likely to be observed, other behaviors may be just as visible and diagnostic. Because they are used to form and cement pair bonds and insure the integrity of the gene pool, mating displays tend to be highly specific and therefore make for valuable identification clues when observed. Most passerines have little in the way of special ritualized displays because song serves the same purpose. However, many larger birds such as grebes, ducks, some raptors, cranes, some shorebirds, and grouse have elaborate and colorful mating displays that are both visual and vocal.

Even some passerines have rather outstanding display behaviors that are diagnostic. Most of these involve aerial singing by the males. This may involve only a short vertical flutter accompanied by a fluffing of throat and breast feathers and a burst of song (Cassin's Sparrow), a more sustained horizontal flight relatively close to the ground (Vermilion Flycatcher, Bobolink), or a very prolonged higher-flight song given while circling or while increasing altitude in step-like fashion (larks and pipits). Male grackles and cowbirds often engage in bizarre posturing and feather erecting when courting females.

Also useful to the identification process are the alarm or escape behaviors of many birds. Most puddle ducks will fly when scared, leaping directly out of the water into full flight. Diving ducks have structural modifications that negate such a fast take-off, and so must get a running start on the surface before getting airborne. Grebes and loons are more awkward still, and usually dive rather than fly to escape. Bitterns freeze with bill pointed to the sky when alarmed, while other herons will fly. When flushed, most grassland sparrows will fly low for a short distance and drop swiftly back into cover. Pipits, larks, and longspurs under the same conditions will often bounce high into the air and circle before returning to the ground.

Not to be overlooked are nest-building behaviors and the form of the nest. The nests of orioles, swallows, woodpeckers, hummingbirds, and others are good indicators of family or group status, while some individual species like the Rose-throated Becard and Altamira Oriole have nests that are impossible to mistake for the nests of any other species.

If you are searching for Cave Swallows in south Texas, a knowledge of nest structure can be an aid to quickly sorting out the Cave Swallow from the very similar Cliff Swallow. Both species will place their mud nests in concrete culverts under highways, but the nests of the Cave Swallows are open cups whereas those of the Cliff Swallows are closed with only a small entrance hole. A quick inspection of the nests clustered on the culvert walls will reveal whether Cave Swallows are present and will save you from vainly sifting through scores of Cliff Swallows.

GESTALT

An important component of identification which has been generally ignored until recent years is the concept of gestalt birding. This concept holds that each species has its own unique elemental character that is more than just the sum of its component parts. This character, in turn, yields a general impression to the birder that may be ill-defined, yet instantly recognizable.

Gestalt, then, combines all of the previously discussed features of structure, flight characteristics, plumage, and behavior into an overall impression that can often be discerned even when specific characters cannot. The British have popularized the term "jizz" which connotes a meaning similar to gestalt.

The approach is essentially the same as that used subconsciously when glancing at a bird and immediately placing it into a family based on a general impression rather than on any specific character(s). As an example, when specific plumage characters are considered, a Ruby-crowned Kinglet is reasonably similar in appearance to several *Empidonax* flycatchers and some vireos (that is, all are olive above, light below, with two wingbars and an eye ring). However, its plump appearance, small bill, and nervous behavior (constant motion and wing twitching) combine for a gestalt that allows instant separation from the other species.

It is this type of impression, then, that allows us to describe a bird as being fierce, powerful, bold, elegant, graceful, delicate, dainty, and so forth. While such an approach and terminology may seem (and is) somewhat subjective, it is, in fact, an extremely useful concept whose value in identification (particularly in certain groups) cannot be denied. When dealing with such difficult-to-identify families as storm petrels, hawks, shorebirds, jaegers, gulls, terns, and flycatchers, gestalt may play a major, or at least initial role in securing the identification.

A ready example is provided by the Mew Gull. There is little in the way of plumage characters to separate adults of this species from several other gulls. Its overall size is smaller than similar gulls, and so is its bill. But size and subtleties of bill shape are relative, and there may be no other gulls nearby with which to compare the bird. This is where the gestalt or jizz of the bird can still make identification easy. Mew Gulls have a small head and a small bill with a gently curved culmen and little gonydeal angle. This, along with the large, dark eye, combines to give the bird a very delicate, almost dove-like look. No direct comparison with other gulls is needed to gain this impression, although it is certainly accentuated when such comparison is possible.

As with other subtleties of bird identification, gestalt is something that can be safely used only with experience. However, the beginning birder can speed his or her progress towards field excellence by remaining cognizant of such advanced techniques. This should not remain a passive back-of-the-mind awareness, but should become an active, diligent search for new ways to recognize birds. When viewing common familiar species, take an extra few seconds to really study the bird—its structure, its plumage, and how it moves. When seeing a species (or other morphological variant) for the first time, make a special effort to register impressions that can aid in its identification the next time. For the true student of bird identification, every sighting should be a challenge to the senses. When this philosophy is assumed, no field trip is a waste no matter how dismal the day's list.

ACCESSORY INFORMATION

Knowledge of a species' life history, distribution, and habitat preferences can serve as valuable accessory information for making identifications. For example, adult shorebirds migrate earlier in fall than do their offspring. Since adult and juvenile plumages are markedly different for many species, a knowledge of migration timetables may provide a clue to the age, and hence to the identity of an unknown shorebird. Dowitchers provide a real problem in identification. There are some reliable methods of separating Long-billeds from Short-billeds (see Chapter 5), but before this can be done you must have some idea of which of the three geographic races of Short-billeds with which you might be dealing. A knowledge of the respective distributions of these three races will allow you to concentrate on the proper set of distinguishing field marks. Looking again at dowitchers, we find that on the West Coast Short-billeds are usually found in saltwater or brackish habitats, leaving the freshwater, inland locales to the Long-billeds. (There are, however, many places where the two species are found together.) Habitat is also a valuable clue when dealing with *Empidonax* flycatchers during the breeding season (see Chapter 5).

IMPORTANCE OF PREPARATION

An underlying thread of this entire chapter has been the need for advance preparation. The need to be cognizant of such points as structure, plumage patterns, molt sequences, age and sex, flight characteristics, behavior, life histories, distribution, and habitat has been pointed out. But awareness of such vital factors of identification should not come after the fact. Birders must become true students to develop real competence in bird identification, and being a true student means doing homework.

Too often one sees birders who only pick up their field guides to identify an unknown bird. They flip aimlessly through the pages until they see something that looks like their bird. By this time, memory of any observed details that might have been important to the identification has become fuzzy, due to the confusion of being presented with a barrage of pictures and information. Many times a field trip participant has come to me with the news that "I don't know what I just saw, but I'll recognize it when I see it in the book." They then proceed to describe it confidently as being "olive above and light below, with two white wing bars and an eye ring." Imagine then their dismay when they come to the page with the *Empidonax* flycatchers (most of which fit the above description), and then follow that with the kinglets, vireos, and fall-plumaged warblers. The common reaction at this point is to either give up in disgust, or make a guess based upon some point in the field guide that was never actually observed in the field.

Such trial-and-error birding may eventually produce real results, but the process is long and arduous. Identification of birds becomes much easier if you have spent hours at home studying pictures and descriptions first. Then when a bird flashes across the trail, you will already have a mental reference collection with which to compare it.

The sighting of a bird often takes place in a matter of a second or two, with visibility obscured by foliage or poor light conditions. In that short time you need to gather enough information to make identification possible. For some species this is not a problem because they are sufficiently distinct from everything else. For many more species, however, accurate identification depends on catching one specific detail that is often obscure. It is not enough to observe the facial pattern, wing bars, and upper and underpart coloration of a bird if the critical mark for separation is the presence or absence of tail spots. The birder who goes to the field without sufficient preparation cannot possibly hope to observe all pertinent details on every bird he or she sees. The prepared birder, on the other hand, will know to look immediately for certain characters depending upon the family or genus of the bird.

Toward this end I have prepared the following list of birds by group (usually by order or family, but often to smaller groups) along with the key characters of identification for each group. The list of characters is by no means comprehensive, and learning such characters should not preclude the acquisition of other information. However, it should provide a helpful starting point for the identification of birds within each group. Indication is also made of the relative difficulty of identifying members of the groups, each of which is characterized as being straightforward, subtle, or difficult to identify. Simple attention to details mentioned in field guides should insure identification of the *straightforward* complexes. *Subtle* implies the presence of distinctive characters that still require attention to minute detail (and possibly some comparative experience) to distinguish. *Difficult* implies that knowledge of complex plumage patterns, geographic variability, and gestalt of structure, flight characteristics, and so forth may be necessary, and even then, identification may not always be possible.

More detailed information on specific identification problems within these groups is provided in the next chapter. Where there are no sympatric members of a group, that group may be excluded from the list because identification may be made on the basis of geography alone.

Loons. Breeding plumages (including bill color) are diagnostic. In winter look at bill shape and color; face and crown coloration; back pattern; size of head, neck, and body; posture on water; and gestalt. Identification of basic-plumaged individuals is subtle-difficult, often depending on viewing conditions.

Grebes. Breeding plumages are diagnostic, and identification is straightforward. Separation in winter is sometimes subtle (mainly for Horned versus Eared). Look at head and neck shape and color, bill shape and color, size, and eye color.

Albatrosses. For adults, bill size and color, combined with mantle/wing/body color is diagnostic, and identification is straightforward. For immatures the critical points are bill size and color and an understanding of plumage sequences. Identification in U.S. waters is fairly straightforward.

Shearwaters. Identifications range from straightforward to subtle. Look primarily at head and rump patterns and colors, underwing patterns, flight characteristics, gestalt, and leg and bill color.

Pterodrama

Petrels. Identification of U.S. species is subtle. Focus on head markings and upper and lower wing patterns.

Storm Petrels. A subtle to difficult group. Concentrate on flight and feeding characteristics, rump markings, tail shape, and gestalt.

Tropicbirds. Concentrate on bill color, pattern of upper and lower wing surfaces, presence or absence of barring on the back (adults), color of tail streamers (adults), and size. Identification is straightforward.

Pelicans. Bill color and overall plumage diagnostic. Identification of all age classes straightforward.

Sulids. A subtle to difficult group to identify. For adults, look at bare part colors (bill, facial skin, feet) and overall plumage (particularly the head, tail, wings, and ventral body). For subadults look at underwing pattern; head, neck, and ventral coloration; presence/absence of white rump, collar, or patch at base of neck; size; and bare part coloration.

Cormorants. Focus on throat pouch shape and color, facial skin color, bill size, body size, and neck thickness. Identification is subtle.

Egrets. Bill/leg combinations are for the most part diagnostic. Look secondarily at plumage, size, facial skin color, habitat, and behavior. Identification is straightforward.

Herons, Storks, Ibis, Cranes, Spoonbills. Look at bill shape, size and build, overall plumage, and soft part coloration (secondarily at feeding behavior and habitat). Identification is straightforward.

Swans. A subtle group. Focus on head/bill profile, facial skin color and shape, posture when swimming, and call.

Geese. Look at overall plumage, leg and bill coloration, and size. Identification is straightforward.

Puddle (Dabbling) Ducks. Focus on colors of head, speculum, rump, and tail coverts. Identification (except for eclipse plumage) is usually straightforward.

Diving Ducks. Most males have distinctive plumages and/or bill colors and shapes (note head/bill profile). For females check head and bill profile and overall color pattern. Identification is straightforward except for scaup, subadult scoters, and female eiders.

Rails. Focus on bill structure and color, overall size and color pattern, calls, habitat, and leg color. Identification straightforward except for King versus Clapper.

Gallinules and Coots. Look at frontal shield color, and body and leg color. Identification straightforward.

Shorebirds. A diverse group with many straightforward identifications, but also with many subtle to difficult ones. Focus on bill structure and length, leg length, overall size, bare part colors, wing and rump/tail patterns, breast/belly plumage, feeding behaviors, and habitat. Knowledge of aging and plumage sequences vital for the separation of some complexes.

Jaegers. The identification of adults is subtle but identification of immatures is difficult. For adults concentrate on tail points (length and shape), flight characteristics, gestalt, upperpart coloration, nature of the breast band, presence or absence of mottling below (light phase birds), presence or absence of contrast on upper wing surfaces, and size. For immatures focus on size, flight characteristics, gestalt, the nature of barring on under and upper tail coverts, the degree of white flash in the wings, and the color tone of the body.

Gulls. The identification of adults is generally subtle, whereas that of immatures can be exceedingly difficult. When dealing with adults focus on bill and leg colors, bill size and shape, upper and lower surfaces of the wings, mantle color, size, presence or absence of a hood, tail shape and color pattern, and (to a lesser extent) iris color and gestalt. Knowledge of molt sequence is critical when identifying immatures. Focus on bare part colors, bill size and shape, wing pattern (particularly the contrast of the primaries with the rest of wing), size, tail bands, gestalt, and flight habits.

Terns. Identifications range from subtle to difficult. Concentrate on bill and leg colors, bill size and shape, size, contrast of upper and under surfaces of primaries with the rest of the wing, the presence/absence of translucent windows in the wings, the presence/absence of a carpal bar (juveniles), head/

face color patterns, the relative protrusion of the head and bill versus the tail, and gestalt.

Alcids. Given good views most identifications are relatively straightforward. Unfortunately, this is often not the case, and identifications can be difficult. Look at bill size, shape, and color (the combination is often diagnostic); size; presence or absence of a crest; head and neck color patterns (particularly eye rings, special plumes in breeding season, etc.); white on wings or scapulars; and overall color pattern (especially if dark to waterline).

Raptors (excluding owls). A diverse group with identification problems ranging from straightforward to difficult. Focus on wing and tail shapes and associated flight habits, color pattern of underparts (belly, wings, and tail), size, and plumage (or bare parts) of the head. To a lesser extent, look at the upper surface of the wings and tail, the scapulars, the rump, and gestalt. Most identification problems are caused by extreme plumage variation within species.

Gallinaceous fowl. Identification is straightforward. Look at overall plumage; presence of special plumes, crests, combs, and so forth; tail shape, bare part colors, habitat; calls; and displays.

Pigeons and Doves. Identification is straightforward. Focus on size, tail shape and color, color pattern of the wings, special marks (bands, spots, scaling) or colors on the neck, bill color, and overall color or pattern (scaled versus plain).

Trogons. Identification is straightforward, made easier in this country by the regular presence of only one species. Note bill and tail color, and presence or absence of a white breast band.

Cuckoos. Focus on bill color, pattern on the underside of the tail, color of the primaries, and call. Identification is generally straightforward but beware of juvenile Yellow-billeds with paler tails and dusky mandibles.

Owls. Identification is relatively straightforward. Note size; the presence/absence of "ears"; eye color; the shape, color, and pattern of the facial disc; breast and belly pattern (i.e., streaked, barred, or spotted); relative length of the tail; habitat; and activity patterns (diurnal vs. nocturnal).

Caprimulgids. Vocal identification is straightforward, but visual identification ranges from subtle to difficult. Focus on wing and tail shape, tail length and color pattern, size, presence/absence of white in wings, warmth or coldness to overall color tone (i.e., rusty or gray), and habit and habitat.

Swifts. Look at size, color, and distribution. Identification is generally straightforward given breeding allopatry of Vaux's and Chimney.

Hummingbirds. Identification of adult males is usually straightforward. Look at face pattern (mask, eyestripe, etc.) and color of gorget, crown, and bill. Look secondarily at size, tail shape, and back and underpart colors. Identification of females and immatures ranges from subtle to inseparable. Note bill color, face pattern, tail shape, size, habitat, and call.

Kingfishers. Identification is straightforward. Note size, back and belly colors, and calls.

Woodpeckers. Identification of most species is straightforward. Note the presence or absence of horizontal barring on the back, head and face pattern, back and rump color, wing pattern in flight, and calls.

Kingbirds. Focus first on the coloration of the underparts. If they are largely white, focus on bill size and the presence or absence and nature of white on the tail. If the underparts are largely yellow, note the presence or absence and nature of white on the tail, contrast of breast with the throat and belly, calls, and size of bill. Separation of all but Tropical from Couch's is straightforward, although these two from Western may be problematical.

Myiarchus flycatchers. Identification is subtle. Focus on voice, head and bill proportions, size, contrast of breast with throat and belly, extent of reddish color on tail, lower mandible color, and range and habitat. A knowledge of plumage sequences is helpful.

Empidonax flycatchers. Identification very difficult. The combination of calls, range, and habitat can make the identification of breeding birds fairly easy. At other times check bill and tail proportions; conspicuousness and shape of the eye ring; size and overall proportions; color of the throat, breast, back, and outer retrices; primary length; and calls.

Pewees. Identification is subtle, but vocalizations generally diagnostic. For visual separation note the presence or absence of conspicuous wing bars; contrast on the ventral surface of the body (particularly the flanks with the breast); size and relative proportions of bill, body, and tail; and the presence or absence of white on the side of the rump. Separation of Eastern and Western Wood Pewees except by voice may be impossible.

Phoebes and Other Flycatchers. Plumages of these remaining flycatchers are generally diagnostic, and identification is straightforward. Beware of confusing Eastern Phoebe with pewees, and tyrannulet with Empids, kinglets, or vireos.

Swallows. Identification is straightforward. Note back, rump, and underpart colors; tail shape; and presence or absence of a breast band.

Jays. Identification is straightforward except for *Aphelocoma.* If the general body color is blue, note the presence or absence of a crest, color of the head and breast, presence or absence of white in wings, face and throat pattern, tail length, and calls. If the bird is not blue, then overall plumage plus bill/tail proportions (nutcracker versus Gray Jay) diagnostic.

Magpies. Identification is straightforward, and the two species are nearly allopatric. Note bill color and the presence or absence of yellow skin around the eye.

Crows and Ravens. Identification is subtle. Note size, call, tail shape, habitat, and distribution.

Titmice. Identification is straightforward, especially given the allopatry of *inornatus* and *bicolor*. Note crest and flank color, presence or absence of a black and white face pattern, and distribution.

Other Parids. Identification is straightforward except for Carolina Chickadee versus Black-capped Chickadee, and young Verdin versus Bushtit. If the bird has a black bib, note the extent of the bib; crown, back, and flank colors; presence or absence of an eye stripe; presence or absence of white edgings to secondaries; and calls and distribution. If the bird does not have a black bib, note head and shoulder color, calls, relative tail length, and habitat.

Nuthatches. Identification is straightforward given the allopatry of *pygmaea* and *pusilla*. Note crown and face color and pattern, color of the underparts, calls, and distribution.

Wrens. Identification is generally straightforward. If an eye stripe is present, focus on size, presence/absence of streaking on the back, underpart color and pattern, relative tail length, presence of white in tail, calls, and distribution. If no eye stripe (or a very inconspicuous one) is present, note throat and belly color, presence or absence and boldness of barring on undertail coverts, voice, and habitat.

Kinglets. Identification is straightforward. Crown color and calls are diagnostic, but the presence of an eye ring versus an eye stripe may be the easiest mark to observe on birds that are seen from below.

Gnatcatchers. Identification is subtle. Breeding-plumaged males are easily separated (except for Black-tailed versus possible Black-capped in Arizona). Note color of crown and underside of tail, habitat, voice, and distribution. Females and winter males can present problems. Note undertail color pattern, voice, habitat, and distribution.

Bluebirds (and solitaire). Identification of males is straightforward. Note overall color, particularly of the throat and chin and central back, but also of the belly and the shade of blue of the upperparts. Identification of females is subtle. Focus on the color of the throat and flanks, wing color and feather edging, and the relative length of the wings. Solitaires are similar to female bluebirds but have wing bars, a longer tail with white outer feathers, and no hint of blue.

Spot-breasted Thrushes. Identification is subtle. A knowledge of the geographical variation present in this group is necessary for accurate identification. Note the boldness and extent of spotting below, upperpart coloration (warm rusty brown, cold gray brown, or intermediate), color of face and flanks, presence or absence of an eye ring, presence or absence of buffy wash on breast, tail or back contrast, and voice.

Shrikes. Identification is subtle. Note size, presence or absence of barring on underparts (adults), back color (juveniles), and range.

Mimids. Identification is straightforward except for Long-billed versus Brown, and Curve-billed versus Bendire's. If the bird is streaked or spotted below, check back and face color, length and decurvature of the bill, streaks versus spots (and how bold) on breast, voice, and distribution. If the bird is plain-breasted, note length and decurvature of the bill, color of the undertail coverts, presence or absence of white in the wings, overall coloration, voice, habitat, and distribution.

Pipits. Identification is straightforward to subtle. Focus on back pattern (scaly, lightly streaked, or strongly streaked), boldness and extent of streaking on breast, face color and pattern, leg color, habitat, range, and voice.

Wagtails. Identification is straightforward except for immature-plumaged Black-backed and White Wagtails, which are indistinguishable. If the bird is essentially black and white or gray and white in plumage, focus on the color of the flight feathers. If the bird is yellow and gray, check the color of the rump. All wagtails occur only as vagrants in the area covered by this book.

Waxwings. Identification is straightforward. Note color of undertail coverts and wings, size, warm or cold coloration to body, voice, and range.

Vireos. Identification is straightforward to subtle. Vireos can be readily divided into two groups, those with wing bars and spectacles/eye rings, and those with plain wings and an eye stripe. If your bird belongs to the first group, note the boldness of the eye markings (and whether it is an eye ring or true spectacles) and wing bars, color of the lores and iris, general coloration, voice, habitat, and range. If your bird belongs to the second group, check the color of the underparts (particularly the throat), crown-back contrast, presence or absence of a black line through eye or bordering eyebrow, eye color, and voice.

Warblers. Identification is straightforward for breeding males, most females, and most fall-plumaged birds. Waterthrushes, *Oporornis,* and some fall birds may be problematical. For breeding males, note overall color patterns (particularly the head and breast); voice; and the presence or absence of wing bars, tail spots, eye stripes, eye rings, and rump patches. For females, immatures, and fall-plumaged males, note color of flanks and undertail coverts; chip notes; and the presence or absence of wing bars, tail spots, eye stripes, eye rings, rump patches, and streaking on the back.

Buntings. Identification of males is straightforward; identification of females is subtle. General plumage patterns of males are diagnostic. For females, note overall coloration, presence or absence of buffy wing bars, rump-back contrast, and the presence or absence of indistinct streaking on the breast.

Towhees. Identification is straightforward with overall plumage patterns diagnostic.

Goldfinches. Identification of males is straightforward, of other plumages somewhat subtle. For males, overall plumage pattern is diagnostic. For females, immatures, and winter males, note color of vent, back, and rump; amount of contrast between throat and lower breast, and between the wings and the rest of the body; wing color; and boldness of wing bars.

Redpolls. Identification is subtle. Focus on the presence or absence of streaking on the rump, bill size, extent of streaking on flanks and undertail coverts, and degree of frostiness to overall color.

Carpodacus finches. Identification is subtle. For males, note the color and extent of red on the head, nape, and breast; the nature of streaking on the vent and flanks; voice; habitat; and distribution. For females and immatures, note the boldness of the face pattern, boldness and extent of ventral streaking (especially on vent), cleanness of the underparts, bill-tail proportions, habitat, and distribution.

Grosbeaks and other finches. Identification is straightforward except for female Rose-breasted versus female Black-headed, and immatures of the same species. For these, focus on degree of streaking below, underpart coloration, underwing coloration, calls, and distribution. For other members of this group, overall coloration is diagnostic.

Sparrows. Identification is straightforward to subtle. Note the presence or absence, boldness, and extent of streaking on the underparts; face, throat, and crown color pattern (presence of median stripes, eye stripes, eye rings, malar stripes, etc.); presence or absence of distinctive central breast spot; back pattern; wing coloration and presence or absence of wing bars; color of lores; size; tail length; voice; and habitat.

Juncos. Identification is straightforward. Eye color is diagnostic for the two species. For racial determination, note back, flank, and belly color; presence or absence of wing bars; presence or absence of a dark hood; and distribution.

Longspurs. Identification of breeding males is straightforward, and separation can be made on the basis of general plumage pattern. For females, juveniles, and winter males, identification is subtle. Focus on the distribution of white in the tail, face pattern, presence or absence of a shoulder patch, bill color and shape, calls, and distribution.

Meadowlarks. Auditory identification is straightforward. Visual identification difficult. Note song, cheek color, amount of white in tail, breeding habitat, and distribution.

Orioles. Identification of adult males is straightforward. Note overall plumage (color and pattern), bill shape, size, and voice. Identification of females and immatures is subtle. Focus on size, overall coloration (particularly contrast of breast with belly, and upperparts with underparts), bill shape and size, presence or absence of streaking on the back, presence or absence and nature of black on the face or throat, calls, and habitat during the breeding season.

Other Icterids. Identification relatively is straightforward. For adult males, check tail shape and length, eye color, color of head and neck, color of gloss (if present) to the body, presence or absence of bright colors in the wings, bill shape, voice, and distribution. For females and juveniles, check the presence or absence of streaking above and below, tail length and shape, eye color, color or pattern of face and breast, size, bill shape, habitat, and distribution.

Tanagers. Identification is straightforward. Overall color is diagnostic for all breeding males except Hepatic versus Summer. For these two note bill color, cheek color, shade of red in plumage, voice, and habitat. For females and juveniles, check overall color, bill color, presence or absence of wing bars, cheek color, calls, and breeding habitat.

PSYCHOLOGICAL INFLUENCES

One of the driving influences behind the sport of birding is the thrill of finding and identifying new or rare birds. The discovery of an unusual bird carries with it not only intrinsic rewards but also extrinsic ones in the form of admiration from peers. This creates a situation which can lead to problems in identification.

We always go afield with the hopes of finding something unusual. But it is easy to let this desire color our judgment when making identifications, particularly when the circumstances of an observation are less than ideal due to distance, light, brevity of observation, and so forth. All too often a bird will flash past your path, giving a tantalizing glimpse of one or two field marks that might indicate a rarity. If the bird is not relocated, frustration takes over, and subconsciously your mind may begin to fill in details that were not seen, thereby pushing the identification in the desired direction.

This kind of situation must be strenuously avoided if we are to maintain high standards of accuracy in the reporting of bird movements and distributions. Although birds are more mobile than most other organisms and are thereby subject to more frequent vagrancy, the odds of finding a rare bird at any point in time are indeed slim. Statistically, then, you are always playing against a stacked deck. Keep this in mind when struggling with an identification. Prove to yourself that the bird in question cannot possibly be an expected species first, before trying to prove that it is something unusual. Avoid single-character identifications. If there remains any sliver of doubt as to the identification, make your uncertainty known when reporting the bird. As for the bird that reveals just enough to whet your appetite before vanishing, remember that birding is a lot like fishing—the big ones often get away!

Such a philosophy will inevitably produce moments of frustration, but the benefits will far outweigh the costs. You will have contributed nothing but "sanitary" records to the literature, your integrity among fellow birders will remain spotless, and you will feel much better about your bird list and about any rarities whose identity you are able to confirm.

Difficult
Identifications:
Beyond the Field
Guides

Although the North American avifauna presents relatively few identification problems when compared to other regions, there still remain many species complexes that present real challenges to birders of all ranks. Birders who are confronted by one of these difficult identification problems often take one of two courses: They either over-extend their abilities and make some sort of guess (likely to be shaped by psychological influences), which often ends in misidentification; or, they give in to confusion and write the bird off as unidentifiable (preferable to the other course, but still unsatisfactory). Either situation results in a clouding of knowledge concerning the true status of the given species in that area.

Fortunately, North American birders are blessed with an abundance of available field guides, which are more than adequate in covering the vast majority of potential identification problems. However, as noted in the last chapter, the field guides have spawned some problems of their own. Some groups or species have been written off as unidentifiable in the field, when this is not the case. Still other groups have received an overly-simplified treatment that makes identification seem easier than it is. Because the guides are often taken as gospel by birders, the printed errors are perpetuated time after time in the field.

Recent years have seen a new approach to field identification by North American birders. This approach reflects a desire to go beyond the field guides, to push our identification capabilities to the limits. Such an attitude has long been in vogue in England where British birders have been subjecting hard-to-identify birds to minute inspection for years. Questions of molt sequence; geographic variation; and subtle behavioral, vocal, and morphological criteria are all being addressed.

The result has been a rapid expansion of our knowledge of identification. Recent years have seen a proliferation of in-depth papers detailing the secrets to identifying some species or group formerly considered next-to-impossible to separate. Unfortunately, these papers are scattered throughout the literature, and many of the advances have yet to be disseminated to the majority of birders.

This chapter attempts to synthesize much of the current knowledge concerning the tougher species of western birds. I have arbitrarily decided which species or groups to include. My decisions are based on many years of leading field trips, editing observations columns, and teaching classes in bird identification. These experiences have given me a feel for which birds are presenting the greatest identification problems. The choices no doubt reflect some personal and regional bias, and other authors would probably produce at least slightly different lists. Some of the more challenging groups are given only minimal treatment (for example, gulls), or none at all (female hummingbirds) because the scope of this book precludes the necessary feather-by-feather treatment.

This chapter, more than any other, is as much written *by* birders of

North American as *for* them. The many "new" field marks presented have been discovered by a multitude of top birders. Some have been published, others just passed by word of mouth. In nearly every case I have extensive experience with the species involved, and have emphasized field marks that I find most useful. Where I cannot vouch for a particular character, I have cited the reference from which it came. Complete references are cited in the bibliography.

Identification problems are presented in taxonomic order. Where illustrations were considered useful, they have been included. You will note the frequent use of photographs of museum specimens to illustrate various species. While dead birds do not reveal such things as posture, behavior, and so forth, they are excellent aids in that they can be conveniently laid side-by-side for comparison. This is especially important when dealing with subtle differences in bill shape or length and other fine distinctions.

Finally, you should not consider any of the following to be the last word in identification. Our knowledge of these groups is still incomplete, and you should constantly look for new field marks to secure difficult identification.

It should also be emphasized that this material is supplemental to (not a replacement for) that found in standard guides. There are many commercially popular field guides available, and nearly all are adequate for beginning-level birders. The one that I recommend most strongly (particularly for intermediate and advanced birders) is the National Geographic Society: *Field Guide to the Birds of North America* (Scott 1983—chief consultants: Jon Dunn and Eirik Blom). This guide incorporates far more of the recent advances in field identification than do the others, and is the most comprehensive in illustrating geographic variation, immature plumages, and so forth. Also recommended is the three volume set *The Audubon Society Master Guide to Birding* (1983, edited by John Farrand Jr.). It too incorporates much of the new information on bird identification.

Peter Harrison's *Seabirds: An Identification Guide* (1983) is also highly recommended for identifying loons, grebes, gulls, terns, and pelagics. Don Roberson's *Rare Birds of the West Coast* (1980) is an excellent book that contains much useful identification information, particularly concerning Asiatic species that appear as vagrants in this country.

BASIC-PLUMAGED LOONS

The world's four species of loons are readily identified in breeding plumage. Basic-plumaged birds, however, present a solvable but subtle challenge to the skills of birders. This problem is of greatest concern to birders on the West Coast (where all four species occur regularly), but should not be ignored by inland birders, since Red-throated and Arctic are regular vagrants to inland bodies of water.

Throughout the interior of North America the Common Loon is indeed the most common loon species. Since it is also common in coastal locales, it will serve as a good yardstick with which to compare the other species.

The Common-Loon is a large-bodied, big-headed, big-billed loon. On the one side it could be confused with the even larger Yellow-billed, and on the other it is comparable to the smaller Arctic. It is not likely to be confused with the much smaller, slender-billed Red-throated, nor is the latter species likely to be mistaken for the relatively massive Yellow-billed. The critical problems then are: (1) Common versus Yellow-billed, (2) Common versus Arctic, and (3) Arctic versus Red-throated.

Common versus Yellow-billed. Most guides tend to stress bill shape and color as being critical field marks in the differentiation of these two species. Indeed, the combination of bill color and structure can be diagnostic for many individuals, but accessory marks should also be examined.

Yellow-billed Loons typically have larger bills than most Commons. The culmen of the Yellow-billed is straight (Common angles to the tip), accentuating the angle of the gonys. This is more pronounced in some individuals, and such birds have a distinctive upturned look to the bill. Such a look is further shown off by the tendency of Yellow-billeds to tilt their heads upward, much like the posture of the much smaller Red-throated Loon. In spite of this, bill shape is an unreliable character for separating the two species because it is subject to some amount of variation. It may be considered an accessory (but not primary) aid in identification.

Likewise, bill color is an important factor but should be viewed with caution. Some Yellow-billeds will show an entirely straw-yellow bill. Such individuals are readily identified. Most others (particularly first-year birds) have paler bills with some duskiness to the base. These birds are not overly dissimilar to many Commons, whose bills may lighten to a very pale gray. The more common error is to mistake light-billed Commons for Yellow-billeds, but the reverse error is conceivable. In any event, you should focus your attention on the color of the culmen. Even the lighter-billed Commons will have dark culmens, while the culmens of Yellow-billeds (at least the distal half) are always light (Figure 5.1). Many Yellow-billeds have dusky coloring on the proximal one-third to one-half of the culmen.

There are some excellent plumage characters that have been largely ignored by most guides. Foremost among these is the pale-headed look of the Yellow-billed. This species is noticeably lighter on the crown and hindneck than it is on the rest of the upperparts. The former areas tend to be pale sandy-brown, and on the face this color typically extends no farther than eye level and often does not reach that far. On most individuals this leaves a face that is mostly pale, except for a conspicuous brown smudge on the auriculars. This smudge can be highly visible on some individuals, but hard to distinguish on others.

FIGURE 5.1. Yellow-billed Loon (basic plumage). Note the massive pale bill, light auricular patch, and the hint of a barred back. Photo by Richard E. Webster.

By contrast, Commons are darker on the crown and hindneck than on the rest of upperparts, and the brown of the crown extends farther into the face, past the level of the eye. The only conspicuous feature of the face is a distinctive white eye ring that stands out well against the brown feathering that borders it. Yellow-billeds also have white feathering encircling the eye, but at most this gives the impression of a crescent above the eye rather than of an eye ring. This is because the feathering in front of, behind, and below the eye is extensively white rather than a contrasting brown.

Some Yellow-billeds show a distinctive pattern of transverse barring of the back. This is especially conspicuous on juveniles. Beware, however, that juvenile Commons, while not as strongly patterned, still show conspicuous cross-barring on the upperparts. In any event, Yellow-billeds average browner on the upperparts, with most Commons appearing darker.

Other differences are structural. Yellow-billeds are larger bodied, with thicker necks and flatter-crowned heads. These are subtle distinctions, however, that may not be obvious except when the two species are in view at the same time.

Common versus Arctic. Most standard guides do little to point out the many differences between these two species. Size and structural distinctions are usually noted, while plumage differences are largely ignored.

Commons are larger, bulkier birds than Arctics. They are thicker-necked and flatter-crowned, and many have a blockheaded look that is created by the steep rise of the forehead from the bill. In flight they appear more hunched with a proportionately larger head and feet. Their wingbeats are noticeably slower. Both species have bills that appear straight, but that of the Common

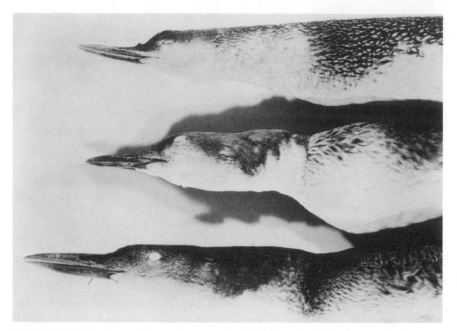

FIGURE 5.2. Basic-plumaged loons (top to bottom: Red-throated, Arctic, Common). Note especially the differences in bill size/shape, and color patterns of the head, neck, and back.

is notably heavier (Figure 5.2). All of these characters are useful and often instantly recognizable to those with much comparative experience. Birders lacking such experience, however, may be misled by individual variation, posture differences, or poor viewing conditions.

Plumage differences lend themselves to more objective discrimination by those with little or no experience with one or the other species.

As pointed out in the preceding account, Commons are darker brown on the crown and hindneck than on the back. They also have conspicuous white eye rings that contrast with the dark crown. Although they lack the extreme patchy look of the Yellow-billed (presented by the white face and dark auricular smudge), Commons still have a somewhat patchy look to the face that results from an uneven, often fuzzy border between the dark crown and white lower face. The lores may be dark or white, but if dark, they are concolor with the rest of the crown. The division between dark and light on the side of the neck is also uneven and somewhat erratic in nature and may show a patchiness that differs from bird to bird. The back appears dark at any distance.

Contrarily, Arctics are lighter on the rear crown and hindneck than on the back. In this species, the crown and hindneck are an evenly colored gray-brown, lending a smooth look. This look is accentuated by a sharp division between white and dark on the side of the neck and on the face. At close range you may see a thin blackish line separating the light from the dark on the sides of the neck. Many Arctics show a row of dark spots across the white throat which form a sort of chin strap. As for the face, the dark color of the crown extends downward to encompass the eye and then breaks off sharply, giving the species a dark-capped look. The area around the eye is typically dark (no white eye ring) and the lores are noticeably blacker than the rest of the face or crown. The back of this species is distinctly darker than either the crown or the hindneck and appears black at a distance or in poor light. Many British birders swear by the presence of a conspicuous white patch on the rear flanks as a diagnostic field mark for identifying Arctic. This mark may be diagnostic only for the nominate race *arctica* because it can be very difficult to see on West Coast birds (*pacifica*).

Some attention has been paid to diving differences between these two species as an aid to identification. Commons tend to slide under the water while Arctics jump up and then under. As with other such behavioral points, this one requires further testing because it could depend heavily on wind and water movements, water depth, and so forth. Another behavioral characteristic that could be considered supplemental concerns flocking behavior. Arctics are often encountered in feeding flocks, while Commons and Red-throateds are rarely found in groups of any real size.

Arctic versus Red-throated. Red-throated Loons in basic plumage are noticeably lighter in overall color than are the other loons and are particularly lighter than Arctics. Like the latter species, Red-throated is lighter on the crown and hindneck than on the back. However, the entire upperparts are a light gray-brown that is very different from the blackish-brown back and lighter (but still dark) gray hindneck and crown of the Arctic. The light appearance of the Red-throated is heightened by a large amount of white speckling on the back, a feature that is absent in Arctics. In juvenile Red-throateds, the division between the gray-brown of the crown and hindneck, and the white of the face and foreneck is often somewhat uneven, and the line of demarcation is not nearly as sharply defined as in the Arctic. (This does not hold for winter adult Red-throateds.) This, combined with the highly speckled back, gives the Red-throated a broken-colored look that is very different from the smooth, evenly-colored Arctic.

Structural differences are also important. Red-throateds are smaller, a difference that is not always obvious in the field. A character that is obvious is the shape of the bill. As already noted, Arctics have straight bills. Red-throateds, however, have a distinctive upturn to the distal end of the lower mandible (See Figure 5.2). The bill of Red-throated is also distinctly thin, almost like that of a large grebe rather than a loon. The upturned bill of the Red-throated is accentuated by its habit of swimming with its bill angled up towards the sky, giving it a snobby look.

HORNED VERSUS EARED GREBES

These two species present an identification problem that is caused mostly by an overemphasis of many field guides on one particular field mark. Most birders have no problem in separating the two species during the breeding season. The problem comes later when the birds are in basic (winter) plumage.

Most guides emphasize the white face and neck of the Horned Grebe as being the best mark for separation in winter. While it is true that Horned Grebes are distinctly whiter in these regions than most Eared Grebes, it is also true that Eared Grebes show considerable variation in the extent of white versus dusky on the face and side of the neck. This has led to many instances of birders reporting numbers of Horned Grebes on lakes in the southwest (where the species is rare) based solely on the presence of white facial areas.

It is much easier and safer to identify the two species by overall structure of the head, neck, and bill, and by the general color pattern of those areas rather than the presence or absence of white in one specific area (Figure 5.3).

The Eared Grebe has a thin neck with a head that often peaks at the mid-point of the crown. When seen in profile this is very apparent. Eared Grebes also have a relatively longer, thinner bill that is slightly upturned at the tip. By contrast, the Horned Grebe has a shorter, thicker neck with a flatter-crowned, triangular-shaped (viewed from above) head that peaks at the rear crown. It is much stockier looking in the head or neck region, and this is accentuated by a shorter bill that is thicker and straight in profile. The flat-crowned, triangular head is almost reminiscent of a pit-viper's head in shape.

The overall color pattern of the two species is also quite different. Although Eared Grebes often show varying amounts of clean white on the face, this white is usually located well below the eye, which is surrounded by dark gray

FIGURE 5.3. Basic-plumaged Horned (top) and Eared (bottom) Grebes. Note structural differences and the distribution of light and dark coloration on the face.

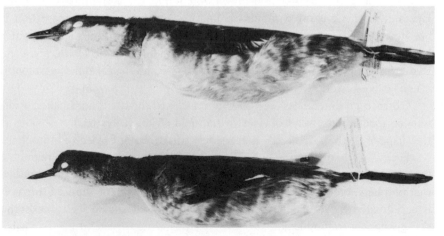

feathers. Also, the line separating the dark color of the crown from the white of the lower face is often uneven and somewhat blurred in nature. Horned Grebes show a clean white face that extends upwards to the eye, where it is sharply demarcated from the dark crown. The amount of white or gray on the sides of the neck is somewhat variable in both species, but Horneds are typically much cleaner looking, and the black of the nape usually forms a narrow line up an otherwise white neck. Eared Grebes typically show a light auricular patch that is not present in the Horned Grebe, whereas the latter species often shows a light spot between the eye and the bill that is lacking in Eareds.

For more information refer to the field notes of Dunn and Garrett (1982).

DOUBLE-CRESTED VERSUS OLIVACEOUS CORMORANT

These are the only two cormorants found in our area away from the West Coast. The Olivaceous is locally common in Texas, Louisiana, and New Mexico but appears to be increasing in numbers at the western edge of its range, and reports from Arizona and southern California are increasing. Certainly it should be watched for in freshwater areas throughout the Southwest.

The Olivaceous is a much smaller bird than the Double-crested, even more in bulk than in length. This size difference is immediately obvious when the two species are side by side and is even quite apparent to experienced observers on lone birds at reasonable distances. However, swimming cormorants of any species often look deceptively small, and observers should not rely on this criterion alone.

In addition to absolute size differences, Olivaceous Cormorants are differently proportioned from Double-cresteds. They are much more slender birds with thinner necks and bills and proportionately longer tails.

The best way to separate the two species is by the shape and color of the gular pouch on the throat (Figure 5.4). In the Double-crested this area of bare skin extends from the eye downward and encircles the throat. In profile it presents a large semicircle outline. Because it covers a large area and is either bright orange or yellow in color, the gular pouch of the Double-crested is usually obvious at even great distances. The Olivaceous, on the other hand, has a much smaller gular pouch that angles posteriorly from the eye and then cuts back sharply toward the chin. It ranges in color from a dull pink-orange to a dull yellow. The combination of dull color with small size makes the gular pouch of the Olivaceous somewhat inconspicuous, especially at longer distances. During the breeding season the gular pouch of the Olivaceous is bordered by a narrow line of white feathers that is diagnostic.

Immatures of the two species are easily separated by the same characters of size, proportions, and gular pouches, but can be additionally identified on the basis of plumage characters. Young Double-cresteds tend to be very pale

FIGURE 5.4. Double-crested (top) and Olivaceous (bottom) Cormorants. Note size differences, differences in the size and shape of the gular pouch, and the white border to the gular pouch of the Olivaceous.

(almost cream colored) on the underside of the neck and breast. This contrasts strongly with the dark brown belly, giving these birds a bicolored appearance. Young Olivaceous are more uniformly dark brown (slightly lighter with buffy tones below) throughout and lack the bicolored look. Young Double-cresteds also have yellowish bills, whereas the bills of young Olivaceous tend to be darker and indistinctly colored.

BRANDT'S VERSUS DOUBLE-CRESTED VERSUS PELAGIC CORMORANTS

West Coast observers have three cormorant species with which to deal. The Brandt's and Pelagic are extremely unlikely to be seen away from the immediate coast or open sea, so any cormorant seen inland is likely to be a Double-crested by default. However, Double-cresteds are routinely seen in numbers at coastal locales, so cormorants in marine environments must be studied before being labeled as to species.

One immediate way to separate the Pelagic Cormorant from the other two species is on the basis of size and shape (Figure 5.5). Double-crested and Brandt's are large, bulky cormorants with thick necks, large heads, and thick bills. The Pelagic, on the other hand, is a small, very slender cormorant, built more along the lines of an Olivaceous. Pelagics have very thin necks and bills, and small heads. When perched on a rock alongside either of the other two species, Pelagics are positively dwarfed. When seen flying over the open ocean, Pelagics can be distinguished by their straight-neck profile tapering to a fine point with very little apparent head (pencil-like).

Pelagic Cormorants have red facial skin that can be seen at close range

FIGURE 5.5. Brandt's (top) and Pelagic (bottom) Cormorants.

(very difficult in winter) and a dull red gular pouch that is relatively inconspicuous. Breeding-plumaged adults show two white oval patches on the flanks that are very conspicuous in flight. Immature birds can be distinguished by their combination of small, slender build and uniformly dark brown plumage.

As stated, Brandt's Cormorants are very large, bulky cormorants built along the lines of Double-cresteds. Breeding adults have beautiful blue-centered gular pouches surrounded by yellow. In other age classes and nonbreeding adults the blue is very dull and inconspicuous, but these birds may be recognized by the dull, yellow-buff throat that is smaller and much paler than the bright yellow-orange throat of a Double-crested. This light buff contrasts as a paler band across the rest of the darker plumage. At very close range note also the clear blue iris. Immature Brandt's show more contrast between upperparts (darker) and underparts (lighter) than do immature Pelagics, but are darker and more uniformly colored than the bicolored immature Double-cresteds. When flying in a straight line Brandt's tends to leave its neck straight out (but not always), while Double-crested routinely flies with its neck crooked. Brandt's are often seen feeding in the nearshore ocean in sizeable flocks (up to several hundred birds). Such occurrences are rare with Double-cresteds.

IMMATURE NIGHT HERONS

This is an identification problem that is of increasing concern to western birders, as more and more Yellow-crowned Night Herons are turning up west and north of their normal ranges. Adult birds of both species are instantly recognizable, but the identification of immatures is somewhat subtle.

Yellow-crowned Night Herons of all ages have positively huge bills that are noticeably thicker than the bills of Black-crowneds (although some experience with the latter species may be necessary to get a feel for this). This look is accentuated by the more slender-necked appearance of the Yellow-crowned. Young Black-crowneds typically have bills that are at least partially greenish yellow, whereas young Yellow-crowneds have all black bills. The latter species also has longer legs that trail well beyond the tail in flight, as compared to Black-crowneds whose feet barely protrude beyond the tail.

A good mark for identifying young Yellow-crowneds is the contrast in the upper surface of the wings, seen when the bird is flying. Young Yellow-crowneds have dark gray flight feathers that contrast strongly with the browner forewing. This gives the wings a distinctive bicolored look that is very conspicuous, and which is somewhat similar to the upperwing pattern of Great Blue Herons. Young Black-crowneds have an essentially uniformly brown wing that looks very different. Yellow-crowneds are generally grayer than the browner Black-crowneds and have upperparts that look smoother in color, due to fewer and smaller white spots on the dark ground color. These smaller white spots (against a grayer background) are almost reminiscent of the spotting on the upper parts of a yellowlegs.

ROSS' VERSUS SNOW GOOSE

These similarly-plumaged geese have been made by many authors to appear more difficult to separate than they really are. Since Ross' Geese are turning up as regular vagrants throughout the west, it is particularly important that birders be aware of reliable easy methods for identifying them.

Because the blue phase of Ross' Goose is extremely rare, it is white phase birds of both species that are likely to be confused. There is nothing in the plumage of adult birds that can be safely used to distinguish between species. Plumage is a helpful cue in identifying immature birds. Young Snow Geese are very dingy looking, with extensive amounts of gray on the wing coverts, back, head, and neck. They also have blackish bills. Young Ross', on the other hand, closely resemble adults in being almost entirely clean white with only small amounts of gray (mostly confined to the crown and nape), and in having pinkish bills.

The clinching characteristics for these geese at any age come from an examination of bill, head, and neck structure, and overall body size. Ross' Geese are decidedly smaller than are Snow Geese. This is usually evident when the two species are side by side but may be very hard to judge on lone birds. Even in mixed flocks size differences can be difficult to judge due to uneven terrain (such as plowed fields) or posture differences.

The best mark by far is the size and shape of the bill (Figure 5.6). Snow Geese have large bills that show a distinct black "lip" at the juncture of the upper and lower mandibles. This mark is extremely prominent and easy to see. Additionally, the culmen of a Snow Goose is slightly humped at the base

FIGURE 5.6. Snow Goose (top) and Ross' Goose (bottom). Note differences in bill size and structure, the dark "lip" of the Snow, and the pattern of feathering at the base of the bills.

and then dips distally. Ross' Geese have *very short*, stubby bills that appear sawed off. The culmen is essentially straight, giving the bill a triangular appearance that is instantly recognizable as being different from that of a Snow Goose. Also, Ross' lacks the conspicuous "lips" of the Snows. One mark that is somewhat overplayed is the presence of warty protruberances at the base of Ross' bills. These are not conspicuous on most individuals unless you are right on top of the bird. What is noticeable, is that this warty area usually forms a distinctive blue-gray band around the base of the bill. This band contrasts strongly with the pink color of the rest of the bill. This blue color is not found in Snow Geese.

Head and neck shape of the two species is also somewhat different. Snow Geese have long necks (beware of postural influences) with heads that are somewhat flat-crowned. Ross' Geese have short, stubby necks with very rounded heads. This, combined with the stubby bill, give Ross' Goose a gentle, cute look that is very different from Snow Goose.

For more information refer to Simon (1978).

FEMALE BLUE-WINGED TEAL VERSUS FEMALE CINNAMON TEAL

Female Blue-winged and Cinnamon Teal are so similar as to be a real identification problem in areas of overlap. Unfortunately, most existing field guides do little to point out the few differences that can be reliably used to sort out these two species.

Female Cinnamons are evenly colored with warm brown tones that tend toward the rusty end of the spectrum. Female Blue-wingeds, on the other hand, have a cold look and are more gray-brown with no hint of rust. Additionally, their dark feathers tend to have broad pale fringes creating a scalloped look that is quite different from the more uniformly-colored Cinnamon.

Likewise, the head and face region of the female Cinnamon is one of fairly uniform coloring with very little pattern apparent. Contrarily, the pale face of the female Blue-winged contrasts rather strongly with a dark crown and dark eye line, thus creating the impression of a bold, light supercilium. Blue-wingeds also typically show a distinct pale spot at the base of the bill. This area may be lighter in Cinnamons as well, but it is much less apparent (Figures 5.7, 5.8). It should also be pointed out that eclipse-plumaged male Cinnamons (which otherwise resemble females) have red eyes, a trait that is not found in any Blue-wings.

Still another character that is useful given comparative experience is the size and shape of the bill. Cinnamon Teal of both sexes have bills that are noticeably longer and more spatulate than the bills of Blue-winged Teal, giving them a more shoveler-like look (although the bill is not nearly as long or as spatulate as in the latter species).

For more information see Wallace and Ogilvie (1977).

GREATER VERSUS LESSER SCAUP

Birders who live in inland areas of the West get few chances to see Greater Scaup, thus making the identification of occasional vagrants a difficult task.

Too many birders rely on the difference in the color of head gloss to separate male scaup. Under many light conditions the heads of both species appear plain black. Worse, the purple head of a male Lesser Scaup may appear green under some light conditions. I have never seen the reverse (that is, a Greater Scaup with a purple head), but it may happen. Head color may be considered an accessory field mark, but should never be the sole basis for identification.

A much better indication is head and bill shape. Greater Scaup of both sexes have heads that are rounded, with proportionately large slipper-like bills (Figure 5.9). The size of the bill combined with the rounded shape of the head tends to deemphasize the size of the head making it appear somewhat smallish. Lesser Scaup, on the other hand, have peaked crowns and smaller, less spatulate bills. This combination makes the head more prominent and appear proportionately larger. The black nail at the tip of the bill tends to be more extensive in Greaters of both sexes but this mark is often hard to see.

Male Greaters that are sitting on the water can often be picked out from a flock of Lessers by their brighter white sides. The whiteness of the sides in male Lessers is quite variable, but many Greaters are a gleaming immaculate white. Again, this is an accessory mark that should not be used alone.

FIGURE 5.7. Female teal (Cinnamon [top] and Blue-winged [bottom]). Note the broader, more spatulate bill, and the lack of facial pattern on the Cinnamon. Blue-winged exhibits a contrasting dark eye line, white loral spot, and smaller bill.

FIGURE 5.8. Female teal (Cinnamon [top] and Blue-winged [bottom]). Note again the differences in bill size, and the contrasting dark cap and eye line of the Blue-winged. Note also the more conspicuous light feather edgings on the upperparts of the Blue-winged.

FIGURE 5.9. Greater Scaup (male). Note the rounded head and large bill. Photo by Alan Wormington.

The often cited longer white wing stripe that is found in Greaters of both sexes is also a helpful accessory mark, but it does show some overlap. Fortunately, most overlap appears to be between male Lessers and female Greaters.

Some female Greaters have light patches on the auriculars, a character infrequently found in female Lessers. Female Greaters also average a paler brown in overall color, with more white around the base of the bill. Both characters are subtle and may show great individual variation. They should therefore be considered only accessory in nature.

FEMALE COMMON MERGANSER VERSUS FEMALE RED-BREASTED MERGANSER

Female mergansers are superficially similar, but their identification has been complicated by most field guides.

Standard guides tend to emphasize the shaggier crest of the female Red-breasted, versus the more pronounced throat and neck contrast of the female Common. While both are usable marks, there are other good characters that in combination can make accurate identification relatively simple.

The head, face, and neck of the female Common are a *bright* rusty brown. Only the chin is white, and the rust-brown color is uniform throughout. The bright white chin does contrast sharply with the rust of the lower throat and neck, but posture of the swimming bird often makes this hard to see. In the same vein, however, the white of the chin encroaches into the face on both sides of the head. The margins of this white area are rounded and sharply demarcated, thus forming distinct white ovals extending from the underside of the bill onto the face. These are very easy to see in profile and contrast greatly with the rest of the rusty-brown head. Additionally, the upperparts of female Commons tend toward silver-gray, which when combined with the snow-white underparts and very contrasty head, give them an overall clean appearance.

Female Red-breasteds have a totally different look to the head, face, and neck. First, the white of the chin is continuous with the white of the breast, with no dark coloring on the underside of the neck or throat. Second, although the white of the throat extends into the side of the face, there is no sharp line of demarcation. Rather, the white fades gradually into the face, as it does on the sides of the neck. Therefore, no distinct white ovals exist, and the boundary between dark and light is blurred and somewhat dingy looking. Overall head and upper neck color is dull brown, very different from the bright rust of the female Common. In addition, the head and face are not uniformly colored, with the face being a lighter buff and the top and back of the head being darker dull brown. All of this, combined with the shaggier crest, gives the female Red-breasted an unkempt, dingy appearance that is very different from the bright, clean look of the female Common. This is accentuated in some birds by upperparts that are more dingy gray-brown than the typical silver-gray of Commons.

An additional point that may prove useful (particularly when light conditions blot out colors) is the structure of the bill and consequent head profile. The bill of the Common is deeper at the base, giving a more pronounced concave slope to the culmen. This slope is continuous with the forehead, giving the entire head a more streamlined profile. The bill depth of the Red-breasted Merganser is shallower at the base, creating a thinner, straighter-billed look. This also gives the impression of a steeper forehead, because the culmen has less upward slope proximally.

SHOREBIRDS

The shorebirds (members of the families Charadriidae, Scolopacidae, Haematopodidae, and Recurvirostridae) present a special challenge to birders everywhere. While several species are distinctively plumaged and easy to identify in all seasons, many others are members of species complexes that involve two or three (or even more) similar species. This is particularly true of members of the genus *Calidris*, the small, brownish-gray sandpipers collectively referred to as peeps in this country and as stints in Europe.

Identification of most shorebirds (but especially the peeps, dowitchers, and yellowlegs) is facilitated by (and in some cases dependent on) at least a basic knowledge of seasonal plumage variation, molt sequences, and patterns of dispersal.

The ability to properly age a shorebird is particularly vital in the identification of many species. Most field guides depict at most only two plumages per shorebird species: a winter or basic plumage and a summer or alternate plumage. In fact, shorebirds have a third plumage—the juvenal plumage—that in most species is distinctly different from either adult plumage. Those species that lack a distinctive juvenal plumage are generally those that pose few identification problems to begin with.

Most north-bound adult shorebirds in spring are in fresh breeding (alternate) plumage as the result of a partial prealternate molt. Fresh breeding dress is characterized by unworn feathers with clean margins and often with sharp, bright feather edgings of white, gold, or chestnut. Except for occasional individuals that retain their winter plumage into summer (usually due to sexual immaturity) all shorebirds seen from mid-April to early June will be in this plumage, or at least molting into it.

This fresh alternate plumage is worn on the breeding grounds and (in most species) on the return migration south in summer or fall. By the time Arctic-nesting species arrive back in the contiguous forty-eight states, their feathers have been subjected to considerable wear and abrasion. This results in a worn alternate plumage that usually looks tattered and dull. Feather margins are often frayed and in all cases lack the brightly-colored edges that were present in spring. Differential feather wear may totally obliterate any real pattern to upperpart coloration. These individuals lack the sharp, natty appearance seen earlier, and thus may totally confuse observers familiar with the other plumage.

Juvenal plumage is acquired by a complete postnatal molt on the breeding grounds and is worn through the southward migration. Because the plumage is only recently attained by the time juvenile birds move south, their feathers have not begun to show the signs of wear that characterize fall-migrating adults. In many species the feathers of the back, scapulars, tertials, and wing coverts are *broadly* edged with white, buff, gold, or chestnut, lending a bold, clean, appearance that is more reminiscent of spring adults than of those in worn alternate plumage. In some species (for example, Eurasian Dotterel, Curlew Sandpiper, Baird's Sandpiper, Ruff, and Buff-breasted Sandpiper) these feather edgings are especially broad and bold, giving a distinctive spangled or scaly look to the upperparts (Figure 5.10). To a lesser extent this is evident in all peeps, and to a lesser extent even in some plovers.

FIGURE 5.10. Juvenal-plumaged Baird's Sandpiper. Note the broad light feather margins, which lend a scaly look to the upperparts. Note also the extremely long wings. Photo by Alan Wormington.

Winter (basic) plumage is typically somewhat plain (although not ratty until late in winter), with most species having grayer feathers with either dark shafts or centers and with little or no trace of light feather margins. This plumage is attained from a complete postnuptial molt by adults, and via a partial postjuvenal molt by juvenile birds. Juveniles of most species retain their scapulars, tertials, and wing coverts from juvenal plumage into first-basic plumage.

Recognition of the three (four including worn alternate) plumage types should go hand in hand with a knowledge of molt-timing and general patterns of movement. For almost all shorebirds adults migrate south earlier than juveniles, this difference sometimes amounting to a month or more. Adults of most species will begin appearing in the contiguous forty-eight states by early to mid July (in some species by the end of June), and for species that winter to the south of us, will have passed through for the most part by mid to late August. Adults typically retain most or all of their alternate plumage until the wintering grounds are reached (Dunlin and Wilson's Phalarope are exceptions). For most species this means that all southward-bound adults will be in worn alternate plumage, and that for species that winter far to the south (for example, Baird's and White-rumped Sandpipers), the basic plumage will almost never be seen in our area.

Contrastingly, juveniles (in fresh juvenal plumage) migrate later in summer and fall, with the earliest individuals arriving in mid to late July, and the bulk movements occurring in August through October. Juveniles also acquire their basic plumage later in fall than do adults, this acquisition often coming from October through November rather than in August. Once again, juveniles of most species do not attain basic plumage until they reach the wintering grounds.

Most areas will show some overlap between migrating adults in worn alternate plumage and migrating juveniles in fresh juvenal plumage. Observers in southern coastal areas need to be particularly alert in late summer through fall because they may encounter three distinct plumages of some species simultaneously. Because these areas serve as wintering grounds for some species (or are at least very close), fall-arriving individuals will be molting into basic plumage. That means that some species (for example, Sanderling, Western Sandpiper) may be present in three plumages: worn alternate, juvenal, and basic, not to mention transitional individuals that are between molts.

For many species there are also sexual differences in the timing of migration by adults. For species with essentially uniparental care, the emancipated sex typically migrates first. These sexual differences do not carry the same importance to birders as do the age differences because most shorebirds are sexually monomorphic (phalaropes are an exception).

Careful attention to details of plumage, as well as to dates of arrival will aid tremendously in the identification of many shorebirds. For the difficult species complexes, a knowledge of molt sequence and migration timing may be critical to accurate identification. In all cases, observers should become thoroughly familiar with all plumage variations of the common or expected species in their area before attempting to identify rare species.

For further discussion of shorebird molts, and migratory patterns, refer to Roberson (1980, 1982).

Peeps. Many a birder has spent hours on end puzzling over the little brown and gray shorebirds that comprise the genus *Calidris*. Indeed, this group presents

many subtle identification problems and offers many opportunities for misidentification by unwary birders. Many of the standard guides are less than adequate
aids in identifying these birds, being characteristically oversimplified in their
discussion of similar species.

The ability to correctly age peeps is of paramount importance to proper
identification. As pointed out in the preceding section, juvenal-plumaged birds
are strikingly different from adults that are present at the same times. Because
most records of rare peeps tend to be of juvenile birds in fall, observers would
do well to pay particular attention to the juvenal plumages of all peeps.

Size, bill structure, wing length, and overall color pattern are also critical
marks in assessing peeps of any age group. Absolute familiarity with all plumages
of the common species in your area is the best foundation for being able to
identify the less common ones. Avoid single-character identifications at all costs.

The following discussion will focus on problems in separating the regular
species of North American peeps. Be aware that the possibility of vagrant peeps
of Eurasian origin can complicate the picture.

Western versus Semipalmated Sandpiper. This is probably the biggest single
problem in peep identification in North America (among regularly occurring
species). Semipalmated Sandpipers are rare but regular migrants west of the
Great Plains (most common in fall), whereas Western (along with Least) is
one of the two most common peeps in this same area. Semipalmated does
not winter in North America (published Christmas Bird Counts to the contrary),
and the Western winters only in southern coastal areas and in a few locales
in the Southwest.

Most discussions of separating these species center on bill length. As a
rule, Westerns have noticeably longer bills that droop more at the tip than
do Semipalmateds. However, bill length in peeps is subject to both sexual and
individual variation, with females of both species tending to be longer-billed
than males. Female Westerns are unlikely to be mistaken for Semipalmated,
but the shorter-billed males may be easily mistaken if bill length is used as
the sole criterion.

More important than absolute bill length is bill shape. Westerns have
bills that are broad-based but which taper to relatively fine points. Many individuals have a noticeable droop to the tip (not unlike Dunlin) but others do not.
In all cases the bill of a Western should narrow conspicuously from base to
tip. Semipalmateds, on the other hand, have tube-shaped bills that are thick
throughout their length, and which do not taper conspicuously. Their bills do
not terminate in a fine point or in a droop, but instead have a blunt look
and may show a somewhat bulbous tip. These shape differences hold for all
Semis and are particularly vital in identifying longer-billed individuals (Figures
5.11 and 5.12).

There are also consistent plumage differences between the two species.

FIGURE 5.11. Semipalmated Sandpiper (juvenile).
Note the tubular-shaped bill (thick to the tip with
little apparent tapering). Photo by Alan Wormington.

FIGURE 5.12. Western (left) and Semipalmated (right) Sandpipers. Note differences in
bill shape. Photo by Richard E. Webster.

Breeding-plumaged Westerns are usually light gray with conspicuous chestnut-colored scapulars, auriculars, and crown feathers, giving them a fox look. Breast spotting extends along the flanks and is shaped like an arrowhead. Breeding Semipalmateds are typically more brownish with only traces (if any) of rust on the scapulars, crown, and face. Spotting is confined to the breast and lacks the pronounced arrow shape found in Westerns.

Juveniles of the two species can also be separated on the basis of plumage. Juvenile Westerns tend to be gray and white with contrasting chestnut-colored scapulars and mantle feathers (as with many other shorebirds, juvenile Westerns retain wing covert feathers along with some scapulars—but not the chestnut inner ones—and tertials when they molt into first basic plumage). The upperpart feathers are neatly edged with white or red. Juvenile Semipalmateds tend toward uniform buffy-brown (not gray) upperparts and lack the distinctive chestnut scapulars of the juvenile Western (traces of this coloration may be present). They typically have a bolder light supercilium that is set off by a more solidly-colored crown (giving more of a capped appearance) and by darker auriculars that extend just above the eye. More striking are the neat, cream-colored edges to all of the upperpart feathers, lending a scalloped or scaly appearance similar to juvenile Baird's (but much less pronounced). This effect is more striking in Semipalms than in Westerns, perhaps due to the more uniformly-colored upperparts and greater contrast provided by the brown feathers with cream edges (as opposed to gray feathers with white edges). Juvenile Semipalmateds frequently show a buffy wash on the side of the breast (usually somewhat smudged looking and often extending as a large wedge from the shoulder midway into the breast). This, however, should not be the basis for identification because similar smudges are often seen on juvenile Westerns. Most far-west records of Semipalmateds are of juvenal-plumaged birds in late summer-early fall, and this plumage should be committed to memory.

Basic-plumaged birds are best identified on the basis of bill shape because many individuals of both species may be virtually identical in plumage. However, as pointed out earlier, adult shorebirds typically delay molt into basic plumage until they reach their wintering grounds. Since Semipalmateds are extremely rare in the United States in winter, this means that basic-plumaged individuals will almost never be encountered. Westerns do winter in southern coastal areas and therefore are commonly seen in basic plumage. This plumage is basically gray and white like the juvenal plumage, but lacks the rusty scapulars and crisp, light edges to the upperpart feathers.

The two species can also be separated by call notes. Westerns give a high, thin "jeet," which is readily separated from the low, grating "jrrt" of the Semipalmated (a call similar to that of Baird's Sandpiper).

West Coast observers should not ignore the remote possibility of vagrant Rufous-necked or even Little Stints, either of which could be mistaken in juvenal or basic plumage for a Western or Semipalmated (given the slim odds of seeing either species and the influences of psychological factors, the reverse mistake is more likely). Juveniles of both of the rare species approximate juvenile Westerns slightly more than they do juvenile Semipalmateds, with more extensive rusty feather edges to the upperparts, and without the buffy scalloped look of juvenile Semipalmateds. Bill lengths of the two Eurasian species average shorter than those of Westerns but lack the tube-shaped bills with blob-shaped tips found in Semipalmateds. Both Eurasian species (especially Little Stint) are sufficiently rare as to require extreme caution in identification and should not be identified in other than breeding plumage by novices or by others lacking comparative experience. Interested birders should consult the European literature on the identification of Palearctic Stints (see particularly Wallace 1974, and Grant 1981). See also Roberson (1980).

Other Peeps. As a general rule, the most common peep across most of the interior West is the Least. As such, observers should make every effort to familiarize themselves with all of its plumages along with all of the plumages of the nearly as common Western. Such familiarization will greatly facilitate the discovery and correct identification of the more unusual species from among the myriads of more common ones.

Let's start with the separation of Least from Western. Least is a smaller bird with a thinner bill. Westerns are larger, with longer, broader-based bills. These differences are especially apparent when direct comparison of the two species is possible. The bills of both species taper to a fine point and may droop slightly at the tips. Standard guides emphasize the greenish-yellow legs of the Least, as opposed to the black legs of the Western. While greenish-yellow legs will confirm the identification of a Least, the fact that such color is not discernible does not eliminate this species from consideration. Light conditions and mud-caking may make yellow-green legs appear dark at any distance.

Least Sandpipers are browner in all plumages than are Westerns (which are gray). Breeding adults in fresh plumage and juveniles are very brown with crisp chestnut and white edges to the feathers of the upperparts. Breeding adults are further characterized by a bold band of blackish streaks (set against a brownish wash) across the breast, whereas juveniles have a buffy wash (with few streaks) across the breast and are more boldly patterned above. Winter adults are dull brown and lack the bright feather edgings. Their breasts are characterized by a band of streaks that is smudged in appearance (not sharp as in spring). Likewise, adults in worn breeding plumage lack the crisp feather edgings and appear dull brown.

Westerns in all plumages are grayer than Least, and breeding adults and juveniles have highly-contrasting chestnut scapulars; whereas breeding adults also have bright chestnut auriculars and crowns. The breast spotting of adult Westerns in breeding plumage is distinctly different from similarly-plumaged Leasts, with arrow-shaped spots against a white (not brown) ground color. These extend down the flanks in Westerns, while being confined to the breast in Leasts.

Least Sandpipers are separated from Semipalmated Sandpipers by a number of characters. Leasts have thinner bills that taper to a fine point, unlike the thick, tubular-shaped bill of the Semipalmated. Like the Western, the latter species has black legs, but again, this mark should be viewed with caution. Winter Semipalmateds are grayer and lack the distinctive breast band of winter Leasts. The buffy, scalloped look of juvenile Semis is also totally different from any plumage of Least.

Two other species of *Calidris* that are likely to be confused with Least, Western, and Semipalmated Sandpipers are the Baird's and White-rumped

Sandpipers. Both species are structurally similar, being noticeably larger than the other species as well as being differently shaped. Baird's and White-rumped are the largest of the small brown and gray peeps, being much larger than Least, and recognizably larger than Western.

Both species have relatively short legs and long wings, which lends a very horizontal (rather than upright) appearance to the postures of the birds. This horizontal look is almost reminiscent of a small tern on land rather than of a small sandpiper. An excellent mark for separating these two from the other species is the length of the folded wings. In Baird's and White-rumped these protrude past the end of the tail, whereas in the other species the wing tips do not even reach the tail tip (Figure 5.10).

The bills of both Baird's and White-rumped are longer than in the other species but are similar in shape to the finely tapering bills of Least. The legs of both species are black, leaving Least as the only small *Calidris* with light legs.

Baird's in all plumages is a buffy-colored bird. Adults in all plumages are somewhat dull (often dull brown due to feather wear) and lack brightly-margined feathers. This is especially true of birds in worn alternate plumage, whose frayed feathers lend a particularly dull, tattered look. Baird's are buffy-brown above and white below with a small band of fine darkish streaks overlaid on a buff-washed breast. This buffy breast contrasts with the white chin. Juveniles are almost unmistakable, with broad light feather edgings giving the upperparts a spangled, scaly appearance that is even more pronounced than in other juvenile peeps (Figure 5.10). Baird's in all plumages have broad, whitish (but not clean white) superciliums.

White-rumpeds lack the buffy coloring of Baird's, being white below and grayer above with some contrasting rusty feather edgings. They have whiter superciliums, and the breast spots are distinctly arrow-shaped and are also heavier and more extensive (extending down the flanks) in distribution. They are overlaid on a white (not buffy) background. In all of these respects White-rumpeds more closely resemble Westerns than Baird's. The clear white rump (not divided by a central bar) of the White-rumped is diagnostic (among peeps) when seen, but reliance on this character alone can lead the observer to confusion with other medium-small shorebirds. Calls of the two species are very different. Baird's has a low, guttural "grrt," whereas White-rumped gives a high, thin "seet" that is almost insect-like.

Juvenile White-rumps lack the distinctive breast spotting of breeding adults, but they can still be distinguished from Baird's by their white rumps, calls, lack of scaly back pattern, and extensively chestnut-edged feathers. The white rump, combined with size and shape are the best features for eliminating other peeps from consideration.

Both Baird's and White-rumped winter far south of the United States (published Christmas Bird counts to the contrary), and as such, are unlikely to ever be seen in basic plumage in our area. Baird's are uncommon to rare spring migrants over much of the West, being more common in late summer and fall. Most White-rumped records west of the Great Plains (where the species is casual) are from spring. White-rumpeds migrate north much later than other peeps and are more likely to be found in the latter half of May and first days of June than at other times.

Yellowlegs. Field guides have traditionally instructed birders to identify yellowlegs on the basis of overall size, bill size and shape, and call, with no attention given to plumage differences. In fact, most guides treat yellowlegs (and other shorebirds) as if they have only one plumage. As with most other shorebirds, the two yellowlegs species (Greater and Lesser) have three recognizably different plumages:

1. basic—attained by adults following breeding and/or fall migration (August to September) and worn until the following April (juvenile birds molt into first basic plumage later—October/November)
2. alternate—worn by breeding adults from April to May through late summer
3. juvenal—worn by young birds from fledging until late fall.

The two species are highly similar in basic plumage and are best identified by structural and vocal differences. Alternate plumages are very distinctive. Upperpart coloration is of little help in identification, but the underparts are radically different. Lessers have finely-streaked throats and breasts with some fine barring on the flanks (may be concealed). Their bellies and lower breasts are immaculate white, and the line of demarcation between streaked upper breast and plain lower breast is sharp (reminiscent of Pectoral Sandpiper, only the streaking is less dense). Greaters are boldly streaked with black on the throat and upper breast, which gives way to dense black spotting and barring on the lower breast, flanks, and belly. They are much more heavily and extensively marked below, and there is no sharp line of demarcation between marked and unmarked areas. Greaters in alternate plumage are actually closer to alternate-plumaged Willets, which have much stouter, straight bills, dark legs, and a bright black-and-white wing pattern.

The two species are also readily distinguished when in juvenal plumage. As a rule, Lessers return south earlier than Greaters (but on the West Coast adult Greaters arrive first), and as in other shorebirds, juveniles follow adults. Juvenile Lessers begin appearing in our area by late July to early August and will greatly outnumber adults by the end of August. Greaters straggle south more slowly (many winter in the southern United States), and juveniles do not typically outnumber adults until October (remember that these dates are averages and will vary somewhat with latitude).

As with the other plumages, the upperpart coloration of the juvenal plumages is of little help in identification. Once again you will have to direct your attention to the underparts. Juvenile Lessers have a grayish wash across the breast and throat. Faint smudgy streaks may or may not be visible against this background. Juvenile Greaters are not similarly washed with gray and instead have white throats and breasts with a distinct bib of heavy black streaks (but with the throat plain, and minus the heavy spotting and barring of the flanks, belly, and lower breast that is seen in alternate-plumaged adults).

In any plumage Greaters will show whitish spots on the inner primaries, whereas the primaries of Lessers are entirely blackish.

None of this is meant to discredit or discourage the use of traditional criteria such as size, bill length and shape, and call notes. Indeed, for basic-plumaged birds these characters are necessary to identification.

Greaters are distinctly larger with longer bills that are often slightly up-turned. Although bill length is variable for both species, Lessers always have very straight bills. Overall size and bill length and shape are easily judged when the two species are side by side (or when other, better-known species are present), but they become less helpful when you are dealing with a single bird, or a monospecific group (Figure 5.13).

Bill color can be helpful because Greaters usually show a bicolored bill (distal ⅔–¾ blackish, basal area yellow-orange, pinkish, or greenish-gray), whereas Lessers have essentially all black bills (sometimes lighter gray right at the base). Leg coloration has been suggested as a useful character, with Greaters often having deep orange legs. This should be considered an accessory rather than primary identification aid, because leg color is subject to great individual variation in both species, and perceptions of it may be easily influenced by light conditions.

FIGURE 5.13. Top to bottom: Willet, Greater Yellowlegs, Lesser Yellowlegs. Note differences in size and bill shape and length.

All calls of Greaters are louder and more resonant than similar calls of Lessers. In addition to the "tu-tu-tu" flight calls described in most field guides, both species have more rapidly delivered alarm notes ("tee-tee-tee-tee . . .") that may be uttered in long series.

As mentioned previously, Lessers winter primarily in South America. A few individuals winter on our southern coasts and at the Salton Sea, but most wintering yellowlegs in the United States should be Greaters. For more information see Wilds (1982).

Dowitchers. Dowitchers probably present the most difficult identification problem among North American shorebirds. Field guide illustrations often disagree in their depictions of the two species (Short-billed and Long-billed), and many birders have long given up identifying silent birds. Fortunately, an excellent paper by Wilds and Newlon (1983) has summarized existing knowledge of dowitcher identification, much of which was known to relatively few birders. Much of the information that follows was first described in their detailed treatment.

As with other shorebirds, dowitchers have three distinct plumages:

1. basic
2. alternate
3. juvenal

Armed with a knowledge of plumage types, geographic variation, and molt sequences, birders can safely identify individuals in all three plumages. However, field identification of basic-plumaged individuals (except by voice) remains tenuous, and the prudent birder will let most individuals go as "dowitcher sp(?)."

Dowitcher identification is greatly complicated by the existence of three distinct races of Short-billeds:

1. *Limnodromus griseus griseus* (mostly migrates along the East Coast, some west to the Gulf Coast)
2. *L. g. hendersoni* (nests in western Canada—migrates from the East Coast west to the Rockies)
3. *L. g. caurinus* (migrates along the West Coast). Of these, *caurinus* is the most variable in plumage, and *hendersoni* mostly closely resembles Long-billed.

Let's start with basic-plumaged individuals. Adult dowitchers molt into basic plumage following nesting. Molt may begin in transit south and be completed upon arrival on the wintering grounds. Short-billeds generally migrate earlier in fall than do Long-billeds, with adults first appearing in the contiguous forty-eight states in late June or early July. Adult Long-billeds follow soon after, with the southward movement of juvenile Short-billeds coming about one month later. Most juvenile Long-billeds don't appear until mid-September. Juveniles of both species do not molt into basic plumage until October or November.

All dowitchers in basic plumage are essentially gray and white. There are no consistent known differences between the three subspecies of Short-billeds in basic plumages, and differences from Long-billeds are few and subtle. Long-billeds usually have the black bars on the tail wider than the light bars, giving the impression of a black tail narrowly barred with white. Short-billeds are the reverse, with the wider white bars giving the impression of a white tail barred with black. Unfortunately, the tail barring is difficult to see unless the bird is preening, and intermediate individuals of both species exist (do not be misled by the barred uppertail coverts, which show black and white bars of nearly equal width).

The only other consistent plumage distinction concerns the distribution of gray on the throat and breast. Long-billeds are typically washed heavily with gray across the throat and breast (whitish on the chin) and show a fairly defined line of separation between the gray breast and white belly. Short-billeds usually have less gray on the breast, and it is distributed more as large smudgy spots than as even wash. The separation of white and gray ventrally on Short-billeds is also less clear. Having said all of this, I would still urge extreme caution in the visual identification of basic-plumaged dowitchers.

Separating dowitchers in alternate plumage is easier but still complex. For one thing, it is in this plumage that the three races of Short-billeds appear different from one another. Also, the alternate plumage of Long-billed overlaps the corresponding plumage of each race of Short-billed in some respect. All is not lost, however, for careful attention to detail will make identification possible.

Long-billeds in alternate plumage have the blackish dorsal feathers *narrowly* edged with rust and tipped with white. Because the rust edgings are narrow, the overall impression given by the upperparts is rather dark (darker than any Short-billed). The underparts are entirely reddish, with the throat, breast, and sides of the neck heavily spotted with black (Figure 5.14). The breast is also typically barred with black as are the flanks and belly (less densely). The undertail coverts are usually barred, but may be spotted. Note that on many individuals of both species the black ventral markings may appear as irregular-shaped marks that cannot be labelled as either bars or spots. As is the case with basic-plumaged birds, breeding Long-billeds have the black bars of the tail wider than the light ones, and the latter are more often orange than white.

The *hendersoni* race of Short-billed is the closest in appearance to Long-billed. Like the latter species, *hendersoni* is mostly or entirely reddish on the underparts (may show some white on the vent). Unlike Long-billeds, they are very *lightly marked* below, typically being lightly spotted throughout (heaviest

FIGURE 5.14. Alternate-plumaged dowitchers. Left to right: Long-billed, Short-billed (*L. g. caurinus*), Short-billed (*L. g. hendersoni*), and Short-billed (*L. g. griseus*).

on flanks and undertail coverts) with some barring on the flanks. Most individuals have the throat, sides of the neck, and central breast virtually unspotted, lending an overall ventral appearance quite different from Long-billed and from *L. g. griseus* and *L. g. caurinus* (Figure 5.14). The black dorsal feathers of *hendersoni* are *broadly* edged with rust, making the upperparts appear brighter than in Long-billed. The light tail bars are wider than the black ones and are most often white (rather than orange) in color.

The nominate race of Short-billed—*L. g. griseus*—is the most different from Long-billed. The throat and breast are a lighter orange than in the latter species, and the belly and vent are *white*. This gives a pronounced two-toned effect to the underparts. The breast is densely spotted with black (much more so than in *hendersoni*) and the flanks are moderately to heavily barred. The undertail coverts are typically white and spotted but may be washed with orange and/or barred (Wilds and Newlon, 1983). The black dorsal feathers have narrow rusty edges, and are closer in appearance to those of Long-billed than those of *hendersoni*. The light bars of the tail are usually wider than the black ones and are most often white.

The most variable race of Short-billed is *caurinus*. They are closest in general appearance to *griseus* (with densely spotted breast and white belly and vent), but many individuals more closely approximate *hendersoni* (more extensively orange underparts with less marking). Dorsal coloration is similar to *griseus*

FIGURE 5.15. Juvenal-plumaged dowitchers (left to right: Long-billed, Short-billed, Short-billed). Note the differences in tail-barring, scapular and tertial edging, and whether or not the tertials bear internal markings.

FIGURE 5.16. Short-billed Dowitcher (juvenile). Note the broad light margins to all of the upperpart feathers as well as the diagnostic internal markings of the tertials. Photo by Richard E. Webster.

FIGURE 5.17. Long-billed Dowitcher (juvenile molting into basic plumage). Note the unmarked tertials and lack of broad light feather edgings to the upperparts. Photo by Richard E. Webster.

or Long-billed, and the light tail bars are usually widest and white in color (sometimes orange).

Degree of feather wear can affect the appearance of alternate-plumaged dowitchers. When in fresh plumage all four forms may show white horizontal bars (feather edges) on the otherwise reddish or orange breasts. Just as these whitish edges fade with wear, so do the rusty edges of the dorsal feathers. This makes the birds progressively darker through the breeding season, and effectively blurs any differences between the two species in upperpart coloration. According to Wilds and Newlon (1983) the black bars of Long-billeds are lost more quickly than the spots of Short-billeds, so that adult Long billeds may be plain orange-red below by late summer.

The two species are most easily separated when they are in juvenal plumage. The three races of Short-billed are inseparable from one another in this plumage, and all are readily told from juvenile Long-billeds. The most obvious differences involve the scapulars, greater coverts and tertials. In Short-billeds the scapulars are *broadly* edged with rust or gold (as are all the feathers of the back and wing coverts) and have conspicuous rust or gold internal markings (giving a "tiger bar" pattern). Likewise, the tertials (which conspicuously cover the primaries when the wing is folded) of juvenile Short-billeds have prominent internal markings of gold or rust, typically shaped as irregular, wavy lines (Figures 5.15 and 5.16). Juvenile Long-billeds have the dorsal feathers (including the scapulars) only *narrowly* edged with rust, and the scapulars *lack* any *internal markings* (Figures 5.15 and 5.17). Similarly, the tertials of juvenile Long-billeds have narrow, pale margins and also *lack internal markings* (some individuals show small light spots at the tips of the tertials—Wilds and Newlon, 1983). Accordingly, if the scapulars and/or tertials of a juvenile dowitcher can be seen well, then it should be identifiable as to species (note that this applies only to juveniles because alternate-plumaged adults of both species have internal markings on the scapulars and tertials. Since juvenile dowitchers (like juveniles of other shorebird species) often retain some juvenal tertials and scapulars along with their remiges when molting into basic plumage (October to November), it may be possible to identify birds on this basis well into winter.

Juvenile Long-billeds are basically washed with gray on the head, neck, and breast (possibly with some buff or orange), and have whitish bellies. Any breast spotting is faint when present. Juvenile Short-billeds tend to be much brighter (orange or buff) below, with some fine spotting or streaking on the breast.

Some mention should be made of structural and vocal differences between the two species. As the names imply, Long-billeds have (on the average) longer bills than do Short-billeds. However, there is enough overlap due to individual variation and to sexual dimorphism (females of both species have longer bills than do males) so as to make bill length an unreliable field character. Extreme individuals of either type are probably separable by bill length alone. The standard guides adequately describe the typical calls of the two species: a yellowlegs-like, mellow "tu-tu" (sometimes with more syllables) for Short-billed, and a high, "kreek" for Long-billed—but beware that Long-billeds almost always string several "Kreeks" together when flushed.

There are some differences between the species in habitat preference, with Long-billed more often preferring inland areas and Short-billed preferring coastal waters, but overlap is extreme. Clearly, hendersoni Short-billeds will be commonly found in freshwater, inland areas, and caurinus is a common migrant at the Salton Sea.

As was previously pointed out, Short-billeds tend to migrate south earlier in summer than do Long-billeds. They also tend to migrate north later in spring. Short-billeds are restricted to coastal locales in winter (primarily at large tidal mudflats) with no verified winter inland records.

Basic-Plumaged Phalarope. Of the three species of phalarope, two (the Red and the Red-necked) are more pelagic in their movements, whereas the other (Wilson's) sticks to inland or coastal locales. Red-necked Phalarope do migrate across much of western inland North America, and in some places may even be locally common during migration. Red Phalarope are almost entirely pelagic but have been found to be regular fall vagrants to inland areas as far east as the Great Lakes. Wilson's remains the common phalarope throughout the West (it breeds over most of our area), and observers at inland locales will be faced with sorting through hordes of Wilson's to find a few Red-necked or a single Red.

Breeding-plumaged phalarope of both sexes (females are much brighter) are generally distinctive. Problems arise with identification of basic and juvenal-plumaged birds in fall.

In all plumages phalarope can be safely separated on the basis of comparative size and structure alone (Figure 5.18). Wilson's and Red Phalarope are essentially the same size but are differently proportioned. Wilson's has a longer, thinner neck, and a long needle-like bill. Reds are stockier-bodied with shorter, thicker necks and big heads. This gives them a chunkier look that is compounded by a short bill that is thicker than the bills of the other two species. Contrary to the way it is pictured in some field guides, basic-plumaged Red Phalarope only occasionally have bills that are yellow at the base. Most individuals will appear entirely black-billed. Red-necked is noticeably smaller than either of its congeners, with a thin neck and tiny head that give it an almost pin-headed look. Their bills are much shorter than those of Wilson's, but with the same thin, needle-like look that is different from Red.

Plumage features are still very useful and are of particular value to birders on pelagic trips when views of phalarope are often limited to several small birds flying rapidly past the bouncing boat.

Basic-plumaged phalarope are all essentially gray and white. In Wilson's

FIGURE 5.18. Nonbreeding phalarope (top to bottom: Wilson's, Red, Red, Red-necked, Red-necked). The Red-neckeds are in juvenal plumage, while the others are in basic plumage. Note differences in bill length/thickness, and in face patterns.

this translates into uniformly dingy gray upperparts (lightest on the nape and crown) and whitish underparts. There is a gray line through the eye setting off a whitish eye stripe, but in general the face is not strongly patterned. The tail is white (seen in flight) and the flight feathers are darker than the rest of the wing, but there are no wing stripes or streaks on the back (Figure 5.19).

The Red-necked, by contrast, is boldly patterned on the back, wings, and head. Like the Wilson's, its underparts are white, but the basic ground color of its upperparts is a much darker, slate gray. This color is darkest on the nape and crown (the extent of gray on the crown is variable—some individuals are white), which contrasts strongly with a white forehead giving a capped appearance. Further pattern to the head is created by a large blackish-gray patch that encloses the eye and extends backward toward the auriculars. Against the otherwise white face, this gives a masked look. Contrast is also found on the back and wings where longitudinal white streaks on the scapulars and back contrast strongly with the otherwise dark upperparts (contrast is strongest in juveniles), and where horizontal white stripes on the wings similarly stand out (Figure 5.19). Occasional individuals are somewhat faded in appearance, and on these birds the pattern may not be obvious. The tail of Red-necked is dark in the center, a mark that sets it apart from Wilson's but not from Red.

Red Phalarope are also more boldly patterned than Wilson's but less so

FIGURE 5.19. Nonbreeding phalarope (left to right: Red, Red, Wilson's, Red-necked, Red-necked). The Red-neckeds are in juvenal plumage, while the others are in basic plumage. Note differences in overall size, bill length and width, and coloration of the upperparts.

than Red-necked. Like the latter species, Red Phalarope have a white face with a bold blackish patch through the eye that extends to the auriculars. Also like the Red-necked, they are darkest on the nape and back of the head. However, in Reds the slate color of the nape typically ends at the rear or midcrown, leaving a more extensively white forehead. This creates somewhat of a balding appearance (but also present in many Red-neckeds). Red Phalarope are somewhat variable in the color of their upperparts. Most individuals are several shades of gray lighter than Red-neckeds, but occasional individuals are nearly as dark (particularly molting adults in fall and juveniles). In any event, they lack longitudinal white streaking on the back and scapulars, leaving a solidly gray back (Figure 5.19). Along with obviously larger size, the lighter, solidly gray back is usually the best mark for separating Reds from Red-neckeds at sea. Another character that is useful is the bold white wing stripe, which against the solidly light-gray upperparts is reminiscent of a Sanderling.

Beware that juvenal-plumaged Wilson's have somewhat buffy breasts, brownish upperparts, and wing and back feathers that are edged with gold. Such birds could be mistaken for juvenile Red-necked, but note the larger size, longer bill, less boldly-patterned face, and absence of bright chestnut or golden stripes on the back and scapulars. Unlike most other shorebirds, juvenile phalaropes molt into basic plumage very quickly, often while migrating.

JAEGERS

This is undoubtedly one of the most difficult groups encountered by western birders. The three species (Parasitic, Pomarine, and Long-tailed) are very similar in plumage and all are polymorphic. In addition to having to contend with a variety of complex plumages, you will often be contending with viewing conditions that are less than ideal. This is because jaegers are highly pelagic away from the breeding grounds (arctic tundra), and most sightings will come from a rocking boat under poor lighting, and often at great distances. Nothing will enliven a dull pelagic trip like the sighting of a distant jaeger, because such an event is likely to throw the entire group into spirited debate over the identity of the bird. Indeed, *many* individuals will have to remain unidentified, especially until you have attained a fair amount of comparative experience.

As already mentioned, all jaegers are polymorphic. There are no known sexual dimorphisms, but there are age distinctions. The ability to correctly age jaegers is often vital to proper identification. There is also a range of variation within age groups. Four distinct types of plumage are recognized.

1. *Adult breeding.* All species have distinct dark and light phases and often a continuum of intermediate phases. All species and phases are characterized by elongated central tail streamers.

2. *Adult basic plumage.* Intermediate between adult breeding and subadult plumages. Lacks the barred underwings of the latter. Tail streamers often reduced or absent. (Harrison, 1983)

3. *Immature (subadult).* Plumage is like dingy adult, with less defined cap and dusky wash on face and neck. There are more scaled upperparts, heavier breast band, shorter tail streamers; and variable amounts of barring on the flanks, underwings, and vent.

4. *Juvenal.* These are darker and more heavily barred, with short tail points. All species are variably polymorphic, often with light, dark, and intermediate morphs. Unlike gulls, jaegers retain their juvenal plumage through the fall until the wintering grounds are reached (Harrison, 1983).

Subadult stages can be particularly complex, with all species requiring three to four years to reach adult plumage. Jaegers undergo a complete molt *after* migrating to the wintering grounds. Therefore, we will seldom see individuals in molt.

In all plumages jaegers are generally separable by jizz (gestalt) and flight characteristics, providing that the observer has sufficient comparative experience with the group. Long-taileds are the smallest and most slenderly built of the three species. They have long, very slender wings and are extremely aerobatic, buoyant fliers. In flight they are almost tern-like. Parasitics are usually larger, but always bulkier, with shorter broader-based wings. Their flight is stronger and choppier (more falcon-like) with less up-and-down motion. They resemble Heermann's Gulls in overall jizz and flight characteristics and are most likely to harass terns or small to medium-sized gulls. Pomarines are the largest, with bigger, stockier heads (more bull-necked) and thicker more deeply-hooked bills. They appear to have a thick heavy undercarriage and in flight are more direct and powerful (reminiscent of small South Polar Skua or Western Gull) than the other species. They will harass the largest of gulls.

The major problems in identification are between Parasitic and Long-tailed on the one hand, and Parasitic and Pomarine on the other. Pomarines and Long-taileds are so different in size, build, jizz, and flight characteristics as to make confusion unlikely. Adults of all species are easiest to identify, whereas juvenal and immature-plumaged birds are most difficult.

Let's begin with the separation of adults. Too many birders rely on the shape and length of the central tail points to identify jaegers. Breeding adult Long-taileds have the longest streamers, and these are pointed at the tips. Parasitics also have pointed streamers, but theirs are typically several inches shorter. Pomarines have streamers that are twisted then flared at the ends (giving a blob-tipped look). These streamers are nearly as long as those of the Long-tailed, something that is not obvious from most illustrations. Unfortunately, tail streamer length is subject to much variation and is largely dependent on age and molt condition of the bird. Adults in basic plumage may have very short projections, whereas other individuals may have the tips broken off. Additionally, streamers are difficult to see against a dark background (such as ocean surface) and may be invisible on low-flying birds at great distances.

Other plumage distinctions are equally or more helpful. Light-phase Long-taileds are immediately separable from the other species if the upperparts can be seen well. They are *light* gray-brown on the back, uppertail coverts, and wing coverts, with *highly contrasting* blackish primaries, and a distinct black trailing edge to the secondaries. Pomarines and Parasitics are an essentially uniform dark brown on the upperparts (except for the blackish cap), with no obvious contrasting trailing edge to the wing. The cap of the Long-tailed is also blacker and more defined than the caps of the other species, and because of the light gray mantle it stands in high contrast.

Underpart coloration is also helpful. Light-phase Long-taileds are typically immaculate white (with some yellow) on the throat and breast. Light-phase Pomarines almost always have a heavy, chocolate-colored breast band. Parasitics are more variable with light birds being white breasted and intermediates having either partial or complete brown breast bands. Long-taileds show some light gray on the flanks. Parasitics have variable amounts of darker brown there, and Pomarine's are often heavily marked with smudgy brown bars. Most light-phase Long-taileds are dusky-colored on the lower breast, belly, and vent. By contrast, many Parasitics are completely white below, and others have white bellies and dusky vents. Pomarines have dusky vents, but again, this color does not extend forward nearly as far as on Long-taileds.

Pomarines of all ages and color morphs have white shafts and bases to the outer five to eight primaries. This creates a distinctive white crescent (seen as a white flash in flight) on both surfaces of the wings. Parasitics have only the outer three to five primary shafts and bases white, and therefore the white flash effect is lessened. Long-taileds have white shafts on only the outer one or two primaries and show essentially no white on either surface of the wings (juveniles do show some white below).

Dark-phase birds present more of a problem, because virtually all plumage distinctions of the light birds are obliterated by dark coloration. Bulk, jizz, flight characteristics, length and shape of tail streamers, and extent of white flash in the wings are the only real clues to identity. The dark phase is rare in adult "Poms" and Long-taileds, but is reasonably common in Parasitics (even outnumbering light-phase birds in some parts of the world).

Juvenile birds are tougher to identify. Both Long-tailed and Parasitics have at least three basic juvenal plumages (light, dark, and intermediate), whereas Poms have only a light and dark phase (although intermediate birds that cannot be pigeonholed exist in all three species).

The three types of juvenile Long-taileds have certain shared characters. All have *distinctively* barred (black and white) undertail coverts, underwing coverts, and axillaries. This barring is most pronounced on light birds and least pronounced on dark ones. Light and intermediate birds have a marbled look to the entire underwing. The upperparts of all juvenile Long-taileds are a cold gray-brown and are narrowly but distinctly barred with white or cream on the scapulars, mantle, and wing coverts. This light barring is more distinct than the similar barring of other juvenile jaegers. The central tail points of young Long-taileds are much shorter than the streamers of adults, and they vary in length. However, they are almost always longer than the tail points of young Parasitics (and much longer than those of young Poms) and are either blunt or round-tipped (not sharply pointed). In fact, the entire tail is longer on juvenile Long-tailed than on the other species. Like the adults, young Long-taileds have only the outer 1 or 2 primaries with white shafts and show little or no white flash on the upper wing. They do show white crescents on the underwing.

Light-phase juvenile Long-taileds have heads and napes that are largely or entirely whitish or buff in color, providing strong contrast with the mantle. Intermediate birds typically have light grayish areas on the nape and side of the head with an indistinct cap. Dark birds are dark or dusky in these areas. Both light and intermediate birds typically have plain whitish bellies, whereas the intermediate individuals often have dusky breast bands and both types exhibit at least some barring on the flanks.

Juvenile Parasitics are equally variable, but again, similarities exist between the different plumage types. Like Long-taileds, Parasitics are barred on the back, scapulars, wing coverts, axillaries, and undertail coverts, with variable amounts of barring on the breast and belly. Likewise, the barring of all surfaces is most pronounced on light birds and least pronounced on dark ones. In virtually all cases, however, the barring is less distinct than on the corresponding areas of Long-taileds. Juvenile Parasitics do not have white bellies (as do light juveniles of the other species), but beware of subadults, which may. The axillaries, underwings, and undertail coverts are barred less heavily and with brown and white instead of black and white. The upperparts are variably and indistinctly barred with buff or chestnut, not the neat whitish bars of juvenile Long-taileds. The basic ground color of young Parasitics is also different from Long-taileds (and Poms), being a warm rufous brown rather than a cold gray-brown. The central tail points are typically short but noticeable, and come to sharp points.

Dark juvenile Parasitics may be either uniform rufous-brown (sometimes blackish) on the underparts (still barred on vent) or have light barring throughout. Light birds are more gray-white below with more distinct barring and also have more distinct caps.

Juvenile Poms are basically either dark or light but with some degree of gradation between. Dark birds are mostly blackish brown with barred undertail coverts, underwing coverts, and axillaries. Light birds are gray-brown or tawny above with narrow (indistinct) light bars. Their underwings are broadly barred on the coverts and axillaries with brown and white. The underparts are more variable and may be uniformly gray-brown, gray-brown lightly barred with whitish, or tawny brown lightly barred with whitish. In general, plumage is somewhat intermediate between the colder gray-brown of young Long-taileds and the warmer rufous tones of young Parasitics. The central tail points of all individuals do not ever protrude noticeably, and these are blunt-tipped rather than pointed.

Both Pomarines and Parasitics are routinely seen on West Coast pelagic trips in spring and fall. Long-taileds are much rarer and are most often found early in fall (August to early September), coincident with the peak movements of Arctic Terns. The status of jaegers off the Gulf Coast is less understood, but Pomarine seems to be the most regular, followed by Parasitic, and then Long-tailed. All three species occur as vagrants to inland areas throughout the West, most frequently to large southwestern reservoirs in fall. Again, Long-tailed is the rarest of the three.

GULLS

Gulls present one of the greatest identification challenges to field birders throughout the northern hemisphere. There are a number of reasons why this is so.

1. Gulls exhibit an extreme amount of both geographic and individual plumage variation.

2. Gulls undergo protracted complex molt sequences which result in as many as three or four basic and alternate plumages per species with which birders must contend.

3. Field guides have generally under-represented the various sources of plumage variation, often illustrating only one or two immature plumages.

4. Hybridization within the group is a frequent occurrence.

Obviously, if one is to become competent at gull identification, a knowledge of geographic variation and molt sequences is an absolute necessity, as is the ability to properly age birds. Even the few guides that give adequate treatment to the various immature plumages can only illustrate discrete points in the molt sequence. No book could hope to cover the range of variation found between excessively worn individuals of one stage, individuals in partial molt, and individuals in fresh plumage.

Although the length of the molt sequence differs from species to species, there are some general consistencies that apply to most gulls. Basic (winter) plumage is attained by a complete molt that takes place about September to November. This is true of all basic plumages except first basic, which juvenal-plumaged birds acquire via a head and body molt only. Alternate (summer or nuptial) plumage is attained about February or March by a partial molt involving only head and body feathers.

Gulls are usually classed as being two-year, three-year, or four-year gulls. This terminology refers to the time required to attain adult plumage. The larger species generally require four years, the intermediate species three, and the smaller species two. There are exceptions, such as that provided by the Yellow-footed Gull, which is a three-year gull in spite of its large size.

Two-year gulls (for example, Franklin's, Bonaparte's, Black-legged Kittiwake) become adult upon molting out of either first alternate or second basic plumage (that is, in their second winter or summer). Three-year gulls (for example, Ring-billed, Mew, Laughing) become adult after molting out of second alternate plumage (that is, in their third winter). Four-year gulls (for example, Western, Herring, California, Thayer's, Glaucous-winged) are not adult until they have molted their third alternate plumage (that is, in their fourth winter).

Because plumage is so variable in gulls, you should pay particular attention to details of bill and head morphology, overall size, and jizz. Such features are of primary importance when dealing with aberrantly-plumaged individuals.

There is no substitute for extensive field experience when attempting to identify gulls. Gull identification is a skill that must be worked at with every opportunity. An intimate knowledge of the variation inherent in the common species will serve well in picking out the rarer ones. A detailed treatment of gull identification is beyond the scope of this book, and indeed, is worthy of an entire book itself. I have dealt with the identification of Thayer's Gull because it is a problem of extreme interest to birders throughout the West. Readers interested in pursuing the group in greater detail are strongly urged to obtain a copy of P. J. Grant's *Gulls: A Guide to Identification* (T&AD Poyser Ltd. Calton, England, 1982). Although its focus is on Atlantic species, many of the birds are shared with the West, and the overall treatment is a model for modern identification study.

THAYER'S GULL

Thayer's Gull, as a full-fledged species, is a fairly recent addition to the American avifauna, having been officially split from Herring Gull in 1972 (it may yet turn out to be conspecific with Iceland Gull). Because of this, and because the bird is rare over most of the West (interior and Gulf Coast), it is of great interest to birders who are looking to add it to their lifelists.

Thayer's Gull breeds in northern Canada, and winters in numbers along the West Coast south to about central California, with numbers decreasing with latitude. They are less common in southern California and are rare but regular visitors over much of the interior West (most regularly in the Lake Superior region of northern Minnesota).

Thayer's (like Herring, Western, Glaucous-winged, California, and Iceland) is a four-year gull, which attains adult plumage after molting its third-alternate plumage. First-year birds represent the bulk of California birds and vagrants found over the rest of the western interior, whereas adults are more common along the Washington and Oregon coasts (Lehman 1980). Second and third-year birds are much less frequently encountered south of Canada (Lehman 1980).

Because of this, the present treatment will focus on first-year and adult plumages only, with the greater emphasis given to first-year birds.

Structural differences are very helpful in the identification of all age classes of Thayer's Gulls. Most Thayer's are about intermediate in size between California and Herring Gulls (but beware of individual variation) and should be noticeably smaller than most Westerns or Glaucous-wingeds. Thayer's tend to have more rounded, dove-like heads (similar to Mew Gull) that are quite different from the flatter-headed look of Herring, Western, and Glaucous-winged. This delicate, rounded look is most evident in female Thayer's.

Bill differences are even more useful. Thayer's have short, almost delicate bills, with gradually-curving culmens and little apparent gonydeal angle. This bill type is very similar to that of Iceland Gull (extremely rare in the West) but quite different from that of Herring Gull, which has a longer thinner bill with a distinctive angling toward the tip. Westerns and Glaucous-wingeds have even more massive bills with sharp gonydeal angles (Figure 5.20). Glaucous-winged X Western hybrids (often encountered), which could otherwise be easily mistaken for Thayer's, likewise have much larger bills.

FIGURE 5.20. First-year gulls (top to bottom: Glaucous-winged, Herring, Thayer's and Western. Note differences in bill size and shape.

Much of the literature stresses the eye color of adult Thayer's as an important field mark. Thayer's of all ages have brown irises, while adult Herring and Iceland have yellow irises. Unfortunately eye color is hard to distinguish accurately, except at close range and in good light. Also, a few subadult Herrings may exhibit essentially adult plumage while retaining the brown irises of earlier stages (some Icelands also have brownish eyes). It should also be pointed out that adult California and Glaucous-winged Gulls and northern Western Gulls also have dark eyes. Therefore, eye color should be considered only an accessory mark in the identification of adults and should never be used as the sole basis for identification.

Leg color of all Thayer's is generally considered to be a deeper, bubble-

FIGURE 5.21. First-year gulls (left to right: Glaucous-winged, Thayer's, Herring). Note the amount of color contrast between the primaries and the rest of the wing.

FIGURE 5.22. First-winter Thayer's Gull. Note the small, all-black bill with gently curving culmen, smallish head, and the darker, but not black, wingtips. Photo by Alan Wormington.

FIGURE 5.23. First-winter Thayer's Gull. Note the translucent look to the underside of the remiges. Photo by Richard E. Webster.

gum pink than the pink leg color of other similar gulls. This is a subjective mark that should also be considered accessory in nature.

First-year Thayer's are fairly variable in overall plumage. Many birds are mostly or entirely dingy, dark brown, with paler edgings to the feathers of the back and wing coverts (giving a marbled look to the upperparts). More commonly, however, first-year birds tend to be buffy in overall coloration but with the same marbled look seen in the darker birds. Some individuals show a noticeably white head (as in young Herring Gulls) but most individuals are very uniform in color.

The best field mark is the color of the primaries. At rest, the folded primaries of a first-year Thayer's should be a medium brown above, and should be at least slightly to moderately darker than the rest of the wing and mantle. The primaries of similarly-plumaged Herring, Western, and California Gulls are more blackish-brown and contrast more strongly with the rest of the wing. The primaries of first-year Glaucous-winged are typically concolor with the rest of the wing or slightly lighter, and those of young Iceland Gulls are even lighter still. Thayer's also tend to have more conspicuous white or buffy edges to these primaries than do the other species (Figures 5.21 and 5.22).

Equally important is the color of the primaries from below. First-year Thayer's have all of the remiges conspicuously lighter than the wing linings when viewed from below. This lends a frosty appearance to flying birds, a trait that is shared with Iceland and Glaucous-winged (Figure 5.23). Contrarily, the outer primaries (at least) of young Herring, Western, and California are darker than the rest of the wing when viewed from below. Young Herrings do show pale windows on the inner primaries. From above, flying Thayer's appear to be nearly concolor on the wings. This is because the more extensive light inner webs of the primaries (concealed when the wing is folded) balance out the thinner, dark outer webs that are so prominent on resting birds. Thayer's does show some contrast on the upperwing between the dusky outer primaries and the paler inner primaries. It also shows a darker secondary bar. These traits may help with eliminating Glaucous-winged, but not with eliminating Herring.

Two further marks that are helpful for first-year birds concern the bill and the tail. All first-winter Thayer's should have entirely black bills from October through February. By February to March some individuals may begin to show some paling at the base of the bill (Lehman, 1980). The tail of Thayer's (from above) is a uniform dark brown, with only a small amount of mottling at the base of the outer tail feathers. This contrasts with the lighter, mottled uppertail coverts and in flight gives the appearance of a wide uniform band. First-year Iceland, on the other hand, has more mottling to its tail, which is lighter and less uniform in color than that of Thayer's.

The color of the primaries is also helpful in identifying adult Thayer's. Resting birds should show clean black wing tips (those of Glaucous-winged and Iceland are lighter) with larger white windows that are found in Herring. From below, the primaries should be mostly light and with only a thin black trailing edge to the outer primaries.

Adult Thayer's typically have mantles that are a shade or two darker than those of Herring (beware the northern population of Western Gulls, which are much lighter-mantled than are southern birds, and which also have dark irises). The possible effects of feather wear should always be taken into consideration, because worn birds in late winter may appear much lighter than normal.

For a more detailed treatment of Thayer's Gull identification (including the identification of second and third year birds), see Paul Lehman's excellent article in *Birding* Volume XII, No. 6 (December, 1980).

COMMON, ARCTIC, AND FORSTER'S TERNS

The Common, Arctic, and Forster's complex of *Sterna* terns has long presented one of the most perplexing identification challenges to birders. The complex breaks down into two real problems: (1) Common versus Forster's, and (2) Common versus Arctic. The first problem is of primary interest in the Southwest and on the Gulf Coast. Common Terns are generally rare at any season over much of the Southwest, and are constantly overreported by observers who are in fact misidentifying the more common Forster's. Commons are expected on the Gulf Coast, except in winter, when all but a few leave the country. In spite of this, they have been regularly reported in large numbers by Gulf

FIGURE 5.24. *Sterna* terns (Arctic left, Forster's right, and Common—wing only—inset center). Note differences in structure and wing color pattern. Artwork by Mimi Hoppe Wolf.

Coast birders in winter. The Common-Arctic problem is mainly of concern on the West Coast, where Arctics are regular but rare (except offshore), and observer interest in them is high.

Although a few marks can be said to be diagnostic for each of these species, observers would do well to avoid single-character identifications and should instead rely on a suite of structural and plumage features. The following discussion is broken down into three categories:

1. Structural differences that apply to all age groups
2. Plumage characters of alternate (breeding) plumaged adults
3. Plumage characters of juvenal and basic (winter) plumaged birds.

Structural Differences. Structural differences are useful in identifying birds of all ages. Common and Forster's are generally more alike with flatter crowns and longer, heavier bills. The overall effect on the flight profile is that the head and bill protrude about equally beyond the leading edge of the wings as does the tail beyond the trailing edge. Arctics have more rounded heads, with shorter more delicate bills. This results in a flight profile that looks sawed-off in front, especially in adult birds with their very long tail streamers (Fig. 5.24). Forster's has a heavier bill than Common, but the differences are less obvious than between these two and Arctic.

Forster's and Arctics have longer tail streamers than Commons. On standing birds the streamers of a Common barely reach the wing tips, whereas those of Forster's and Arctics extend well beyond the wing tips. This applies only to breeding adults because juveniles and winter birds lack the streamers. Juveniles typically have shorter, more rounded wings than do adults.

A final structural characteristic that is somewhat difficult to judge (and which should be considered an accessory character only) is tarsal length. Forster's have much longer legs than Arctics, with Commons being intermediate. This is sometimes apparent in mixed flocks that are standing on level terrain.

Adults in Breeding Plumage. The best plumage characters on breeding adults concern differences in color pattern on both surfaces of the wings.

On the upper surface, Commons have the outer five to seven primaries extensively blackish, forming a conspicuous dark wedge on the wing tip (sometimes just on inner primaries). From below, the outer five to seven primaries are extensively tipped with black. This forms a large, smudgy, and ill-defined, black trailing edge to the wing tips. The remainder of the underwing is opaque, except perhaps for the inner primaries, which may be translucent.

Forster's has an upper wing that looks entirely different. The outer webs of the outer primaries are only narrowly dark, while the inner webs of all of the primaries plus the entire outer secondaries are broadly white. This creates a silvery-white flash to the upper wing surface, making the wing tips the lightest part of the wing (in contrast to Commons, where the tips are the darkest part). From below, the outer primaries are broadly tipped with blackish-gray, creating an ill-defined, smudgy trailing edge similar to that of Common (but not as dark, nor as extensive).

Arctics have perhaps the most diagnostic, recognizable wing pattern of the three species. The upperwing is more uniformly colored than that of Common or Forster's, being essentially plain gray with a hint of a thin dark trailing edge to the outer eight or more primaries. From below, these outer eight or more primaries are finely tipped with black, creating a narrow, well-defined black pencil line to the trailing edge of the primaries. Arctics also have noticeably translucent primaries and secondaries when viewed from below (sometimes seen from above), creating the impression of large translucent triangles in the wings.

Forster's has the whitest underparts of the three, while Arctic is the darkest gray below. The gray on the underparts of an Arctic often extends to the face, where it is separated from the black cap by a white facial stripe. This should be considered an accessory mark at best, since many Commons are similarly colored below.

Forster's shows little contrast to the upper body, since both the back and rump are gray, as is the tail (white outer edges). Arctics and Commons have white rumps that contrast strongly with their gray backs. Their tails are also largely whitish with gray outer edges.

Bill color has been stressed in many guides, but is not diagnostic due to its variability. In general, Forster's has an orange bill, Common a redder one, and Arctic the deepest red of all.

Juvenal and Winter Plumages. Juvenal and winter-plumaged Forster's largely have white heads with black confined to a large eye patch on each side. Their napes are usually light but are often streaked or smudged with dark gray; these markings often reach nearly to the eye patches (pushing the resemblance toward Common and Arctic). Similarly plumaged Commons and Arctics have white foreheads with black surrounding the eyes and extending onto the hind-crown and nape (more extensively black than most Forster's).

Commons have a distinct blackish carpal bar (extends from the shoulder to the wrist on the leading edge of the wing) that contrasts strongly with the gray inner wing panel. This mark is even conspicuous on standing birds and immediately eliminates Forster's. The secondaries of juvenile and winter Commons are gray. Arctics have a less distinct carpal bar that may or may not show on standing birds. Their secondaries are distinctly whitish. Forster's lack the carpal bar altogether and have essentially uniformly gray upperwings.

The underwing differences of breeding adults generally hold in these plumages. Forster's and Common have broad, short, black trailing edges to the primaries, with the remainder of the wing opaque. Arctics have the well-defined, narrow black "pencil-line" to the trailing edge of nearly all primaries, and the secondaries and primaries form conspicuous translucent triangles (more noticeable than in the adults, and often seen easily from above).

Bill color may serve as a final distinction between juveniles. Juvenile Arctics and Forster's have entirely black bills, whereas juvenile Commons usually have some flesh coloring at the base.

For further discussions see Russell (1976), Grant and Scott (1969), Scott and Grant (1969), and Hume and Grant (1974).

ELEGANT VERSUS ROYAL VERSUS CASPIAN TERNS

The Elegant, Royal, and Caspian Terns, the largest of North American terns, are often somewhat confusing to beginning birders or to those who haven't dealt with one of the species before. With experience and the knowledge of what to look for, they can be readily separated.

The three species form a size continuum with Caspian being the largest, Royal the intermediate size, and Elegant the smallest. Size as a distinguishing character is most obvious on Caspian Terns, which are positively massive, and in fact, approach Herring Gulls in size. Both the Royal and Elegant are much smaller and more slender in build. Elegant is decidedly smaller and more slender than Royal, but this distinction is used safely only when the two species are side by side. When such comparisons are possible, an additional character that may prove useful on standing birds is relative leg length. Royal shows little visible leg above the ankle, giving it a squat, closer-to-the-ground look. Elegant shows more leg above the ankle, giving it a longer-legged look.

Bill structure and color is a more reliable character for identifying these terns. Caspians have a very stout bill that is enormous by comparison with Elegant and still conspicuously larger than that of the Royal (Figure 5.25). Bill color in Caspian Terns is a deep, blood red, with a blackish tip that is not always conspicuous. The other two species have bills that are more orange (less red) and each lacks the dark tip. Elegant Terns have proportionately longer bills than Royals, and their bills are distinctly thinner with more of a droop to the tip. In color they tend more toward a yellowish-orange (more yellowish still in juveniles), whereas Royal has a deeper red-orange color.

Face and head pattern are also of prime concern. All three species attain full black caps during the breeding season, but show varying degrees of whitening to the forehead and crown later in the year. The black cap is most short-lived in the Royal Tern, which is white-crowned for most of the year. Elegants too will whiten on the forehead and crown following breeding, but they retain more black, making them look less bald than the Royals. At least one of the standard guides has reversed the face patterns of nonbreeding Royals and Elegants. In nonbreeding Elegants the more extensive black of the rear head and nape extends forward to encircle the eye, making it fairly inconspicuous (Figure 5.26). In nonbreeding Royals, the black of the rear head usually stops just

FIGURE 5.25. Terns (top to bottom: Caspian, Royal, Elegant). Note differences in bill size and shape.

FIGURE 5.26. Basic-plumaged Elegant (left) and Royal (right) Terns. Note the distribution of black on the face. Artwork by Mimi Hoppe Wolf.

short of the eye or meets it posteriorly, making the eye conspicuous against the more extensively white face. Note also the shaggier rear crest of the Elegant. Caspian Terns lighten on the forehead only enough to give a salt-and-pepper impression, but never attain the pure white forehead and crown found in Royals and Elegants.

Wing and tail pattern and structure is also a useful aid. Caspians have the widest wings and the least fork to the tail. The outer several primaries are blackish, creating a large dark wedge on the underwing that is prominent when viewed from below. Royals and Elegants by contrast have more slender wings that show mostly white primaries from below and tails that are much more deeply forked. Juveniles of these two species show a dark carpal bar on the upper surface of the wing, which contrasts well with the light panel posterior to it. No such carpal bar is evident in Caspians of any age.

CRAVERI'S VERSUS XANTUS' MURRELET

The Craveri's and Xantus' Murrelets, being very similar species of small alcids, present a difficult identification problem to West Coast observers, a problem that is compounded by normally less than ideal viewing conditions.

Xantus' Murrelet is represented by two subspecies: a southern breeding form (*hypoleucus*) that nests on islands off the coast of Baja and western Mexico, and a northern breeding form (*scrippsi*) that nests on islands off the coast of southern California. The former very rarely shows up in our waters in fall as the result of post-breeding dispersal, while the latter also disperses northward (regularly to Washington) in late summer and fall. Craveri's Murrelet also breeds on islands off the coast of Baja and in the Gulf of California, and disperses northward in small numbers to southern California (regularly to Monterey) following breeding.

All three forms are very similar in general appearance. They are small alcids that are dark above and light below and lack the white scapulars of the Marbled Murrelet. All three ride low in the water, but when feeding, keep their necks held high (not tucked as in other murrelets). Contrary to the way they are pictured in many guides, these murrelets swim so low that they are dark to the waterline, often concealing their white sides.

Xantus' Murrelets of the *hypoleucus* race are readily identified by their

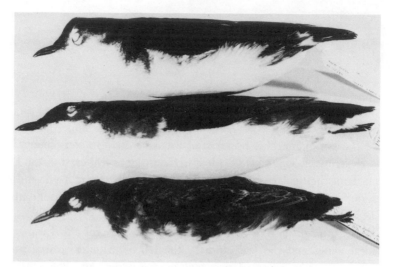

FIGURE 5.27. *Synthliboramphus* murrelets. Top to bottom: Xantus' (*S. h. hypoleucus*), Xantus' *(S. h. scrippsi)*, and Craveri's. Note the dark half-collar of Craveri's and the conspicuous eye ring of *S. h. hypoleucus*.

large, broken white eye rings that are conspicuous even at great distances (Figure 5.27). The other two forms have incomplete white eye rings that are much smaller and which can usually be seen only at close range.

The main problem for U.S. birders comes in trying to separate *scrippsi* Xantus' from Craveri's. Most guides emphasize differences between the two in underwing color. Xantus' typically have bright white underwings, whereas those of Craveri's are variable but always much duskier (lightest on the axillaries). Unfortunately, small alcids typically fly at great speeds with whirring wings, making underwing color a difficult character to judge. The task is made harder by the tendency of small alcids to jump from the path of the boat and fly straight away.

One plumage character that can be helpful in identifying flying or sitting individuals is the dark half-collar of Craveri's that juts down on the side of the neck into the white breast (Figure 5.27). This mark is reminiscent of the similar half-collar seen in winter-plumaged Spotted Sandpipers, and is not found in Xantus' Murrelets. Another character that may prove helpful at close range is the position on the face of the line of demarcation between black and white feathering. In Xantus' the black of the crown extends only as far as the gape line of the bill. In Craveri's the black extends to the bottom side of the bill. Craveri's also averages slightly darker and browner above than Xantus'. The latter mark is readily observable in the hand, but may be of dubious utility under most field conditions.

A structural difference that is valuable is the length of the bill. Xantus' has a relatively stubby bill, whereas that of Craveri's is longer and thinner.

For more information see Dunn (1978) and Roberson (1980).

IMMATURE EAGLES

Although adult Bald and Golden Eagles are immediately separable species, immature birds of both species are similar enough as to warrant confusion. This confusion is enhanced by a less-than-adequate treatment of subadult plumages in most guides. Most of the problem stems from attempts to pigeonhole immature eagle plumages into a single illustration per species. Because eagles take several (three to five) years to attain full adult plumage, such attempts are not only untenable but misleading.

Because Golden Eagles have the simpler plumage pattern, let's start with them. Birds of all ages have wider wings than Bald Eagles, with heads that do not project as far beyond the leading edge of the wings. Their tails appear relatively shorter in flight, and their bills are less massive. All of these features are somewhat hard to judge, particularly by those lacking comparative experience. Fortunately, several aspects of plumage are more diagnostic and much more objective to judge.

Golden Eagles of all ages have entirely brown bodies. Birds molting worn feathers may show assymetrically scattered white feathers, but these are neither extensive nor prominent. Birds of all ages show a tawny gold nape and a tawny bar across the upper wing coverts that contrasts slightly with the darker brown remiges. Young birds have clean white spots at the base of the inner primaries but no white on the coverts or axillars (these white spots become smaller with age and eventually disappear). Immature birds have tails that are white at the base and broadly-banded with dark brown at the terminal end. The line of demarcation between white base and dark terminal band is always sharp, and the white is clean and bright in color. The tail becomes progressively darker with age. The bill of Golden Eagles at any age is bicolored (black at the tip and gray basally), with the cere being yellow.

Bald Eagles of all ages have thinner wings with the leading and trailing edges being more nearly parallel. Their heads project more beyond the leading edge of the wings, and along with the bills, are more massive. Again, such structural characters are hard to judge.

Plumage pattern in this species is more complex, with birds requiring four to five years to attain adult plumage. The bill and cere of subadult birds are concolor (slate gray). Young Balds lack the tawny gold nape of the Goldens, and have more extensive pale brown upperwing coverts (not reduced to a tawny bar). More diagnostic is the pattern of the underwings. All immature Balds show dirty white patches near the axillars and white diagonal ulnar bars, along with a variable number of white remiges. This is very different from the clean white patches found at the base of the primaries on Goldens.

Second and third-year birds show more extensive white to the tail, remiges, belly, and wing coverts than do first-year birds. Most second-year birds have extensively whitish (dirty-white) bellies that contrast with the dark brown head, throat, and breast. This creates a distinctive hooded effect. Many third-year birds are so extensively off-white on the underwing coverts as to present a negative underwing pattern (light linings, dark remiges) reminiscent of Swainson's Hawk (but not nearly as clean or bold). Where extensive white is present in the tail it is less clean, more irregular, and less sharply demarcated than the white found on the tails of young Goldens. Second and third-year birds also show a variable amount of whitish mottling on the upper back as well as a light eyebrow above dark auriculars.

For more information see Clark (1983).

ACCIPITERS

The three species of U.S. Accipiters (Sharp-shinned Hawk, Cooper's Hawk, and Northern Goshawk) present one of the most difficult field problems in North America. Only adult Northern Goshawks are readily identified by plumage alone. The rest must be identified by a suite of subtle structural, plumage, and flight characteristics, many of which require some comparative experience to use properly. Even the best birders must be content with recording "*Accipiter* sp. (?)" occasionally.

These birds present a size continuum, ranging from the small Sharpshinned to the large Northern Goshawk, with Cooper's being intermediate. Females of all three species are distinctly larger than males, but there is no overlap in size between species. Female Sharpies may approach male Cooper's in size, whereas female Cooper's approach male Northern Goshawks.

Sharpies are the lightest in weight, and relative to body size have proportionately long wings and short tails. The wing loading (weight distribution/ surface area of wing) that results from these structural features produces a buoyant flight pattern with much flapping.

Cooper's Hawks are heavier, with proportionately short wings and longish tails (relative to body length). This results in a more powerful flight pattern, with fewer strokes and greater speed.

Northern Goshawks are heaviest of all, with proportionately long wings and short tails. Their flight is extremely fast and powerful with fewer required flaps. Because of their size and the few strokes/unit time, it may appear that Goshawks are slow fliers compared to Sharpies. This is illusion rather than fact, because flight speed of Accipiters is proportional to size.

While flight characteristics provide a good clue to the identity of an Accipiter, they should be used with caution. Individual birds will adjust their flight behavior to existing wind conditions, creating exceptions to every rule.

The real problem identifications in this group are between Sharp-shinned and Cooper's Hawks of all ages, and between immature Cooper's and immature Northern Goshawk.

Most guides point to the difference in tail shape as the best separator of Sharp-shinned and Cooper's Hawk. Cooper's have rounded tails while Sharpies have tails that are typically either squared or notched at the end. While such distinctions are often useful, they are far from diagnostic. Many Sharpies have tails that are slightly rounded, especially when fanned. A distinctly squared tail will probably allow elimination of Cooper's, but a rounded tail does not safely eliminate Sharp-shinned. Cooper's of all ages have a broader, more defined white terminal band to the tail.

Cooper's Hawks of all ages have relatively massive heads (most apparent on perched birds), but the heads of Sharpies are relatively small. In flight, this results in the head of Cooper's extending much farther forward from the leading edge of the wing. Relative to head size, the eye of the Cooper's appears small, lending a fierce look. Contrastingly, the eye of the Sharp-shinned is large relative to head size, giving a more gentle look.

Adult Cooper's have very blackish caps that show a sharp line of contrast with the slate gray backs. Adult Sharpies are not nearly as dark-capped and show little or no cap-back contrast.

Juvenile Cooper's tend to be very buffy or tawny on the head and neck, whereas juvenile Sharpies are whiter. Breast streaking on young Cooper's is finer and sharper and does not extend to the belly. Young Sharpies are more extensively streaked below, and the streaks are larger and blurrier in nature. Both species typically have unmarked white undertail coverts.

There are fewer plumage characters that are useful in the separation of immature Cooper's and immature Northern Goshawks. Size alone will probably do except for young female Cooper's versus young male Goshawk. Immature Goshawks have more pronounced white eyebrows (widest posterior to the eye), much heavier breast streaking, and narrower white terminal tail bands than young Cooper's. All of these features may be subject to considerable variation and are at best subjective to judge. Immature Goshawks do have dark spotting on their crissums (young Cooper's are typically clean white), but this is often hard to see. Relative wing/tail proportions, and size with related flight characteristics may prove to be the most reliable characters. Calls of the two species (a loud series of "kaks") are separable with practice.

Both Cooper's and Sharp-shinned tend to stick to denser cover than do Goshawks. This is most pronounced in Sharp-shinned, but both species will pursue prey by climbing through dense brush. Contrary to the claims of at least one guide, Sharpies will perch on telephone poles, although such behavior is more common in Cooper's.

For contrasting discussions on this group refer to Mueller et al. (1979) and Clark (1979).

BUTEONINE HAWKS

Because there are so many species of *Buteos*, and because there are several possible avenues of misidentification for each species, I have broken with style by treating each species separately.

Red-tailed Hawk. The Red-tailed Hawk is probably the most common and most variably-plumaged *Buteo* in the United States. The best path to true competency in identifying *Buteos* is to carefully study every Red-tail seen. More than a few birders have misidentified immature, dark-phase, or rare variant Red-tails for almost every other species of *Buteo*. Typical adults are identified by the combination of orange or rust tail, distinct brown belly band on otherwise white underparts, large buff or white patches on the scapulars (an excellent mark for perched birds), and a black bar from the shoulder to the wrist on the underwings.

There are countless exceptions to the above generalizations. Many Southwestern birds have even brown upperparts without the distinctive light scapulars. Furthermore, many of these same birds lack any trace of a belly band. Many Great Plains birds are extremely pale above, with tails that are only lightly washed with orange. These individuals are often mistaken for Ferruginous Hawks but can be identified by light, gray-brown (not rust) shoulders; white (not rust) feathering above the tarsi; a dark carpal bar; lack of prominent white patches on the upper surface of the primaries; and dirtier underwings.

Dark-phase birds are common in some areas and are frequently misidentified as the rarer Harlan's race, or even as other species. These birds typically have entirely dark brown bodies (usually with rufous tones, seldom blackish like Zone-tailed, Black, or dark-phase Rough-leg) with dark wing linings, light remiges with some barring (from underneath), dark undertail coverts, and reddish tails with a darker subterminal band. Harlan's Hawks are usually a darker sooty brown (not rusty) with dusky gray-white tails (sometimes with a rusty cast) that are often mottled with dark vertical streaking. The tail has a vaguely-defined dark terminal band, and the entire underparts of the bird are often mottled with white spotting.

Immature birds are also highly variable and lack the distinctive reddish tails of most adults. The best identifier of most immatures are the large white or buff patches on the scapulars, which form a light "V" on the back when the wings are folded. The color of the head (which may range from dark brown to white) and the amount and distribution of dark streaking below are highly variable.

Ferruginous Hawk. The Ferruginous Hawk is a large *Buteo* with long broad wings, which appear more narrow than they are due to the bird's longish tail. Birds of all ages are best identified by the large white patches on the upperside of the wings (base of primaries). These create a bold white flash in flight (reminiscent of Caracara) and are larger and more conspicuous than the white windows often seen in the wings of other *Buteos*. Birds of all ages have a large gape that lends an almost owl-like look when the bird is flying straight at you screaming.

Adults are further distinguished by generally rusty upperparts, whitish head, rusty tarsal feathering forming a dark "V" in flight, largely immaculate white underwings with blackish crescents at the carpals, and a white tail (sometimes light pink or orange) with a variably-thick rusty band at the distal end.

Immatures are variable but are typically darker brown above, often with a buffy head. They lack the rusty leggings of adults but retain the white underwings with black carpal crescents and show some dark spotting on the leggings.

Dark-phase birds are usually a darker brown than like-plumaged Red-tails. They can also be distinguished from other dark *Buteos* by the entirely light tail (sometimes with diffuse rusty terminal band) and by the less apparent dark border to the tips of the remiges.

Flight characteristics can be helpful. Ferruginous frequently hover (like Rough-legs), and when soaring they are usually intermediate in wing dihedral between Red-tail (flatter) and Swainson's (more pronounced).

Swainson's Hawk. Best told by a combination of wing structure and underwing pattern. Birds of all ages have long narrow pointed wings that are unlike those of any other *Buteo*. These appear relatively long on perched birds, extending to or past the end of the tail. Flight attitude is typically a pronounced dihedral, and it is common for the birds to teeter back and forth like a Turkey Vulture.

Adults have a strong "negative" pattern of contrasting light wing linings with blackish flight feathers (reverse of normal raptor underwing pattern). They are evenly brown above, without the white mottling of the scapulars that is found on Red-tails. A brown bib encircles the throat and breast, leaving a white chin.

Immatures are variable, with heavy brown streaking below (against a usually bright buffy ground color). Heavy dark malar streaks combine with upper breast streaking to form large blobby blotches on the sides of the breast. A bold, buffy eye stripe is usually present, although it may be inconspicuous on birds with largely pale heads. The upperparts are still more evenly colored than those of Red-tails, and the underwing pattern, although less pronounced than in adults, is still evident. Given the variable nature of plumage in young Swainson's, it is best to concentrate on wing shape and pattern.

Dark-phase and reddish intermediate birds exist. The former is rare and is told from other dark *Buteos* by shape, lack of sharp contrast to the underwing (remiges are dingy gray, not white), grayish tail without bright white bands, pale undertail coverts, and a generally dingy dark-brown body coloring.

Rough-legged Hawk. The Rough-legged Hawk is a long-winged, long-tailed *Buteo* (similar in shape to Ferruginous Hawk, but with slimmer wings) that is extremely variable in plumage. While most guides depict typical light and dark-phase birds, there actually appears to be a color continuum from very light to very dark individuals (for details see Cade 1955). The so-called "light-phase" birds shown in most guides are actually intermediate in plumage. All individuals habitually hover when hunting.

Perhaps the best mark in any plumage is the white tail with a broad brownish-black subterminal band. Adult males have multiple thin bands proximal to the wide one (many individuals have tails that are off-white with somewhat smudgier bands). Lighter birds of all ages are also characterized by large black marks at the carpals (seen from below), small white patches at the base of the primaries on the upperwing (much smaller than similar patches of Ferruginous), a broad dark belly band (typically darker and more solidly-colored than in Red-tails) contrasting with light head and breast, and conspicuous leggings that are light in color and which also contrast with the belly band. Many adults (particularly males) lack any real belly band.

Immature birds are often extremely buffy on the head, breast, and leggings, and are particularly striking. Dark-phase birds are blacker in general coloration than dark individuals of many other species and have light remiges (from below), dark wing linings with a distinct blackish trailing edge to the wings, and a tail similar to light-phase birds.

White-tailed Hawk. Birds of all ages have a unique wing shape, with the wings both very long (project beyond the tail on resting birds) and pointed, and very broad (second only to Common Black-Hawk). The tail appears relatively short.

Adults are beautiful hawks, with silver-gray upperparts, bright rusty shoulders, immaculate white underparts (sometimes shadow-barred with light gray), and white tails with a single black sub-terminal band. Most obvious in flight is the "negative" underwing pattern (dark gray remiges with contrasting white linings) reminiscent of Swainson's. Immatures are mostly dark brown, heavily streaked/mottled below (suggestive of young Bald Eagles) and are best identified by shape.

Common Black-Hawk. This striking bird is readily distinguished from all other dark *Buteos* by its incredibly wide wings. These are much broader than in any other U.S. hawk, and are suggestive of Black Vulture. The tail appears very short, and the dangling, bright-yellow legs are usually prominent on flying birds.

Zone-tailed Hawk. The Zone-tailed Hawk is slender-winged, and is given to soaring with the wings raised in a dihedral like the Turkey Vulture (birds flying at high altitudes can be easily passed off as the latter species). Told from Common Black-Hawk by the very different shape, distinct bicolored effect to the underwing (like Turkey Vulture), smaller bill, lack of yellow skin between the bill and eyes, and long, multibanded tail (beware that only one band may be visible under many conditions).

Harris' Hawk. Adults are unmistakable. Immatures resemble Red-Shouldereds, but the white at the base of the tail, bright rusty shoulders, and different underwing pattern will secure identification.

Gray Hawk. Adults are nearly unmistakable, but in south Texas confusion with male Hook-billed Kite is possible. The latter has more oval-shaped wings, a longer tail, an absurdly-hooked beak, white irises, more coarsely-barred underparts, and lacks the neat black border to the underwings. Immatures are similar to immature Broad-wingeds and Red-shouldereds (see below).

Red-shouldered Hawk. The Red-shouldered Hawk is a slender, long-winged, long-tailed *Buteo*. The wings are distinctly rounded at the tips. Adults are readily identified by the black-and-white checkered wings, heavily banded tail, rusty shoulders, orange underparts (very pronounced on California birds), and pale windows at the base of the primaries. Individual hawks of many species show pale windows that are typically oval or rectangular in shape, but those of the Red-shoulder are crescent-shaped. The only similar species is the Broad-winged Hawk, which lacks the checkered flight-feathers, rusty shoulder, and pale windows, and which has a totally different jizz.

Immature Red-shouldereds are similar to young Broad-wingeds, but wing/tail shape, wing windows, tail pattern (Red-shouldereds have evenly-thick bars throughout, Broad-wingeds have a wider subterminal bar), and the lack of a defined black trailing edge to the wings will prove diagnostic. Broad-wingeds are also whiter below with less marking, and have more uniformly colored upperwings with whitish or pale buff underwing linings. For further information see Dunn (1979) and Clark (1982).

Broad-winged Hawk. The Broad-winged Hawk is a small, chunky *Buteo* with broad wings that are pointed at the tips. The tail appears relatively short. The underwings are pearly-white (linings occasionally buff) with narrow but distinct, neat black borders and tips. Proportions and flight pattern (along with underwing coloration) will allow separation from the remotely similar Accipiters.

Immatures are very similar to young Red-shouldereds (distinguished by shape; absence of pale, crescent-shaped wing windows; more uniform upper wings; whitish or pale buff underwing linings; tail pattern; whiter underparts; and neat black edge to the underwings) and are even more similar to young Gray Hawks (but rump is darker, malar stripes wider, and the black border to the underwings is more evident). For further information see Dunn (1979) and Clark (1982).

COMMON VERSUS LESSER NIGHTHAWK

Most birders rely solely on voice or geographic range to identify nighthawks. While both methods are often the easiest identifiers, neither is of any help when silent birds are encountered in regions of sympatry. Nighthawks can be identified visually, although the characters used are subtle and may require some practice.

The only visual mark pointed out by most guides is the position of the white bar in the wing. In Lesser Nighthawk it is closer to the tip, but in the Common Nighthawk it is more proximal. This distinction is fairly subtle and may require some experience to be used with confidence.

Much more distinctive (and totally unmentioned in most field guides) is the difference in wing shape (Figure 5.28). Common's have the outer primary as the longest, giving a very pointed look to the wings. Lessers typically have the outer primary shorter than the adjacent inner one, giving a more rounded appearance. Although the difference is noticeable, beware that it is also relative— that is, Lessers will still look pointed-winged compared to Common Poorwills. Beware also that there is much individual variation in wing shape among nighthawks, and that while most birds of both species will conform to the above patterns, there are many exceptions. These differences are accentu- ated by the wing lengths of the two species—longer in Common, shorter in Lesser. The structural differences of the wings result in different flight charac- teristics. Commons tend to fly higher and with deeper, more emphatic strokes (reminiscent of Black Tern). Lessers typically cruise lower with a shallower, more fluttery stroke. Again, these distinctions are relative and require some practice to discern.

Other plumage distinctions are complicated by sexual differences in both species, and by geographic variation in the Common. Males of both species have white tail bands that are lacking in females. Males also have white throats while females have buffy ones. Males of both species have white wing bars, a trait shared by female Commons. Female Lessers have buffy wing bars that are less distinctive. In general, Lessers are more brownish, while Commons are more gray. This is subject to geographic variation in Commons, with eastern birds being darker brown, and many western birds being lighter gray. Lessers are more evenly-colored above, whereas Commons show contrast between the paler wing coverts and darker back. The two species also differ slightly in under- part coloration. Commons have a whiter base color to the belly and vent with more strongly contrasting barring. Lessers are buffier in those regions, and the barring is less distinctive.

FIGURE 5.28. Nighthawk wings (upper left—Common, lower right—Lesser). Note structural differences and position of the white bars. Artwork by Mimi Hoppe Wolf.

Calls are the most obvious difference, with the Common giving a loud, nasal "peent," and the Lesser a wavering trill that often varies in pace and intensity. In the Southwest (where the two species overlap), habitat differences are also helpful. Lessers are more common in arid deserts, and Commons are typical of more mesic, usually montane areas. The two often overlap in lowland riparian settings that are bordered by desert. Common is the more likely species to be seen flying about in the daytime, but Lessers are occasionally seen cruising in the first few hours of daylight.

See also Garrett and Dunn (1982).

YELLOW KINGBIRDS

Four species of kingbirds (genus *Tyrannus*) whose underparts are largely yellow occur in the western United States. These are: Western, Cassin's, Couch's, and Tropical. All are superficially similar to one another and can cause problems for the unwary birder. A knowledge of key field marks makes identification of these birds straightforward.

As is so often the case, the best way to learn to identify the various yellow-bellied kingbirds is to become thoroughly familiar with the species that is most common in your area, and use it as a measuring stick with which to mentally compare the other species. For most people, this common species will be the Western Kingbird, which is the most common and widespread of the four.

Westerns are overlapped most widely in range by the Cassin's. A look at the underparts should readily separate the two. Both are yellow on the belly, flanks, and lower breast. However, the Western has a light gray-white throat that fades gradually into the yellow around the upper breast. The Cassin's, on the other hand, has a *dark* gray breast that nicely separates the yellow belly from a very white throat. The throat itself contrasts sharply with the gray breast. Overall, the Cassin's is a darker bird, particularly on the head and neck. The darker gray of the head, neck, and breast, contrasting with the white throat, gives the Cassin's a hooded appearance that is totally lacking in Westerns. Other differences include the tail, which is laterally edged with white in the Western (usually conspicuous), but terminally banded with buff in the Cassin's (often hard to see). Calls of the two species are very different. The Cassin's has a sharp "chi-queer," while the Western gives a "whit" or series of the same, often strung together in an excited chatter.

Most problems with this group result from the recent separation by taxonomists of the Tropical Kingbird complex into two species: (1) an essentially west Mexican form *T. melancholicus* that barely reaches the U.S. as an uncommon to rare summer resident in southeast Arizona and as a rare fall and winter vagrant to coastal California and (2) an essentially east Mexican form *T. couchii* that is a common summer resident of southernmost Texas. The former species has retained the common name of Tropical Kingbird, while the latter is now known as Couch's Kingbird. The two species can be readily separated from Western and Cassin's by visual marks, but are best separated from one another by calls.

The underparts of both the Couch's and the Tropical are very different from Cassin's in that they lack the dark gray breast band. They more closely resemble the Western, but the yellow is brighter and extends farther toward the throat. Both species have a noticeably darker face patch than is seen in either Western or Cassin's. The tails of both Couch's and Tropical are more brownish than the tail of the Western and are slightly forked rather than squared at the end. The emphasis placed on the forked tail by some field guides has often led to misidentifications. In late summer many Western Kingbirds will show a forked tail due to post-nuptial or post-juvenal molt. Reliance on this mark is most dangerous.

A good way to separate the Couch's and Tropical from both Western and Cassin's is by the size and structure of the bill (Figure 5.29). The bills of both Couch's and Tropical Kingbirds are *very* long, and *very* thick, giving the birds a noticeably big-billed look. This is not quite as pronounced as in the Thick-billed Kingbird, but it is very apparent to one who is familiar with the smaller bills of the Western and Cassin's.

As mentioned earlier Couch's and Tropical Kingbirds are best separated from one another by voice. The bill of the Tropical is slightly thinner (accentuating its length), and its back is less olive (more gray) than that of the Couch's, but these are extremely subtle differences that require comparative experience. More noticeable is the proportionately shorter bill of Couch's. The calls of

FIGURE 5.29. Western (top) and Couch's (bottom) Kingbirds. Note the longer, thicker bill of Couch's.

the two species are noticeably different. The Tropical has a twittery "pip-pip-pip-pip . . ." that is given very rapidly. The Couch's has a sharper "kip, kip, kip" that is strung together in a usually slower sequence and that is often punctuated by a loud "breer" (as in "kip, kip, kip breer!"). The "breer" call is sometimes given separately.

Of course, range is an immediate clue to the identity of these latter two species, since they are allopatric in the U.S. However, members of this complex are regular fall vagrants to the West Coast, and at such time, range is of little help in making the specific identification. All such vagrants that have been identified to species have proven to be *melancholicus*.

MYIARCHUS FLYCATCHERS

The genus *Myiarchus* contains four U.S. representatives of medium to large flycatchers that differ only subtly from one another in both plumage and structural characters. One species (Great Crested) is essentially eastern in distribution, while the others are essentially western. In some areas as many as three of the species may be sympatric, and vagrant individuals of all four species have been found well outside their normal ranges. For these reasons it is essential that birders be aware of species differences within the genus, even if they live in areas inhabited by only one *Myiarchus*.

The Great Crested Flycatcher is a common summer resident of deciduous woodlands, orchards, and tree claims throughout the eastern United States. It breeds regularly west to the west-central Great Plains and central-south Texas. In the latter region it overlaps the breeding ranges of the Ash-throated and Brown-crested Flycatchers. It is an occasional vagrant (mostly in fall) to areas farther west.

The Ash-throated Flycatcher is the most widespread of the three western species. It ranges south from southern Washington along the West Coast to

San Diego and east through Nevada, Utah, Arizona, New Mexico, portions of Idaho, Wyoming, and Colorado; and the western two-thirds of Texas. It overlaps the range of the Great Crested in central Texas and is an occasional vagrant to both the east and the upper northwest. It winters in the extreme southwest corner of Arizona and southeast California (rare). Habitat preferences of this species are more varied than those of its congeners. It may be found in sparse shrub-desert, the thorn-scrub saguaro deserts, lush lowland riparian forest, and dry oak woodlands of low to middle elevations.

The Brown-crested Flycatcher has a disjunct distribution in the United States. In extreme southeastern California, the Morongo Valley (California), southern Arizona, and southwestern New Mexico, it is a fairly common but local summer resident of saguaro deserts, lowland riparian forests, and streamside deciduous growth in lower montane forests. It is absent from most of southern New Mexico and west and central Texas but is a fairly common summer resident of live oak groves, thorn-scrub, and subtropical forest in south Texas. In this latter area it is sympatric with both Great Crested and Ash-throated, whereas in the Arizona and New Mexico portions of its range it is sympatric with Ash-throated and Dusky-capped.

The Dusky-capped Flycatcher has the most restricted United States range, being limited to southeastern Arizona and extreme southwestern New Mexico. Here, it is a common summer resident of lower montane pine-oak woodlands and lush, lowland riparian forests. It is a casual late fall and winter vagrant to coastal California (Roberson, 1980).

Separating the four species in the field is not easy, but it can be done by using a suite of plumage, structural, and vocal characteristics. It is vital to be aware of a few general trends of molt common to the four species. Breeding plumage is attained by a partial pre-alternate molt, and basic plumage is attained by a complete molt following breeding. Summering adults are therefore more worn and paler in color than are fall adults, which are usually brighter yellow on the belly and darker gray on the throat and breast. Juvenal-plumaged birds resemble adults but are generally browner on the back, *much* rustier on the wings and tail, and paler below. These seasonal differences are important because they affect characters that differ subtly between species. By October juveniles will have molted into first basic plumage and will essentially resemble adults.

Bill color and structure is one of the most useful characters in the field identification of the genus (Figure 5.30). Ash-throated, Brown-crested, and Dusky-capped typically have entirely black bills. Great Crested shows a pale (fleshy or yellow) base to the lower mandible. Although this mark is diagnostic, it may be difficult to see on some individuals, and is usually lacking on juveniles, which are black-billed. Beware also that occasional Ash-throateds and Brown-cresteds can have some paling at the base of the lower mandible (although this is typically not as bright nor as extensive as in the Great Crested). Southwestern Brown-crested (*M. t. magister*) have relatively massive bills that are noticeably

FIGURE 5.30. *Myiarchus* flycatchers (top to bottom: Brown-crested, Ash-throated, Dusky-capped, Great Crested). Note differences in overall size and bill size.

longer and thicker than the bills of the other species. The Brown-cresteds found in south Texas (*M. t. cooperi*) are smaller billed (closer to Great Crested). Great Crested has a smaller bill that is still longer and thicker than that of the Ash-throated and Dusky-capped. The bills of the latter two species are closest in size (Ash-throated being slightly larger), but because the body size of the Dusky-capped is distinctly smaller, its bill appears relatively larger in the field. Caution must be used in judging bill size, since all *Myiarchus* will appear large-billed to those lacking comparative experience.

Brown-crested is also the largest and most robust in body size, followed by Great Crested, Ash-throated, and the distinctly smaller Dusky-capped.

Plumage differences are complex and multidirectional (Figure 5.31). In

FIGURE 5.31. *Myiarchus* flycatchers (left to right: Great Crested, Great Crested, Ash-throated, Ash-throated, Brown-crested, Brown-crested, Dusky-capped, Dusky-capped). Note differences in overall size, bill size, and contrast between breast color and belly color.

general, Ash-throated is the palest below, being very light gray (often whitish) on the throat and breast, and pale yellow on the belly and vent. (Remember, however, that birds in fresh basic plumage are brighter.) Brown-crested is generally darker gray on the throat and breast and brighter yellow on the belly and vent than Ash-throated, but lighter and duller in these areas than either Great Crested or Dusky-capped. The latter two species are darker gray on the throat and breast, and brighter yellow on the belly and vent than either Ash-throated or Brown-crested. These color differences make for a highly contrasting line of demarcation between the dark gray of the breast and the bright yellow of the belly in both Great Crested and Dusky-capped. This contrast is strongest in the Great Crested. In Ash-throated and Brown-crested the lighter colors fade into one another, and the demarcation of gray and yellow is much less pronounced. Once again, it is important to note that fresh fall adults will be darker and brighter below, whereas juveniles will be paler and duller.

Upperpart coloration differs even more subtly. Great Crested and Dusky-capped are more olive on the back, but the other two are slightly browner. Dusky-capped is the darkest above, being especially dark on the crown and nape. Great Crested shows the most rufous in the primaries and retrices, but the adult Dusky-capped shows almost no rufous coloring in either area (juveniles have tails that are largely rufous). Ash-throated and Brown-crested are comparable in the amount of rufous on the primaries, but the former species is more extensively rust-colored on the retrices. Great Crested, Ash-throated and Brown-crested all have thin whitish wingbars and conspicuous whitish margins to the wing coverts and tertials. The wingbars of Dusky-capped are rustier and inconspicuous, and the tertials and wing coverts are less distinctively margined.

Vocalizations are extremely useful for birds on the breeding grounds, less so for the often silent fall migrants. All species have a commonly heard one-or-two-note call, a longer and less commonly heard dawn song, and a variety of rolling notes that are most often given during intra-specific encounters.

Brown-crested sings a loudly whistled "will-for-you." Great Crested sings a two-phrase song consisting of a low "wheeyer" followed by a pause and a higher "wheeyer." Dusky-capped sings a varied "whip, weoo, wee hoo." The song of the Ash-throated is three-syllabled, with a rising then falling inflection. All song descriptions are from Davis (1962).

Call notes are more commonly heard and just as useful. Brown-crested delivers a loud "whit" (either singly or in rapid succession); Great Crested a loud, uprising "wheep"; Ash-throated a two-syllabled "ka-brick" or "ka-wheer" that is similar to the "chi-queer" of Cassin's Kingbird and a single-syllabled "pyrrt"; and Dusky-capped a mournful whistled "peeur" (reminiscent of Say's Phoebe).

Foraging differences may be useful secondary clues, but are often meaningless for migrating or vagrant individuals. In general, Dusky-capped is the only species prone to hover-gleaning insects from vegetation, although the other species may do so opportunistically. Also, Ash-throateds tend to forage lower in the canopy than do the other species.

Habitat overlap in regions of sympatry is often broad; however, some generalizations are possible. Dusky-capped typically ranges to higher elevations than either Ash-throated or Brown-crested and consequently is the most common species in areas where pines grow among live oaks and deciduous species. Brown-crested is more restricted to lowlands and ranges upslope only along water courses that provide significant stands of deciduous trees (particularly sycamores). It avoids the sparse, low-shrub deserts that are often occupied by the Ash-throated and in such areas occupies only lush riparian groves of trees or saguaro deserts (which are closer to thorn-forest than other American deserts). In Texas, Great Crested typically occupies more shaded woodlands, Brown-crested the drier forest and thorn-scrub, and Ash-throated the most arid mesquite brushlands. Again, some overlap is found.

For further information see Dunn (1978, 1979) and Roberson (1980).

CONTOPUS (PEWEES)

Four species of pewees (genus *Contopus*) are found in the United States: Eastern Wood-Pewee, Western Wood-Pewee, Greater Pewee, and Olive-sided Fly-catcher. The Eastern Wood-Pewee breeds across the eastern United States, west to the Great Plains, where it barely overlaps the range of its western counterpart, the Western Wood-Pewee (which breeds throughout the west). The Olive-sided breeds in appropriate montane forests and conifer bogs through-out much of the West and migrates across the Great Plains and points east. The Greater Pewee is very restricted in range within this country, being found only in the mountains of southeastern Arizona (and rarely southwestern New Mexico). It is also a casual fall through winter vagrant to California.

All four species are similar in general appearance, and two (the Eastern and Western Wood-Pewees) are probably inseparable in the field except by voice.

The two Wood-Pewees resemble one another most closely and are notice-ably smaller than the other two species. Both can be told from *Empidonax* flycatchers by their calls, larger size, longer wings, lack of tail-wagging, and lack of eye rings (but beware of Willow Flycatchers). Both species exhibit sufficient individual variation so as to make field identification (except by voice) nearly impossible. Some generalizations with respect to species differences may be made, but readers should be mindful of the problem of individual variation and should base extralimital sightings on vocalizations.

Easterns tend to be more olive-green above, with a somewhat olive-gray cast to the breast. Westerns are grayer above and on the breast without the olive tones. The white belly of the Western intrudes into gray breast so as to form a distinctive inverted "V," the sides of which are formed by the gray flanks. This pronounced vested look is usually lacking in Easterns, which nonetheless have extensive dusky olive washes across the breast region. Easterns typically have lower mandibles that are dark at the tip and yellow/orange for at least the basal one-half to three-fourths (immature birds have entirely black bills). Westerns are more often entirely dark-billed; however, *many* individuals have up to one-half of the lower mandible (basal portion) light colored. Having said all of this, it should be reiterated that these are only generalizations, and as such, do not hold for many individuals. Individual variation and overlap in morphology is so prevalent in these two species as to demand confirmation by vocalization prior to identifying either species outside of its normal range. Songs of the two species are diagnostic, with Easterns giving a plaintive, whistled, "pee-a-weee" (upslurred, but sometimes followed by a descending "pee-ur") and Westerns a repeated, harsh, "zheer." Both species have sharp chip notes. Westerns can also give a soft, Say's Phoebe-like note.

The Greater Pewee is superficially quite similar to the preceding two species, and is sympatric throughout its U.S. range with the Western Wood-Pewee. It is recognizably larger than the latter species (Figure 5.32), but field judgments of size are often misleading. When heard, the pretty whistled "ho-say-marie-ah" song is unmistakable. The call note is a "pip," given either singly or strung together in rapid succession. One of the best marks for identifying the Greater Pewee is its entirely orange-yellow lower mandible. Even light-billed Westerns have the distal half of the lower mandible dark. The Greater is structurally different as well, with a tail that is both proportionately and

FIGURE 5.32. Top to bottom: Olive-sided Flycatcher, Greater Pewee, Western Wood-Pewee. Note differences in overall size, bill size, and relative wing/tail length.

FIGURE 5.33. Left to right: Greater Pewee, Olive-sided Flycatcher, Western Wood-Pewee. Note differences in overall size, bill size, relative wing/tail length, and underpart coloration.

absolutely longer. Greaters also have larger bills and heads, and their heads often show a more conspicuous pointed crest.

There are several plumage differences that are also useful in separating the two species. Greaters have less distinctive wingbars and are much more evenly-colored below (Figure 5.33). Their throats, bellies, and vents are conspicuously lighter than their breasts and flanks but are seldom as white as the corresponding areas of Westerns (and may even be somewhat yellowish). The Greater is often more olive-gray on the breast and flanks than is the Western which is typically plain gray. In any event, the inverted white "V" or vested look of the Western is not seen on the Greater.

Olive-sided Flycatchers are probably the easiest of the group to identify. They are about equivalent in size to the Greater Pewee but are conspicuously larger than the other two species. They are more stockily built than any of their congeners, with more of a bull-headed look. This is accentuated by a large bill and a very short tail (Figure 5.32). The short tail, coupled with the big head and bill, results in a silhouette that is markedly different from the other species (especially from the Greater Pewee, which is longer-tailed).

Plumage characters are equally helpful. Olive-sideds have two bright white patches located at the sides of the rump. These are typically concealed but when visible are diagnostic. The throat, central breast, and belly are white (sometimes tinged yellow), whereas the flanks are dark olive-gray and streaked. The darker color of the flanks intrudes ventrally enough to create a narrow corridor of white (or "zipper") down the center of the breast that opens on the throat and belly (Figure 5.33). The patches and streaks on the flanks are much darker than anything on the underparts of the other species and show much greater contrast with the rest of the underparts. The white corridor effect is superficially similar to the inverted "V" of the Western Wood-Pewee but shows greater contrast and breaks through to the throat instead of just intruding into the breast before stopping (some individuals have flank streaks extending into and meeting at the center of the breast, but the darker, streaked look is still easily distinguished). Juvenile Olive-sideds are more brownish above (as opposed to dark Olive-gray) and their flanks are more extensively streaked.

The bill of the Olive-sided is typically light in the center of the lower mandible but is not nearly so conspicuous in this respect as is the Greater Pewee. Call notes (a repeated "pip") are similar to those of the latter species, while the song is a distinctive "quick-three-beers!"

Additional treatment is given by Roberson (1980) and by Dunn and Garrett (1983).

EMPIDONAX FLYCATCHERS

Flycatchers of the genus *Empidonax* have traditionally been a source of frustration to field birders. The standard advice given to most beginners is, "Don't identify them unless they sing." While this approach may work well on the breeding grounds during the peak of territorial activity, it offers little during the migratory periods when the birds do not sing. When faced with the dilemma of identifying silent *Empids*, cautious birders often throw in the towel and label them simply as "*Empidonax* species (?)." Less cautious or knowledgable birders often make specific identifications based solely on subtle coloration differ-

FIGURE 5.34. Extremes in *Empidonax* flycatcher bill length, as demonstrated by Gray Flycatcher (top) and Hammond's Flycatcher (bottom).

FIGURE 5.35. *Empidonax* flycatchers (left to right: Dusky, Hammond's, Gray, Least, Western). Note the shorter-billed, shorter-tailed look of Hammond's and Least; and the longer-billed, longer-tailed look of Dusky and Gray. Note also the thin bill of Hammond's vs. the wide, triangular bills of Least and Western.

ences pictured in their field guides. Such an approach is often useless and may lead to serious errors in presumed knowledge of *Empid* species distribution and abundance at the local level.

In recent years active field birders have made great strides in the techniques of identifying species of this genus. Armed with the knowledge of what to look for, it is now possible to accurately identify most silent *Empidonax* species occurring north of Mexico. Caution must remain the watchword, however, because the new techniques demand that the observer have a fair amount of comparative experience with all members of the group. Even then, if the birds are seen under less than ideal conditions, positive identification may be impossible. This is clearly a case where a little bit of knowledge is dangerous. *Empids* should be identified using a suite of morphological, behavioral, and vocal characters, and even then many birds will have to be identified to genus only. Single-character identifications should be strictly avoided. Observers should use extreme caution in identifying vagrant *Empidonax*, such identification coming only after the expected species has been systematically eliminated from consideration.

As mentioned previously, coloration is often useless as the sole means of identifying these flycatchers. The only western species that can always be safely identified on the basis of general coloration is the Buff-breasted, which is found only in a few mountain ranges in southern Arizona and New Mexico. Many species exhibit extreme individual variation in color that may be further influenced by lighting and by age of the bird and feather condition. Habitat preference is often fairly useful in separating species on their breeding grounds, but is useless during migration.

Perhaps the best approach is to look first at head versus tail proportions. *Empids* fall into two basic structural groups: those with proportionately large heads and short tails, versus those with smaller heads and longer tails. Birds of the first group have a big-headed, sawed-off look, whereas birds of the latter group are more normally proportioned and have a more slender appearance (Figures 5.34 and 5.35). Once a bird is mentally placed in one of these two categories, the observer needs to turn to a combination of bill proportions, plumage, and behavioral and vocal characteristics.

The big-headed, short-tailed group includes the Western, Hammond's, Buff-breasted, Least, and Yellow-bellied Flycatchers. The latter two species occur only as vagrants throughout much of the West but are regular in many areas from the Great Plains south to the Gulf Coast.

Western Flycatcher. This is probably the most widespread of the western *Empids*, and as such provides a good basis for comparison with other members of the genus. This species has a particularly large, broad bill, which further accentuates the big-headed appearance. The lower mandible is entirely yellow-orange in color, and is often quite bright. An excellent plumage characteristic is the shape of the eye ring, which is fairly diagnostic. Other *Empids* have a circular eye ring, whereas the Western has a tear-drop look with the point of the tear trailing posteriorly from the eye. This mark is very distinctive when seen at close range (but beware of occasional Yellow-bellieds, which can also share this mark). Less diagnostic, but still helpful is the usually extensive yellowish coloration of the underparts, including the throat. While other *Empids* often display some yellow to the breast, flanks, and/or belly, it is usually not as bright nor as extensive as in the Western.

The eye ring and wing bars (both of which are conspicuous) are often yellowish or buffy, as opposed to dull white in other species. Back color tends toward more olive and less gray or brown. The call heard on the breeding grounds is a rising, whistled "zu-weep" (coastal populations) or a clearer "whee-seet" (interior populations) or, less commonly, a somewhat squeaky "squeet." All of these are quite distinctive from any other western *Empid*. In migration it more often utters a high but soft "peet" very different from the lower "whit" given by many members of the genus. This species is fairly active and frequently flicks its wings, a trait not often seen in other *Empids* (except Hammonds).

Yellow-bellied Flycatcher. This species is very similar to the Western Flycatcher but is more strongly yellow below and green above. The eye ring is usually circular (rarely tear-drop shaped), and the wings are more blackish which gives greater highlighting to the contrasting white feather edgings. The tail is slightly shorter than in the Western, which heightens the stubby appearance. The bright yellow or flesh color of the lower mandible is similar to that of the Western. This species is less vocal than the Western during migration, and utters a sneezy "chew."

Hammond's Flycatcher. This species is often said to be virtually impossible to distinguish from the Dusky Flycatcher, and in plumage the two species may show much overlap. Again, structural differences are more important, with the Hammond's being a small, big-headed, short-tailed bird, and the Dusky being larger, longer-tailed, more slender in appearance, and smaller-headed.

Probably the best mark of the Hammond's is the positively *tiny bill* compared to its congeners. The bill is both short and thin, a distinction that is immediately obvious to observers with much comparative experience with the genus (Figures 5.34 and 5.35). The lower mandible is sometimes flesh-colored along the basal third but is most commonly black or dusky throughout its length.

Plumage is variable but tends to be more olive-gray above, as opposed to green in the Western and gray-green in the Dusky. This contrasts with the grayer head, giving Hammond's a saddled look to the back (often found in Dusky as well). The underparts frequently show some yellow on the flanks and belly (but not the throat), but this is highly variable (most conspicuous on fresh fall-winter birds). The throat is usually dusky with a darker grayish-green breast band which extends down the sides of the breast, giving the bird a vested appearance. The wing bars and eye ring are conspicuous and may tend toward a cream color rather than white. The wings are dark, and light feather edgings often contrast more strongly than in the Dusky. When viewed from below, the outer retrices may appear lighter gray than the others, a mark that is more pronounced in the Dusky and Gray Flycatchers.

Of much use is familiarity with the call note, a high, sharp "peek" that is often compared to the similar note of the Pygmy Nuthatch. This note is distinctly different from the calls of all other *Empids* (except Alder). Like other *Empids*, Hammond's frequently jerks its tail. Unlike other congeners (except Western), Hammond's is an habitual wing-flicker, giving it a nervous, hyperactive look. Other *Empids* (including Dusky) flick their wings from time to time, especially upon changing perches. However, Hammond's does it much more frequently and in more exaggerated fashion (the wings often raised nearly to the level of the head). On the breeding grounds it shows a tendency to forage from perches high in the canopy, a distinction that is not maintained during migration.

Least Flycatcher. Like the Hammond's, the Least looks small even for an

Empid. Unlike the Hammond's, it has a short bill that is *very broad* at the base (Figure 5.35). The lower mandible is more extensively yellow or flesh colored.

Underpart coloration may vary considerably between individuals. Many birds are quite whitish below (especially on the throat) whereas others may show a dusky upper breast and some hint of yellow on the lower flanks or belly. Most individuals are decidedly olive above (some are fairly gray), with very conspicuous whitish wing bars and eye ring. The wings are typically blackish with strongly contrasting white feather edgings.

This species is very active and often flicks its tail. Vocalizations include a sharp "whit" or "pit" ("harder" than the mellow "whit" common to several members of the genus) and the more familiar "che-bec" song, which may be repeated continuously on the breeding grounds. The call note has been compared to the chip of a distant "Audubon's" Warbler.

The small-headed, long-tailed group includes the Dusky, Gray, Willow, Alder, and Acadian Flycatchers. The Acadian is a vagrant in the West, except for eastern Texas where it nests.

Dusky Flycatcher. The dusky appears more symmetrical in shape than any of the big-headed, short-tailed species discussed earlier. The head is small and the bill is long and of medium width. The lower mandible varies from being almost entirely orange or flesh colored to being mostly blackish.

This is another species which is somewhat variable in plumage. Some individuals may closely resemble Hammond's while others approach typical Gray Flycatchers. Dusky tends to be gray-green on the back, with the shade of gray exhibiting much variation. Darker individuals usually have a darkish wash across the breast with a gray throat but lack the vested appearance of the Hammond's. There may be a fair amount of yellow on the lower flanks and belly (especially in fall) or these may be a dirty white. Lighter individuals often have very light gray backs and light gray smudging on the breast, with little or no yellow below. Such birds may be mistaken for Gray Flycatchers, although the reverse mistake is harder to make. Most Duskies show conspicuously lighter outer retrices when seen in proper light. The contrast is stronger than in Hammond's but not as pronounced as in the Gray.

The typical call is a mellow "whit," common to several members of the genus. Duskies flick their tails upwards, as do all other *Empids* except the Gray. In areas where the breeding range of this species overlaps that of Hammond's, habitat preference and foraging mode may also prove useful. Duskies tend to occupy drier forests at lower elevations and often forage low among the inner branches of trees. Hammond's prefer wetter, higher elevation forests, and more often utilize the upper strata of the canopy. Duskies also occupy some of the drier, highest-elevation forests near timberline.

Gray Flycatcher. The Gray Flycatcher is often one of the easiest *Empids* to distinguish visually. The general impression one gets is that of a largish but slender and evenly-proportioned *Empidonax.* The bill is long and somewhat narrow (Figures 5.34 and 5.35) and often shows much orange to the lower mandible.

Many individuals are almost strikingly pale, with silver-gray upperparts and clean white underparts with only a hint of light gray wash on the breast. The general color is reminiscent of Lucy's Warbler. The eye ring and wing bars are clean white, and the whitish outer retrices usually contrast conspicuously with the rest of the tail.

The common call-note is a "whit," similar to that of the Dusky and Willow Flycatchers. A behavioral trait that is diagnostic is the downward wagging of the tail. Other tail waggers in the genus flick their tails up. Gray Flycatchers typically perch and forage close to the ground, but, as with many behavioral traits, this is a generalization that often may not hold. Habitat on the breeding grounds (sagebrush desert and foothills, often with pinyon and juniper present) is useful in identification.

Willow and Alder Flycatchers. These two flycatchers may be indistinguishable in the field except by voice. Prior to 1973 they were considered to be two different song variants of the same species (Traill's Flycatcher). Because of the recentness of the split of these two species by taxonomists, much remains to be learned about their respective geographic ranges. In general, the Alder breeds in Canada and Alaska, and the Willow breeds as far south as the U.S.– Mexican border.

Both species are somewhat largish *Empids,* with longish tails; small heads; and long, broad bills. The lower mandible is often orange or flesh-colored, at least along the basal two-thirds.

Plumage is distinctive, mostly due to an absence of bright colors or distinguishing marks. The upperparts are dark (brown in Willow, more olive in Alder), with faint wing bars and on many birds an almost *indistinguishable* or *absent* eye ring. This, combined with the larger size, make both species easy to pass off as pewees. Pewees have different calls, a high-crowned head shape, are larger, don't wag their tails, and in the case of the Western Wood-Pewee, have a dusky brown breast and flanks with the white of the belly intruding to form an inverted "V" in the center of the breast. The underparts of the Willow and Alder are dirty white with a dusky bib and often a more contrasting white throat. The flanks may be dusky brown as well.

The nature of the eye ring in these two species is complex, and needs further investigation. Most western Willows lack an eye ring altogether. Alders almost always have at least a faint eye ring (variable), and eastern Willows can apparently go either way.

Call notes may be the best means of separating the two species away from the breeding grounds. Willow gives a "whit" (similar to Dusky but more liquid), whereas Alder gives a sharper "pic" (not unlike Hammond's). On the breeding grounds the Willow has a sharp, buzzy "fitz-bew" song that is both diagnostic and oft-repeated. The Alder has a three-syllable song that is often denoted as "fee-be-o." Breeding habitat is also fairly distinctive with both species preferring brushy bogs. The Willow is usually found in brushy, wet meadows throughout much of its range. In the Southwest, it more often inhabits riparian areas (along river, streams, irrigation ditches, etc.) with a thick growth of shrub willows.

Acadian Flycatcher. This is a large, evenly-proportioned *Empid* that does not easily fit into either of the two major structural divisions of the genus. The bill is large with a largely orange or flesh colored lower mandible.

Upperpart coloration tends to be very greenish with blackish wings. Feather edgings on the wings are very white, and contrast sharply with the rest of the wing (similar to Least). The underparts are fairly clear in appearance, with a whitish throat, breast, and belly. The flanks and belly are often yellowish, particularly in fall.

The common vocalizations are a high "seep" (call), and an explosive "peet-suh" (song).

Most *Empids* do not molt into basic plumage until after they have migrated to their wintering areas. Adults of these species will look particularly pale from feather wear in late summer and fall. Juveniles will be less worn, and therefore brighter in color. Acadians, Hammond's, and Buff-breasteds all molt prior to migrating. Fall migrants of these species will therefore appear much brighter (greener above and yellower below for Acadian and Hammond's) than they do on the summer breeding grounds.

For more detailed discussions see the series by Dunn (1977), and Roberson (1980).

APHELOCOMA JAYS

There are two species of jays belonging to the genus *Aphelocoma*. They are the Scrub Jay (*A. coerulescens*) and the Gray-breasted Jay (*A. ultramarina*). The former is found throughout much of the West, whereas the latter is restricted to the mountains of southern Arizona and New Mexico, and the Chisos Mountains of southwest Texas.

These jays present an identification problem in the zone of sympatry to many beginning birders. Field guide illustrations are probably the primary cause of confusion. Most guides picture Scrub Jays as having distinctive brown backs, but depict the Mexican Jay as being gray-backed. Although this is generally the case, back color in Scrub Jays is subject to much variation depending on subspecific race, age, and the individual bird. California birds are particularly brown while those from southern New Mexico and Arizona are often quite gray. This has led to many Scrub Jays being misidentified as Gray-breasted Jays purely on the basis of back coloration.

Better field marks are provided by contrast or lack of contrast on the face, throat, and breast (Figure 5.36). On most Scrub Jays the throat is several shades whiter than the belly, and this is set off by a necklace of blue streaks that separates the two areas in the middle of the breast. Once again, however, this is subject to variation, and many birds lack the well-defined necklace and separation. One mark that seems to remain constant is the face pattern. Scrub Jays have a blackish face patch that is set off by a thin, white eyebrow stripe. This gives the face a patterned look. Gray-breasted Jays show some blackish color to the face, but this is typically limited to the lores and post-ocular area and is not bordered by a white eyebrow. At the same time they are uniformly dingy gray on the entire underparts.

Overall, the Gray-breasted Jay is a larger, more robust jay that is a fairly uniform blue-gray in color. Scrub Jays are smaller, thinner, and show more contrast to the face, breast, and often to the back. The calls of the two species are very different. The Scrub Jay has a variety of harsh, raucous calls, all of which are readily distinguishable from the upslurred, less raspy "weenk, weenk, weenk" of the Gray-breasted Jay.

The two species can usually be separated by habitat also, although some overlap does occur. Gray-breasted Jays are typical of open oak (Arizona) or pine-oak (New Mexico, Texas) woodlands at low to intermediate elevations.

FIGURE 5.36. *Aphelocoma* jays (top to bottom: Gray-breasted, Scrub, Scrub, Gray-breasted).

In the zone of sympatry, Scrub Jays are usually found in drier pinyon-juniper forests, or dense oak-chaparral covered hills.

Scrub Jays in western North America are monogamous breeders. Gray-breasted Jays, on the other hand, are cooperative breeders—nonbreeding birds share in the care of young that are not their own—and live in groups of two to fifteen birds throughout the year. Therefore, one would expect to find Gray-breasted Jays in groups all year, and Scrub Jays in pairs through the breeding season. Scrub Jays do occasionally indulge in winter flocking that is usually coincident with irruptive movements into low-lying areas during periods of severe food shortage and/or cold.

The sociobiological behaviors of Gray-breasted Jays would seem to leave them as unlikely vagrants to areas outside of their breeding range because groups maintain and defend territories the year-around. Thus, any fall or winter records from outside the known breeding range should be considered as suspect unless extreme care has been exercised in making the identification.

CATHARUS THRUSHES

Thrushes of the genus *Catharus* constitute one of the more troublesome complexes to identify in North America. They are a constant bane to Christmas Bird Count compilers, who must annually wrestle with erroneous reports of Swainson's and Gray-cheeked Thrushes and Veery when only Hermit is likely in winter. Much of the confusion stems from the over-reliance on one or two field marks and from the fact that field guides have traditionally ignored the problem of geographic variation within the genus. These thrushes can be readily identified if the observer uses a suite of characters and remains cognizant of intra-specific variation and how it changes with geography.

Of the five United States species (Wood, Hermit, Swainson's, Gray-cheeked, and Veery) only the Wood can be readily dismissed as being easily separable from the others. The remaining species are all composed of at least two distinct races, and different characters must be used in different regions to separate congeners. On the breeding grounds, both song and habitat are usually diagnostic, so the following discussion is centered on migrant or wintering birds.

Hermit Thrush is the most widespread member of the genus, and is the *only* one likely to be seen in winter. It is the smallest *Catharus,* and the only one that habitually flicks its tail (or that pumps its tail while actively flicking its wings). It is geographically variable, but all plumages show a rusty-reddish tail contrasting with a grayer-brown back. The contrasting rusty tail does not show up well when the bird is in the shade. All races are boldly spotted below with thin (but conspicuous) light eye rings (almost always whitish) and a light line from the eye to the bill (usually whitish). Flank color and ground color of the breast are particularly variable. Eastern races tend to have buffy flanks, and western races have grayish flanks. Individuals may have whitish or buffy breasts—this may vary both within and between populations. Hermit has a light bar under each wing (as do other *Catharus*) that is conspicuous in flight. The call note is a low "chup" (often doubled), quite distinct from the calls of the other species. Also commonly given is a harsh, ascending call similar to that given by western Rufous-sided Towhees.

Swainson's Thrush is also geographically variable. Most observers will be familiar with the eastern/central races (*swainsoni* and *almae*), which have dark, olive-brown upperparts and are colder looking than the rusty-tailed Hermit Thrush. West Coast birds (*ustulatus* and *oedicus*) are rusty-brown above and look warmer than Hermit Thrushes. These are not pictured in most guides and could easily be mistaken for Veeries by unknowing observers. Individuals of both races are larger and more robust than Hermits, and are unicolored above, without the tail-back contrast. All Swainson's Thrushes have a prominent *buffy* eye ring and a *buffy* line running from the eye to the bill (similar to Hermit but more striking and buff, not white). They are buffy on the face, underwings, throat, breast, and flanks, with only moderate breast streaking/spotting. In general they are much buffier below and on the face than Hermits. The call is a soft "wink," which has been likened to a drop of water hitting a pool (Dunn and Garrett, 1983).

Gray-cheeked Thrush is another large *Catharus*. Birds occurring in the West are not racially distinct. They have evenly-colored gray-brown upperparts that are even colder in appearance than those of *C. s. swainsoni* and *C. s. almae*, and much colder than those of *C. s. ustulatus*. One of the best features for separation is the lack of any distinct eye ring or line from the eye to the bill (some individuals may have a *very* thin partial white eye ring). As the name implies, the cheeks are a slate gray, and almost concolor with the crown— very different from the buffy face of Swainson's. The breast is more heavily spotted than in coastal Swainson's, perhaps equivalent to or less than Hermit's and inland races of Swainson's. Most birds will be quite whitish below, but some have the breast lightly tinged with buff (richer in fall), which may lead to confusion with Swainson's. The flanks are gray, as are the underwings. The call note is a downslurred "wheer," similar to that of the Veery (Roberson, 1980). Note that the foregoing discussion does not pertain to the New England mountain form of Gray-cheeked (*C. m. bicknelli*).

Veery is a small *Catharus*, closest to Hermit in size. Two races, the eastern (*fuscescens*) and the western (*salicicolus*) are very different in overall coloring. The former is extremely rusty above (almost orange), while the latter is much darker and duller. Both races are minimally spotted on the breast (heavier in *salicicolus*), much less so than any congeners. Only the thinnest of white eye rings is ever visible, while the cheek may be light gray or brownish (but not contrasting buff as in Swainson's). The breast is often washed with buff, while the flanks are gray (a mark that will aid in separation from *C. s.*

ustulatus). Beware, however, that the lower flanks can be tinged with buff, especially in the nominate race (*fuscescens*). The call is a downslurred "teeur," similar to the call of Gray-cheeked.

For more information see the excellent four-part series by Dunn and Garrett (1983).

FEMALE BLUEBIRDS

Although the range of Eastern Bluebird with respect to both Western and Mountain is largely allopatric, there is still enough distributional overlap as to make careful identification of bluebirds a concern in many areas. Males of all three species are so distinctively plumaged as to make identification straightforward. The spotted juvenal plumage of all three species is retained for only a short time and is lost prior to fall migration. Thus, it is seen only on the breeding grounds where the habitat overlap of any two species of bluebirds is minimal. Females present the only real problem in the group, but most standard guides are of little help in separating them.

Easterns and Westerns are structurally and behaviorally more similar to one another than either is to Mountain. Mountains have longer, thinner bills than either of the other species, with proportionately longer tarsi and wings (Figure 5.37 and 5.38). These features combine to give Mountains a leaner, more elongated look. Easterns and Westerns have shorter, thicker bills and proportionately shorter wings and tarsi, giving them a more rotund or dumpy shape that is accentuated by their hunched posture when perched. The difference in relative wing length is most striking between Mountain and Eastern. The wings of Mountain extend to or beyond the tip of the tail. The wings of Eastern are very short, always falling well short of the tip of the tail. Westerns are intermediate in wing length but are still noticeably shorter in this respect than are Mountains.

The feeding behaviors of Easterns and Westerns are also similar, and both differ markedly from Mountains. The former two species feed extensively in trees (both the crowns and inner branches), but also commonly drop to the ground. Mountain Bluebirds do little foraging in trees, preferring instead to feed mostly on the ground. They differ in their ground feeding from Easterns and Westerns in that they frequently hunt from a low perch (fence post or vine) and make repeated short forays, during which they hover over potential prey for several seconds.

Details of plumage provide less subjective clues to species identity. Females of all three species are duller in color than their respective males. Female Easterns are a dull blue-gray above with a brownish wash across the back that contrasts with the rump and back of the head. Female Westerns are similar (subtly darker) but with stronger brownish overtones to the central back. Female Moun-

FIGURE 5.37. Female bluebirds (top to bottom: Eastern, Mountain, Western). Note differences in bill length and shape, and in relative wing and tail lengths.

FIGURE 5.38. Female bluebirds (left to right: Mountain, Eastern, Mountain, Western, Eastern). Note bill length and relative wing and tail length.

tains are a lighter blue-gray than the other species and lack the brown back and consequent crown-back contrast.

All three species show extensive blue in the wings and tail, but this blue is darker in Eastern and Western and closer to turquoise in the Mountain. An excellent mark of female Mountains is that most of the wing coverts and secondaries have grayish centers with distinct white edges. This is most pronounced in fall after the molt and provides much contrast in the wing. Females of the other species generally lack the light fringes, but when present they are buff rather than white and not nearly as noticeable.

Of particular importance is the color of the underparts. Easterns are largely reddish brown below (breast and flanks) with strongly contrasting, clean white vents, bellies and chins. The throat may be either white or reddish brown. Westerns also have somewhat rusty breasts and flanks, but these are more dingy buff as opposed to the brighter reddish colors of the Eastern. In addition, Westerns have a dingy gray or blue-gray throat and chin, and the belly and undertail coverts are a dirty white. This results in underparts that lack the sharp contrast between flanks and belly, and between breast and chin that are so conspicuous in female Easterns. In general, then, Easterns have a sharper, cleaner look to the underparts than do Westerns.

Female Mountains differ from the other two species in having generally gray or gray-brown underparts. Their chins are paler than surrounding areas, but the throat, breast, and flanks are concolor, and this color generally matches that of the back and head (very different from the contrast of dorsal and ventral surfaces found in the other two species). Mountains have clean white vents and bellies that contrast sharply with the flanks and breast (like the Eastern), but the contrast is between gray and white as opposed to red-brown and white.

An additional mark noted by Dunn (1981) that sets female Easterns apart from the other two species in the intrusion of reddish-brown from the breast into the neck region. This intrusion of rust coloring has the effect of setting off the bluish auricular region from the back of the head, thus creating an auricular patch that is absent in the other bluebirds.

Be aware that bluebirds undergo only one molt per year, this being a complete postnuptial molt following breeding in late summer. Southbound birds in fall will be in freshest plumage, which may differ somewhat from the more faded plumage worn in spring and summer. Mountain Bluebirds of both sexes tend to be somewhat buffier (rather than blue-gray) on the underparts when in fresh plumage, and this should be kept in mind.

Vocalizations can be helpful, with Westerns giving a mellow "pew" note, Easterns a two-syllabled "chur-lee" (Dunn 1981), and Mountains a note similar to Westerns but which is flatter in tone.

Mountains and Easterns are more highly migratory than are Westerns, which still show altitudinal migration into the lowlands each winter. Least migratory of all is the highly localized southwestern subspecies of the Eastern

(*Sialia sialis fulva*), which is found at high elevations in the Chiricahua, Santa Catalina, and Huachuca Mountains and low, along Sonoita Creek (Arizona). This race is not known to migrate (Females of *S. s. fulva* resemble those of the nominate eastern race, while the males of this subspecies are slightly buffier— less red—below than their eastern counterparts).

All three species may be found in open or semi-open habitat during winter and migration, but this tendency is most pronounced in Mountain Bluebirds, which are often seen in large flocks in the middle of treeless prairies, deserts, or cultivated fields.

BENDIRE'S VERSUS CURVE-BILLED THRASHERS

This is another instance in which information presented in many field guides is misleading and results in much confusion in the separation of the two species.

The two marks emphasized by most guides for separating these species are bill shape and length, and eye color. Neither mark is infallible, and identifications in the area of sympatry should not be made solely on these features.

While a bird with a long, distinctly decurved bill will immediately rule out Bendire's, the reverse situation does not automatically eliminate Curve-billed. Bill length and degree of decurvature is highly variable in Curve-billed Thrashers, and birds located at the opposite extremes of the spectrum can look very different. Young (recently fledged) Curve-billeds can have particularly short and straight bills that resemble exactly the bills of adult Bendire's (Figure 5.39). More than one birder has joyfully checked off his or her first Bendire's Thrasher, only to watch with dismay as an adult Curve-billed flies up to feed it a grub. Some Bendire's also have a slight droop to the tip of the bill, thereby creating more potential confusion.

FIGURE 5.39. Thrashers (top to bottom: adult Curve-billed, Bendire's, juvenile Curve-billed).

FIGURE 5.40. Bendire's (top) and Curve-billed (bottom) Thrashers. Note the finer breast markings of Bendire's.

Likewise, eye color can be used as an accessory aid to identification, but should not be considered diagnostic. Most field guides stress the orange or red eye color of Curve-billeds as opposed to the yellow eye of the Bendire's. This mark has probably resulted in more misidentified thrashers than any other. Curve-billeds often show an orange or red iris, but individuals with yellow eyes are also routinely seen. This yellow tends to be more of a golden color than the yellow of the Bendire's, but such impressions are subject to error depending on viewer distance and light conditions. For the most part eye color is useless (at best), and is often misleading.

What characters, then, should be used to separate the two species? There are several marks that when used in concert can provide an accurate identification. One is general body color. Bendire's is a light, sandy brown above, giving a warmer appearance (especially on the flanks). Curve-billeds tend towards a grayer shade of brown, giving a colder appearance. Bendire's is lightly streaked below with small chevrons. These are crisper and more defined than the more smudgy spots found on Curve-billeds (Figure 5.40). The gray, smudged breast of the Curve-billed is set off by a white throat, that contrasts more strongly than in Bendire's. Curve-billeds of the race *palmeri* have spots that are often indistinguishable. One mark that is diagnostic but difficult to see is the color at the base of the lower mandible. In Bendire's this is pale, contrasting with the remainder of the bill, which is black. Curve-billeds have the entire lower mandible black. Body size is also suggestive of species status with Curve-billeds being larger and more robust.

Vocalizations are also very useful. Curve-billeds frequently whistle a loud, sharp (almost human-like) "whit-wheet" that is instantly recognizable. Bendire's have a low "check" that is infrequently given. The songs of the two species are also different, with that of the Curve-billed being separated into distinct trills and warbled phrases, and that of the Bendire's being more of a continuous warble.

None of the above is meant to disregard bill length or shape as a useful character in separating these two species. Indeed, it is probably the most recognizable feature in the majority of instances. However, accessory information should be verified before finalizing the identification.

SPRAGUE'S PIPIT

Sprague's Pipit is not a particularly difficult bird to identify. However, it has not received adequate treatment in most field guides, and in some cases, field guide illustrations have not even remotely resembled the real bird. Most books also fail to point out the geographic variability of the related Water Pipit, thus increasing the likelihood of observer confusion where these species are concerned.

Three races of Water Pipits (*Anthus spinoletta*) are currently recognized by the A.O.U. (American Ornithologists Union) as occurring in our area (a fourth race, *A. s. japonicus*, reaches islands in the Bering Sea). These are:

1. *A. s. pacificus* (West Coast race breeding from Alaska south to California)
2. *A. s. alticola* (Rocky Mt. race)
3. *A. s. rubescens* (eastern race breeding from Newfoundland west to Alaska).

These races differ most conspicuously in alternate plumage. Individuals of *alticola* are the brightest pinkish buff below (with very pinkish buff eyestripes), and are almost entirely lacking in breast or flank streaking. Individuals of *pacificus* represent the other extreme of moderate-heavy breast and flank streaking with yellowish to white (not pink) eye stripes and underparts. Typical Eastern birds (*rubescens*) are intermediate with respect to amount of streaking and degree of pinkish buff coloring (Parkes, 1982). All races are somewhat light gray or gray-brown above with fairly indistinct (often smudge-like) streaking on the back, crown, and nape. In all cases the supercilium (be it buff or white) contrasts sharply with the darker face and crown.

In basic plumage (which is attained in fall) the distinctions between the races of Water Pipit are less conspicuous (except in *japonicus*, where they are more pronounced). All individuals are darker (more brown) above and much more heavily streaked below. The streaking takes the form of a broad necklace that extends down the flanks on the sides. Excluding *japonicus*, upperpart coloration is darkest brown in *rubescens* and lightest gray in *pacificus* (Parkes, 1982). The latter race shows reasonably distinct blackish streaking on the crown at this time (Parkes, 1982). Underpart coloration is subject to much individual variation, with *alticola* averaging buffier and *pacificus* whiter (Parkes, 1982). The most important features to note (regardless of race) are the strongly contrasting superciliary (with darker face), indistinctly streaked back, and heavily streaked underparts (including flanks).

FIGURE 5.41. Sprague's Pipit. Note the prominent dark
eye against the pale, unpatterned face and the scaly
back pattern. Artwork by Dale A. Zimmerman.

In contrast, Sprague's Pipit is a warm sandy buff (not pinkish buff) color
in all seasons (worn birds are darker, particularly on the upperparts). The back
and crown are *strongly* streaked with black and buff, giving it an appearance
that is very different from the cold and indistinctly-streaked upperparts of any
of the Water Pipits. The distinction between upperpart coloration of the two
species is heightened in juvenal plumaged Sprague's, which have regular buff-
gold margins to the black back and scapular feathers, thus giving these birds
a scaly look.

Equally distinctive is the nature of head-face coloration in Sprague's. Although a faint buff supercilium and eye ring are present in this species, the
lores and auriculars are almost equally light buff, thus eliminating the impression
of any facial markings (except at very close range). This unmarked, buffy face
causes the dark eye to look very prominent, a feature that is recognizable at
great distances and that is reminiscent of Upland or Buff-breasted Sandpipers
(Figure 5.41). This lack of facial pattern is clearly different from the strong
eyebrowed appearance of Water Pipits.

Sprague's Pipits are streaked below only on the breast, and even here
the streaks are confined to a narrow necklace and are finer in character than
the breast streaks of Water Pipits. Sprague's also displays greater amounts of
white in the tail (when seen flying) than does Water Pipit.

Much has been made of leg color differences between the two species,
with Water Pipits typically having blackish legs and Sprague's having pinkish
legs. Over-reliance on this single character often results in misidentification
because leg color in Water Pipits is highly variable and can at least approach
the light color of Sprague's (although even light-legged Water Pipits tend toward
yellowish rather than pinkish legs).

Because the two species are essentially allopatric with respect to breeding ranges, and because breeding habitats are entirely different (Sprague's nest in prairie grasslands, Water Pipits in alpine or arctic tundra), confusion on the nesting grounds is unlikely. Hence, the entirely different songs of the two birds are of little help in making the separation. Call notes are useful, however, with Water Pipits giving an oft-repeated "pi-pit" or "pip-pip-it" and a "pseet" (both typically uttered in flight), and Sprague's giving a loud, squeaky "squeet" (either singly or doubly repeated).

Habits of the two species are also distinctly different. Water Pipits (in winter and migration) frequent open areas such as plowed fields, mud flats or sandbars, and athletic fields. They are often seen in large flocks and frequently pump their tails up and down. When flushed from cover Water Pipits bound high in the air and return to the ground via a bouncing stair-step descent. Sprague's Pipits frequent grasslands or agricultural fields with greater cover (such as alfalfa) and tend to creep furtively about through the vegetation. On the ground they tend to move quickly away from you with their head and neck held low in front and parallel to the ground (much like longspurs). From time to time they will pause, straighten up, and strain their necks to look around. In this respect they are reminiscent of Buff-breasted Sandpipers or many plovers. They are more solitary (although frequently migrating in small flocks) and rarely or never pump their tails. When flushed they fly high and then drop rapidly to the ground in a straight descent (not bouncing).

For more information see King (1981) and Parkes (1982).

BELL'S VERSUS GRAY VERSUS SOLITARY VERSUS HUTTON'S VIREOS

There are four species of somewhat drably-colored vireos whose ranges overlap principally in the Southwest. These are the Bell's, Gray, Solitary, and Hutton's. All are some combination of gray, white, and/or olive; all have wing bars and some sort of eye ring; and the plumage of three of the species is geographically variable. These factors combine to make for a group that confuses many beginning birders.

Gray Vireos have the most restricted ranges and are (generally speaking) the hardest of the four to find. Birders who are eagerly seeking their first Gray Vireo commonly mistake both Bell's and Solitary Vireos for their bird. Much of this problem can be attributed to a lack of information in standard guides, and to the plumage variability of both the Bell's and Solitary Vireos.

Let's start with the Solitary. Eastern birds have olive backs, white throats, highly contrasting blue-gray heads, yellow-olive flanks, yellowish wing bars, and bold white spectacles. Western birds are less richly colored and show some variability even within a given region. West Coast birds tend toward dull olive upperparts with bold white spectacles, white wing bars, and a variable amount of dull yellow on the flanks. Head and back color are consistent, lacking the contrast of eastern birds. Western interior birds (particularly of the Rockies and adjacent ranges) are much grayer, and it is these individuals that are often mistaken for Gray Vireos. Typical individuals are entirely gray above and clean white below (usually some gray on the flanks), with two white wing bars and bold white spectacles. However, many birds are somewhat olive-gray above and may even show slight contrast with a grayer head (although not nearly to the degree of eastern birds) and a faint yellow wash on the flanks.

Gray Vireos are entirely gray above and clean white below, with two white wing bars and a white eye ring. The upperparts are generally a lighter gray than those of gray Solitarys, and the flanks usually have less gray and more white. The wing bars of Gray Vireos are typically fainter (particularly the upper bar) than those of Solitarys, but many individuals of the latter species also have somewhat inconspicuous upper bars. The wing coverts of Solitarys are blacker and the tertials are more conspicuously edged with white, providing more contrast than is found in Grays (which have more brownish wings).

The two species are best separated by the markings of the head. Solitary Vireos in any plumage will show bold, highly conspicuous white spectacles with dark lores. Grays have inconspicuous white eye rings (not complete spectacles) and light lores.

Habitat preference is a generally useful clue, with Grays preferring drier foothills where open pinyon-juniper and/or live-oak woodlands meet more xeric desert brushlands. Solitarys tend to inhabit more mesic mixed forests, but both species may overlap in dry, oak woodlands. In these cases Grays will usually stick to drier slopes and leave the canyon bottoms to the Solitarys.

Gray Vireos typically forage very low in the interior canopy, seldom venturing into the open or above six feet in height. Solitarys tend to forage higher, but again, some overlap occurs. Gray Vireos have proportionately long tails (in contrast to shorter wings) which they flick habitually, a habit generally not demonstrated by Solitarys.

Songs are also useful in the discrimination of the two species, with Solitarys giving a deliberate "chu-wee, cheeyou," and Grays a faster "chu-wee chu-weet."

Bell's Vireos may also pose a source of confusion with Grays. This species is highly variable in plumage and is not adequately treated in most guides. In general, West Coast and Southwest birds are grayer, and eastern and central interior birds more olive, but local variation between individuals is also found. Eastern individuals on the one extreme are entirely olive above with variable amounts of yellow wash on the flanks and breast. These individuals most closely approximate the illustrations in most guides. At the other extreme are birds that are entirely light gray above (slightly olive on the rump) with white flanks. In the Southwest (where confusion with Gray Vireos is most likely) most individuals are somewhat intermediate with light olive-gray backs, lighter gray heads (showing some contrast) and whitish or only faded yellow flanks. Where variations from this average occur, it is usually toward the grayer end of the spectrum.

Like the Gray Vireo, the Bell's does not have conspicuous spectacles or wing bars. Often, only the lower wing bar is evident at any distance, and it is not even conspicuous. Bell's do have spectacles, but they are faint and the portion that encircles the underside of the eye is often so light as to be nearly invisible. This often lends Bell's Vireos more of an eye-striped (albeit faint) appearance than a spectacled one. An excellent mark for many Bell's that is usually not mentioned nor depicted is a lower mandible that is largely yellowish or tan in color (this is particularly conspicuous from below). Some individuals may show entirely dark bills.

The Bell's shares with the Gray a proclivity for constant tail-pumping, and tail-fanning (particularly when disturbed) is also common. Bell's are typically found at lower elevations than Grays, being especially characteristic of riparian thickets of mesquite, shrub willow, salt cedar, and cottonwoods. Bell's is a persistent singer (even during the hottest hours of the day) and its song is unmistakable. Typically it sings a rapid, speeded-up "cheedle cheedle chee" (upward inflection as if asking a question) followed by an equally rapid "cheedle cheedle churr" (downward inflection as if answering its own question). On many occasions only half the song (usually the second part) is given. Like other vireos it has a variety of harsh, scolding notes. Bell's is typically very nervous in its actions and will often flit constantly through the underbrush while singing or scolding, without coming into the open.

Bell's Vireos may also be confused with Lucy's Warblers, which share the same habitat in the area of sympatry. The warbler is entirely gray above (except for a brick-red rump patch and crown patch that are usually concealed) and white below, and shares the light-faced and faint eye-striped look of the vireo. However, it lacks spectacles and any real wing bars, has no trace of yellow on the flanks, has a big-eyed look (large dark eye against pale face), and a thin, black bill that lacks the vireo-hook.

Hutton's Vireos are probably more likely to be confused with Ruby-Crowned Kinglets than with other vireos. Once again, Southwest birds are grayer (with olive-gray flanks), whereas West Coast individuals are brighter olive with more yellowish flanks. All members of the species are suggestive of kinglets in being small, plump, olive-gray above and lighter below, with an olive or yellow wash on the flanks, a white eye ring, two white wing bars, and dark wings with contrasting white or yellowish edges to the tertials, secondaries, and coverts.

Contrary to the claims of some guides, Hutton's Vireos do not have true spectacles. Rather, they have whitish lores and white eye rings that are broken at the top. The white lores and broken eye ring are one of the better characters for separating this species from the Ruby-crowned Kinglet, which has dark lores and a bolder, complete eye ring.

A mark that is equally as good concerns the color of the wings and the boldness of the wing bars. Kaufman (1979) pointed out that Hutton's have both wing bars equally conspicuous, with the area between the bars standing out as the blackest portion of the wing. The kinglet, on the other hand, has a posterior bar that is much bolder than the anterior one, and the blackest portion of the wing is a narrow panel posterior to the trailing bar.

Bill structure is an excellent separator. The vireo has a thicker, slightly hooked bill that is somewhat typical of the family. The kinglet has a tiny, straight little bill that looks entirely different.

The vireo is the more sedate of the two species, although it is quite active by vireo standards. Although it does not match the hyper behavior of the kinglet (perpetual motion, with constant wing and tail flicking), the vireo does twitch its wings and tail sometimes, particularly when alarmed. Kinglets seem to chatter constantly, whereas the vireo utters a shorter harsh, scold note (not unlike that of other vireos), and a repetitious "zu-wheet."

WARBLING VERSUS PHILADELPHIA VIREO

Distinguishing the Warbling Vireo from the Philadelphia Vireo is an identification problem that is not even addressed in many field guides. Breeding birds are easily distinguished, but most people are not aware that fall Warbling Vireos can look very similar to Philadelphias. This has doubtlessly led to the misidentification of many Warbling Vireos as the much rarer Philadelphias.

Fall-plumaged Warbling Vireos tend to show more olive upperparts than they do in spring and summer, and also tend to have varying amounts of yellow on the underparts. In many individuals this yellow is quite extensive, being distributed on the breast, flanks, and undertail coverts. Such individuals are easily mistaken for Philadelphia Vireos.

A point that should be noted immediately when dealing with a yellowish vireo of this type is the brightness of yellow on the throat and upper breast (centrally, not on the sides). In Philadelphia Vireos this is the area of brightest yellow (along with the undertail coverts) and it is solidly colored. Warbling Vireos tend to be palest (even white) on the throat and center of the upper breast, while being brightest on the flanks. Even when yellow is present in these areas on a Warbling, it tends to be faded or washed, and not evenly colored.

Crown-back contrast is another important point to note. Philadelphia has a darker gray crown and a more olive back, creating more contrast between the two regions. Warblings are more evenly gray colored over both areas and thus exhibit less contrast.

Philadelphia Vireos have a dark eye line that extends forward through the eye to the bill. This gives this species dark lores, whereas the lores of Warbling Vireos are light. The shape of the white eye stripe is also helpful. In Warbling it is noticeably arched above the eye, while in Philadelphia it is straighter. Warbling Vireos tend to be flatter-crowned than the more round-headed Philadelphias and frequently erect their crown feathers into a bushy crest (especially when agitated). This behavior is less frequently seen with Philadelphias, but should certainly not be used as the sole criterion in making an identification. Philadelphias also have blacker primary wing coverts than do Warblings.

Overall proportions also differ between the two species. Philadelphia is smaller with a shorter bill and relatively shorter tail. When these are combined with the more round-headed look, the result is a very chunky stubby vireo that is much different from Warbling.

For more information see Dunn (1978), Roberson (1980), and Terrill and Terrill (1981).

WATERTHRUSHES

Although their breeding ranges are largely allopatric, the Northern and Louisiana Waterthrushes present a difficult identification problem throughout their extensive migratory zone of overlap. Both species are also at least occasional vagrants west and south of their breeding ranges, where identification is seldom aided by song.

Most guides point to the larger bill and unspotted white throat of the Louisiana as being the best marks for identification. Although both of these characters can be good, neither is infallible due to a wide range of individual variation. Out-of-range individuals in particular should be identified on the basis of a suite of subtle characters (Figure 5.42).

Bill size is a good indicator of specific identity, since Louisianas have bills that are both absolutely and relatively longer and heavier. However, the distinction is subtle enough that observers should seek confirmation from other marks.

Most Louisianas have unspotted, unstreaked throats, whereas *most* North-

FIGURE 5.42. Northern (left) and Louisiana (right) Waterthrushes. Note the differences in bill size, undertail coverts, distribution of streaks on the underparts, and shape of the supercilium. Artwork by Dale A. Zimmerman.

erns are streaked or spotted on the throat (note that the streaks or spots are often absent from the chin). Variants are found in both species, and thus this field mark cannot be considered safe (although once again it is a good indicator). When viewed head on, the white, unspotted throat of the Louisiana dips into the streaked area of the breast, creating the impression of a white oval. Louisianas always have immaculate white throats (even when spots are present) in contrast to the typically off-white or yellowish throats of Northerns.

One very good mark is the shape and color of the supercilium. In Northerns it is either uniform in breadth throughout its length, or else *narrows* conspicuously behind the eye. Its color is typically buffy to yellowish (although in some birds it may be cream or even whitish). Louisianas have a supercilium that *broadens* conspicuously behind the eye. Anterior to the eye it is washed with buff or gray, but behind the eye it is gleaming white.

Another excellent mark is the color of the flanks in contrast to the rest of the underparts. The flanks, belly, and undertail coverts of Northerns are typically yellowish, or off-white, and are in any case concolor. Many Louisianas, by contrast, have a distinctive patch of pinkish buff color on the flanks that extends almost to the shoulder. This patch contrasts markedly with the remainder of the clean white underparts. When present this patch is probably diagnostic, however, its absence does not eliminate Louisiana.

There may be some general differences in the nature of the breast spotting, although again, individual variation is rampant. Generally, the spotting of Northerns is more dense and tends to cluster strongly on the upper end at the throat. Louisianas typically have more diffuse spotting and lack the cluster effect.

Leg color may also be useful because Louisianas tend toward brighter pink while Northerns are dull pinkish in color.

For further discussion see Binford (1971), Wallace (1976), Dunn (1979), and Roberson (1980).

BLACK-HEADED VERSUS ROSE-BREASTED GROSBEAKS

Females and immature Black-headed and Rose-breasted Grosbeaks are presenting an identification problem of increasing importance. Black-headeds are becoming regular vagrants to the midwestern states, while Rose-breasteds are making numerous incursions far to the west of their breeding range. In the Great Plains (where the breeding ranges of the two species overlap), even the birds can't seem to identify one another because hybrids are common.

Adult males of both species are unmistakable. Although female and immature Black-headeds are not as likely to be mistaken for similarly plumaged Rose-breasteds, the reverse mistake can be easily made.

Females of both species are mostly brown above with strongly striped heads, light underparts, yellow wing linings, and at least some streaking on the breast and flanks. Female Black-headeds are typically very buffy throughout the head and underparts, while female Rose-breasteds are typically very white in the same areas. This general coloration is subject to some variation, however, with many female Rose-breasteds being somewhat buffy and with worn Black-headeds being more whitish. The picture is clouded by the appearance of first-fall male Rose-breasteds, which are strongly buff colored (often pinkish-buff) on the face, throat, and breast. These birds can be eliminated from consideration by checking the amount of breast streaking and the color of the wing linings, which are pinkish-red.

In general, female Rose-breasteds have whitish head stripes, whereas those of female and immature Black-headed are distinctly buff-colored. Once again, feather wear and individual variation can cause overlap. Rose-breasteds are usually more heavily streaked on the breast, and the streaks themselves are somewhat broad. Black-headeds have finer streaks that are more sparsely distributed (usually only on the sides of the breast). This is particularly true of immatures, which are virtually unstreaked below. Black-headeds also have buffier rumps that contrast more strongly with the rest of the back than does the darker olive-brown rump of the Rose-breasted.

With practice, call notes can be diagnostic. The Black-headed gives a sharp "ik" or "eek" that is lower than the very squeaky "eek" of the Rose-breasted.

For more information see Dunn (1977).

FEMALE BUNTINGS

Female buntings (genus *Passerina*) present a real identification problem, particularly in the Southwest where at some times of the year all four species may occur. Of the four species (Painted, Indigo, Lazuli, Varied) Painted is the easiest to identify, being bright green above and yellow-green below (juveniles are much duller). It presents no real problem. The remaining species, however, epitomize the concept of the "little brown bird" and can cause difficulty in areas of sympatry.

Lazuli Buntings breed in open deciduous (especially riparian bottomland) or mixed woodlands and in brushy foothills throughout most of the West, excepting Texas, and the extreme Southwest (through which they migrate). They range east to the central Great Plains, where they coexist in a broad zone of sympatry with Indigo Buntings, which breed in forest-edge and secondary growth habitats throughout the East (west to the Great Plains). In recent years Indigo Buntings have become increasingly common summer residents of riparian forests throughout the Southwest. Varied Buntings have a very limited breeding range in the United States, being present in localized mesquite/acacia brushlands (primarily in arroyos and canyons) from southeast Arizona south and east to the southern tip of Texas. They are rarely seen in migration.

Indigo versus Lazuli. Breeding-plumaged female Lazulis are essentially plain brown above, with a rump that is lightly tinged with blue. Their throat and breast are a light to deep buff (similar to female Blue Grosbeaks) and contrast with a white belly and vent. Two narrow, buffy wing bars and a light eye ring can usually be seen. Breeding female Indigos are similar but lack the bluish rump. Their wing bars are less evident, and their breast is washed with a dull brown that is less warm in appearance than the buffy breast of the Lazuli. This wash extends down the flanks and is usually overlaid by darker (but smudgy and inconspicuous) streaking on the breast. The colors of the throat and breast are not uniform, with the throat of the Indigo being more whitish. Also, the Indigo lacks the noticeable division between white belly and buff breast found in the Lazuli and instead has a belly that is washed with dingy gray-brown. On the average, Indigos are a richer brown on the upperparts, whereas Lazulis are more of a gray-brown. The wing bar situation can be complex in female Indigos. Most have buffy bars, but others have white ones. The degree of barring can vary from distinct but thin bars to just lighter edges, to nothing at all.

The picture is complicated by juveniles and first-winter males, which are similar to adult females in appearance. Juvenile Indigos are not appreciably different from adult females. Juvenile Lazulis, on the other hand, do differ from adult females in two important respects—they possess breast streaking and contrasting throats like female Indigos. There are still differences, however. Juvenile Lazulis have even more pronounced breast streaking (almost forming a necklace of faint streaks) than do female Indigos, and this streaking is set against a warm buffy background (not dull brown). The throat is grayish, as are the belly and vent (both of these are paler in Lazuli than in Indigo). The head is a gray-brown that contrasts with the buffy wash to the breast, a contrast that is not so evident in the Indigo.

Further complicating the picture in the Great Plains is the presence of numbers of hybrids that possess characters of both species.

Varied. The problem of separating this species from the preceding two is limited in geographical extent. The breeding range of Varied does not overlap that of the Lazuli, but it does at least potentially overlap that of the Indigo. Both of the widespread species migrate through breeding areas of the Varied.

Much of the difficulty surrounding the identification of female Varieds stems from the field guides themselves. Nearly all guides describe and depict female Varied Buntings as being dull gray-brown with no trace of streaking, wing bars, or distinctive marks of any kind. Although a fair case can be made for the lack of any distinctive marks, the overall representation (both pictoral and verbal) of female Varieds is misleading.

Female Varieds are actually more richly colored than female Indigos. Rather than the gray-brown shown in field guides, they are a tawny, cinnamon brown that gives a much warmer appearance than the dull brown of the Indigo (some Fall Indigos are a fairly rich brown). The head and face are particularly tawny/cinnamon in color, and the underparts are much lighter but still tawny (the degree of lightness of the underparts seems to be subject to some individual variation). The back is a grayer brown than the head and face but is still just as richly colored as in the other two species. Female Varieds have uniformly-colored upperparts (lacking the bluish rump of the Lazuli) and underparts (lacking both the breast streaking of the Indigo and the contrasting white belly of the Lazuli). At close range a thin, light cinnamon eye ring, and narrow cinnamon wing bars may be seen. The lower mandible is distinctly pale (almost straw colored on some individuals), whereas the upper mandible is more grayish. (Juveniles, first-winter males, and first nuptial males are all similar in plumage to adult females but may be less rusty in color, with scattered purple flecking throughout.)

With practice, "chip" notes may be of use in separating the three species. Indigo has an emphatic "pit," as well as a sharper, more metallic "chick." Lazuli has a sharp "pink" that is not as hard, nor as metallic as the similar note of Indigo. Likewise, Varied gives a sharp "chip" that is lower than the note of the Lazuli and less metallic than that of the Indigo. Both Indigo and Lazuli (and possibly Varied) also have identical "psit" calls that are thinner and less metallic, but which are still emphatic.

BAIRD'S SPARROW
VERSUS SAVANNAH SPARROW

In the Southwest many birders routinely mistake Savannah Sparrows for wintering Baird's. Such errors result less from similarity of the two species than from a combination of three factors:

1. field guide emphasis on one or two marks,
2. the extreme variability of Savannah Sparrows,
3. the fact that few Southwestern birders have had field experience with Baird's Sparrow.

Savannah Sparrows breed over most of North America, and winter in large numbers across the southern tier of states. By contrast, Baird's Sparrow is an uncommon summer resident of the Dakotas, Montana, and the prairie provinces of Canada. It winters only in west Texas, southern New Mexico and Arizona, and Northern Mexico. It is seldom easy to find on its U.S. wintering grounds.

Habitat should provide an immediate clue to the identity of a suspected Baird's. Baird's Sparrows are birds of the grasslands. This is as true in winter as it is on the breeding grounds. Savannah Sparrows also inhabit grasslands

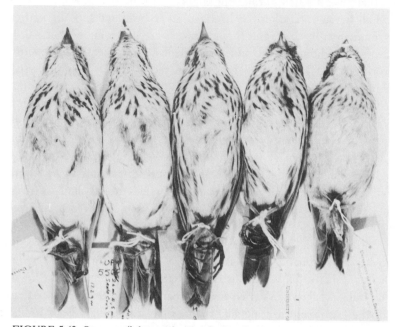

FIGURE 5.43. Sparrows (left to right: Baird's, Baird's, Savannah, Savannah, juvenile Grasshopper). Note the more extensive breast and flank streaking of Savannah, and the double whisker mark of Baird's (best seen on left-most bird).

but are equally or more common in a variety of agricultural habitats. It is highly unlikely that you will ever find a Baird's Sparrow along a drainage ditch, in a plowed or stubble field, or along a grassy right-of-way, while such habitats may be brimming with Savannahs.

Habitat considerations aside, the two species are not as difficult to separate as one might think. Most confusion results from the concentration of standard guides on only one or two marks of the Baird's Sparrow.

The feature that is most cited in erroneous reports of Baird's (and one of the two marks most mentioned in field guides) is the necklace of streaks on the breast. Baird's does have finer breast streaking than does Savannah, and in the former species the streaking is limited to a narrow necklace across the upper breast and some residual streaking that tightly borders the sides and flanks (Figure 5.43). The extent to which the streaking extends posteriorally varies somewhat, but in all cases it fails to extend inward to the central belly or undertail coverts. Savannah Sparrows typically have thicker breast streaks that are blurrier at the margins, and these streaks are usually more widely distributed across the upper breast and down the sides. Many individuals have a convergence of streaks in the center of the breast to form a small but distinct stickpin. Be aware, however, that Savannah Sparrows are among the most variable of all birds, and that many individuals not only lack the stickpin but also show

FIGURE 5.44. Sparrows (left to right: Baird's, Baird's, Savannah, Savannah, juvenile Crasshopper). Note the broad median crown stripe of Baird's, as well as its generally brighter and more contrasty upperparts.

a necklace effect similar to that seen in Baird's. The nature of breast streaking should never be the sole criterion for separating these two species.

The field guides also mention the orange median crown stripe of the Baird's (an excellent mark), but usually fail to illustrate it to full advantage. Baird's has a broad orange-buff stripe that covers most of the crown and that is bordered by a broad blackish stripe on each side (Figure 5.44). The orange crown may have some fine dark streaks in the center, but these are not obvious, and do little to blunt the conspicuousness of the crown. The nape too is orange, and is margined posteriorly by a broken border of blackish streaks. The contrast between the color of the nape and back is obvious. Juveniles tend to be lighter buff on the crown and nape with more streaking. Savannah Sparrows typically have a thinner median stripe that is cream or light-gray in color, and that more often (but not always) has small dark streaks overlaid on the light stripe. On many birds, the light median stripe is laterally bordered by thick, dark-brown stripes. If the median stripe is unstreaked, the general appearance is not totally dissimilar to the crown pattern of Baird's. In all cases, however, Savannahs lack the obvious contrast between the nape and the back that is found in Baird's.

Further characters that are highly useful but infrequently mentioned are the color of the upperparts and the facial pattern.

Baird's has back feathers that are dark in the center, with thin chestnut inner edgings and broader cream-buff outer edgings. The scapulars and wing coverts have chestnut centers with broad cream-buff fringes. The net effect is a very contrasting back that has a dark stripes on light background look (Figure 5.44). The chestnut adds richness to the overall impression of upperpart coloration. Juveniles have a scalier, more scalloped look, but still retain the light and dark contrasting appearance of adults. By contrast, Savannahs have dark back and wing feathers that are thinly edged with gray or gray-brown, lending a darker, duller, more uniform appearance to the upperparts. The tail feathers of Baird's are edged with cream-color on both sides (even the innermost retrices), giving a much lighter look to the tail that is lacking in Savannahs. Upperpart coloration can be of great importance, because these two species are often only seen flying quickly away just over the tops of the grasses.

The face pattern of the two species is also very different. Baird's has a very golden-buff color to the face (not orange like the crown) that is accentuated by the broad, dark lateral crown stripes. The face patch is noticeably light and is outlined by a thin, dark border. The posterior border is often reduced to double spots. The anterior border of the face patch stands out well, and is situated virtually parallel to a thin, dark malar streak. The result is a double malar-stripe appearance that is very distinctive. Savannahs have a single dark malar stripe on each side that is wider and less crisply-defined than either malar streak of Baird's. The face patch is finely but densely streaked with brown, giving the face a darker look. Baird's, then, has a light buff cheek patch that is outlined by a thin, dark border, whereas Savannah has a dark patch that is more outlined by white or buff. Savannahs typically show some yellow on the lores (Baird's doesn't), but the extent and intensity of this yellow can vary tremendously.

CHIPPING VERSUS BREWER'S VERSUS CLAY-COLORED SPARROWS

The separation of these three members of the genus *Spizella* is a subtle problem that is exacerbated by illustrations and text in some of the standard field guides. This group presents a problem primarily in the Southwest, where both Brewer's and Chipping Sparrows winter in large numbers, and where most birders are unfamiliar with both the plumage and the true pattern of occurrence of the Clay-colored. Identification on the breeding grounds is seldom a problem, because song, and to a lesser extent habitat, is diagnostic for each species. Additionally, Chipping Sparrows in breeding plumage are impossible to confuse with the other two species.

Winter birds and fall migrants present more of a problem. As is usual in such cases, most misidentifications involve mistaking the more common species (in this case Chipping or Brewer's) for the rarer one (Clay-colored). Clay-

FIGURE 5.45. *Spizella* sparrows in winter plumage (left to right: Chipping, Clay-colored, Brewer's). Artwork by Dale A. Zimmerman.

colored Sparrow winters primarily in Mexico, regularly remaining as far north as south Texas. It is rare in winter elsewhere in the West. In spite of this, the species is routinely reported on Christmas Bird Counts, often in large numbers. This perpetuates the idea that the species is to be expected in winter, thus compounding the problem. Most legitimate sightings of the species for California and the Southwest represent fall (September to October) records of immature birds, and records outside of this time span should be approached with caution.

For the most part, field guides have failed to point out the distinctiveness of Clay-colored Sparrows, particularly of first-winter and basic-plumaged birds. Compared to the other two species, Clay-colored is a very bright, sharp, and warm-appearing bird. The difference is most apparent on the head and upper breast, but is also noticeable on the back, wings, and scapulars. Clay-colored has a sandy brown facial patch that is sharply outlined by a thin, dark brown border. Further isolating and highlighting this patch are a broad, cream-white eye stripe above, and an equally broad, cream-white mustache stripe below. The latter, in turn, is margined by a thin dark malar streak that divides the mustache stripe from the even whiter throat. The crown is sandy brown with blackish streaks overlaid, and a very noticeable cream-white median crown stripe dissecting it. The entire head is set off from the body by a very broad, well-defined gray nape that is unstreaked, and very noticeable. This nape creates the same effect as would a large collar (Figure 5.45).

The gray collar of the Clay-colored serves to isolate the head, which gives the general impression of being boldly striped with buff and white. Clay-coloreds typically show a buffy wash of variable intensity to the breast that contrasts sharply with the white throat and adds to the contrasting buff and white pattern of the head and face.

The back and scapulars of the Clay-colored are also quite buffy, with strongly contrasting blackish streaks. This adds to the warm appearance of the bird. The rump is unstreaked but does not contrast with the back (as does the gray nape).

Chipping Sparrows in winter and juvenal plumage share the light median crown stripe, unstreaked rump, and grayish collar with the Clay-colored. However, the median stripe tends toward light gray or grayish-white rather than cream-white, and the gray collar is not as broad nor nearly as obvious as in the latter species. Part of the reason for the less conspicuous collar is that Chipping Sparrows in fall and winter are typically very gray on the breast and face, and therefore the gray of the collar presents little contrast. Also, while both species have unstreaked rumps, the rump of the Clay-colored is essentially concolor with the back, while that of the Chipping is medium gray and contrasts strongly with the rust-brown back.

In general, fall and winter Chippings are dark grayish birds that lack the bright buff and white overtones of the Clay-colored. On both the back, and the crown and face they tend toward a reddish brown color that is very different from the colors of either Clay-colored or Brewer's. Juvenile Chippings have very obvious breast streaking, but this remains only until the post-juvenal molt in mid-fall. While Chippings show more contrast in plumage than do Brewer's, the effect still does not approach the bold, striped look of the Clay-colored (Figure 5.45).

Brewer's is almost more readily identified by a lack of characters. It is a very dull bird with a sandy gray-brown overall coloration that is noticeably different from the warm-buff of the Clay-colored or the cold dark-gray-and-rust of the Chipping. Most conspicuous is the general lack of pattern to the face and head (Figure 5.45). Although Brewer's has a brownish, darkly-outlined face patch, the stripes on either side of it (eye stripe above, malar stripe below) are dull gray rather than cream-white, and therefore do not stand out like the stripes of the Clay-colored. Also, the throat and breast are the same light-gray color, leaving virtually no contrast in those areas either.

Unlike the other two species, Brewer's lacks the light median crown stripe, and in the field the impression given is of a sandy-brown crown with many fine, darkish streaks. These fine streaks continue on to the nape and then onto the back, eliminating the collared look of the other two species. Often the rump (which is concolor with the back) is streaked, too. One feature that does set Brewer's Sparrow apart is the presence of a white eye ring (more conspicuous on some birds than on others), that is almost reminiscent of the eye ring of Vesper Sparrow.

In general, an absence of real contrast anywhere on the body suggests Brewer's Sparrow, whereas a gray-and-rust look with a strongly contrasting rump points to Chipping Sparrow. Clay-coloreds are distinctly buffy and clean. This look is so different from the other species that if you find yourself wondering whether or not a given *Spizella* is a Clay-colored, the chances are that it's not.

Calls of the three species are separable with practice. Both Clay-colored and Brewer's have a "tsee" that is thinner than the Chipping's single note. These calls are often heard in migration and winter. Wintering flocks of Brewer's will often engage in sporadic song bouts which include a variety of prolonged buzzy trills.

For further discussion see Simon (1977).

WINTER-PLUMAGED LONGSPURS

Winter-plumaged longspurs cause birders fits. Although the four species (Lapland, Chestnut-collared, McCown's, and Smith's) fit nearly everyone's definition of "little brown birds," that is not the worst of the problem. Most of the difficulty surrounding the identification of winter-plumaged longspurs stems from the difficulty in seeing them well. They usually occur in flocks, either with other longspurs or with Horned Larks. On the ground they tend to crouch down and blend in, to the point that they become nearly invisible. Most views consist of a swirling mass of birds bounding high in the air before settling back into the grass, where they become invisible once more.

Aside from these difficulties, it is possible to see wintering longspurs well. Unfortunately, most of the standard guides offer little help in identifying them once seen.

Tail patterns are helpful in at least narrowing the choices. McCown's and Chestnut-collared show much more white than the other two, which have their white restricted to the outer two pairs of retrices (much like a Vesper Sparrow). McCown's typically has an inverted, black "T" at the end of its tail, while Chestnut-collared has a centrally located black triangle. The distinctions between the two are frequently obvious, but just as often, are not. It is especially hard to see the exact pattern on an individual that is bouncing around in the middle of a nervous flock. The overall amount of white in the tail is helpful for breaking the four species into groups of two.

Bill size and structure are helpful to identifying sitting birds. McCown's has the heaviest, thickest-based bill of the four. It is somewhat different from the more slender bill of the Chestnut-collared (its closest partner on the basis of tail pattern). Likewise, Lapland has a stouter bill than Smith's, which is its closest partner on the basis of tail pattern alone. Adult McCown's also have mostly pale-colored (pinkish or yellowish) bills, while those of other longspurs tend to be dark.

Lapland is the only one of the four with truly black legs. Smith's has the lightest, with the other two being somewhat intermediate.

Overall body structure can also be useful. McCown's has proportionately long wings that nearly reach the end of the tail. This, combined with the big bill, gives McCown's a stocky, somewhat dumpy build. The wings of the other species are proportionately much shorter, leaving plenty of tail exposed.

Plumage distinctions are probably easiest to make among males, which show traces of their breeding colors. McCown's, Chestnut-collared, and Lapland often have some black smudging on the breast. Laplands will display some trace of their rusty nape, as will Chestnut-collared (but less conspicuously). McCown's will still have the bright-rusty median wing coverts, a mark that is seldom seen on flying birds. Likewise, Smith's and Chestnut-collared will show their white shoulder patches, but only at rest.

Laplands of both sexes share some distinctive plumage characters. They are fairly dark above and are whiter below than the other species (being almost entirely white, with perhaps some buff on the breast and flanks). They have darkish, heavily-streaked crowns, with the streaks often merging in places to give the impression of a dark cap. Their flanks are usually heavily streaked, whereas females may also show some streaking on the breast. More than any of the other species, Laplands have strong, rust-colored edges to the tertials, greater wing coverts, and (to a lesser extent) the scapulars. Most distinctive is the face pattern, which is similar in both sexes. The face (auriculars) is a unique golden-buff color, not unlike the faces of Baird's Sparrow or winter-plumaged Harris' Sparrow. The auricular patch is boldly outlined in black, and highlighted by a bold, buffy eyestripe. There is also a dark malar streak that combines with the outlined, buffy auriculars to yield a facial pattern reminiscent of Baird's Sparrow. No other longspur is similar.

Male McCown's is distinctly grayer below than the other species, and also has a grayer rump. Female McCown's is more buffy, and often shows little or no rusty wing coverts. It is closest to Chestnut-collared in appearance, but can be distinguished by its heavier bill, longer wings/shorter tail, broader buffy eye stripe, and general lack of streaking below. Another difference is the color of buff tones on the two birds. McCown's of both sexes have buffy regions that are best compared to the buff of a female House Sparrow. Chestnut-collared is a lighter, sandier buff color. Female Chestnut-collared can also be separated from McCown's by its lighter nape (contrasting more with crown and back) and its finer dark crown and back streaking. McCown's has blurrier dark streaking on the upperparts, again reminding one of female House Sparrow.

Smith's of both sexes are somewhat similar to Chestnut-collareds (mainly to females). All are quite buffy, but this color is much stronger on the underparts of Smith's. The whitish chin of Smith's contrasts with the buffy breast, but this pattern is often seen in Chestnut-collareds as well. Smith's generally have broader buffy eye stripes and better defined auricular patches. Their breast streaking also tends to be finer and more gingerly distributed (mostly on the flanks). If there is doubt in your mind in choosing between these two, try flushing the bird, since the tail patterns are very different.

Call notes can be helpful. Chestnut-collared has the most distinctive call— a finch-like "kittle, kittle," often repeated several times. The other three have a dry rattle (Chestnut-collared sometimes gives a soft rattle), while Smith's has a hard, sharp rattle that may be best compared to the winding of a noisy watch. Laplands may also intersperse "tew" notes between rattles.

Further treatment is provided by Dunn (1976).

EASTERN VERSUS WESTERN MEADOWLARK

The Eastern and Western Meadowlark are sympatric across much of the eastern edge of the Great Plains, Texas, New Mexico, and Arizona. They are easily distinguished by song, which in the Eastern consists of two penetrating whistles ("seeyou, seeair"), and in the Western of a variable, liquid series of warbles, gurgles, and whistles.

Many people consider the two species to be inseparable by visual characters. Most guides pay token homage to the more extensive white in the tail of Easterns and the more extensive yellow on the cheek of Westerns but still suggest using song as the primary criterion. Although this may be all that can be said of Eastern-Western differences in the eastern edge of the sympatric zone, the situation is different in the Southwest.

Eastern Meadowlarks show considerable geographic variation, with eastern populations (*Sturnella magna argutula*) being darker and more richly colored, and southwestern populations (*S. m. lilianae*) being lighter and more similar in general appearance to Westerns. Southwestern birds do show one excellent mark that is consistently different from Westerns, and that is a cream-colored or white, unstreaked cheek patch. Westerns typically show a brown, streaked cheek patch. Although Westerns are somewhat variable in this respect, they are never as clean on the cheek as the Easterns (Figure 5.46). Another good

FIGURE 5.46. Orioles (top to bottom: male Streak-backed, female Streak-backed, female Hooded, male Hooded, Altamira). Note differences in bill size and culmen shape.

mark is the color of the dark stripes on the head. In Western, these are dark brown with even darker thin streaks overlaid, and are not much different than the coloring of the cheek. In Eastern, these stripes are more solidly colored, and are much darker black-brown. This darker-striped look really stands out due to the contrast of the very white cheek.

Habitat differences during the breeding season are also important clues to meadowlark identity in the Southwest. In Arizona, New Mexico, and west Texas, Eastern Meadowlarks (*lilianae*) typically dominate grassland areas during the breeding season, while Westerns tend to settle in agricultural lowlands. Even in winter Easterns are most likely to be found in grasslands (or in grassy swales or playas in the middle of more arid areas), while Westerns are common in both more mesic farmlands and more xeric creosote deserts.

ORIOLES

As a rule, adult male orioles provide few problems in identification. For example, male Orchard, Audubon's, Scott's and Northern (both Bullock's and Baltimore), are all virtually unmistakable. Many birders do have problems, however, in distinguishing between Hooded, Streak-backed, and Altamira. Because Altamira is found only in south Texas (where it is nonmigratory), while Streak-backed is a very rare visitor to southern Arizona and California, the problems come

FIGURE 5.47. Orioles (left to right: immature male Streak-backed, immature male "Bullock's," immature male Streak-backed, adult female Streak-backed, adult male Hooded, adult male Streak-backed, adult male Streak-backed). Note particularly the resemblance of immature male "Bullock's" to female and immature Streak-backed.

FIGURE 5.48. Meadowlarks (top to bottom: Eastern, Eastern, Eastern, Western, Western, Western). The Easterns are all of the southwestern race *lilianae*. Note the differences in face patch coloration and boldness of the lateral crown stripes.

in separating each species from Hooded, which occurs from Texas to California.

Altamira is a much bigger, heavier bird than Hooded. Particularly apparent is the difference in the size and shape of the bill (Figure 5.47). Hooded has a long, narrow bill, with a distinctly downcurved culmen. Altamira has a much heavier bill with a culmen that is essentially straight. While the plumages are very similar, there are two differences that may be helpful. Altamira has orange lesser and median wing coverts, forming a shoulder patch that is not found in Hooded. Hoodeds have more extensive black in the malar region (Altamira is more orange), which lends a slightly different look to the face. The call notes of the two birds are also quite different, with Hooded giving a "wheet" that is very similar to the call of a House Finch.

Like the Altamira, the male Streak-backed can be separated from the male Hooded by its larger size, heavier bill with straight culmen, and more extensively orange malar region. Breeding plumaged birds are immediately separable on the basis of back pattern. Streak-backed has an orange or orange-yellow back with distinct vertical rows of black streaks (Figure 5.48). The back of

Hooded is entirely black. The problem comes from winter-plumaged Hoodeds, which are rarely seen in this country, and are therefore unfamiliar to most birders. Kaufman (1983) pointed out that male Hoodeds in fresh basic plumage have mostly buffy backs due to the broad buffy tips of the feathers. The black that is visible may reveal itself as irregular barring or spotting (but not as neat vertical rows of streaks), thus giving the impression of a streaked back. Feather wear brings about a gradual darkening of the back until it becomes solidly black. The Streak-backed Orioles that have been seen in the U.S. are of the west Mexican race (formerly known as Scarlet-headed Oriole), males of which are usually much deeper orange-red on the head than on the rest of the body. Hoodeds are typically uniformly colored, although some adult males may be deeper orange on the head.

Female and immature orioles present greater problems in identification. Scott's, Orchard, and Hooded fall into one group, with each species having uniformly colored yellow or yellow-green underparts. The Streaked-backed, "Baltimore," and "Bullock's" have more orange-yellow tones below, and have bellies and vents that are gray, buffy, or whitish, contrasting with the color of the breast. There is little or no sexual dimorphism in either Audubon's or Altamira, so they provide no problem.

Let's start with the first group. All are essentially greenish above and entirely yellowish below. Scott's is the largest of the group, with a heavy bill that is long and slightly decurved. It is the darkest of the three species, being more of a gray-green, without bright yellow. The throat is usually barred or spotted with black (absent on juvenile males and immature females), whereas the back has thin, but noticeable black streaking. The call note is a harsh "chuck." Hooded is much smaller, with a thinner bill and a distinctly curved culmen. It is greenish-yellow below (brighter than Scott's) and lacks the black markings of the throat and the streaking on the back. The House Finch-like "wheet" call is different from anything uttered by the other species. Orchard is the smallest, with a shorter bill that is less distinctly curved than that of the Hooded. It is more purely yellow below (brighter than the other two species) and shares the habit of jerking its tail sideways with Hooded. Its sharp "chuck" is quite unlike the call of Hooded. Beware however, that young Hoodeds may "chuck" for a short time after fledging. Some young Hoodeds also have shorter bills than adults, and can be a real source of confusion.

Female "Baltimores" are brownish-olive above, with orangish breasts that fade to buff, white, or gray on the belly. The undertail coverts typically match the orange of the breast. The white wing bars are more evident than in "Bullock's," as are the light edgings to the other wing feathers. Female "Bullock's" are more yellowish on the breast, with a more extensively light (grayish) belly. It is also grayer above, with a fairly noticeable gray-green eye stripe. The biggest confusion is likely between "Bullock's" and Streak-backed, which can even be difficult to distinguish in the hand. Contrary to the illustrations in most guides, female and immature-plumaged Bullock's may show dusky streaking on the olive back, thus leading to possible confusion with Streak-backed (Figure 5.48). The latter species is larger with a heavier bill, and has more contrast between the brighter orange on the side of the face and the duller yellowish of the breast. These are somewhat subjective distinctions, however, and female Streak-backeds should be identified in this country only with utmost caution.

See also Dunn (1975).

FEMALE CARPODACUS FINCHES

Females of the three species of *Carpodacus* finches (Purple, Cassin's, and House) provide western birders with a challenging identification problem. The challenge also applies to immature birds of both sexes, because male Purple and Cassin's Finches retain a female-like plumage until their second fall. This group is of particular concern in parts of the Southwest, where Cassin's Finches are typically uncommon and irregular winter visitors, Purple Finches are rare but regular vagrants, and House Finches are abundant residents.

Both the Purple and Cassin's Finch show a more strikingly patterned face than does the House Finch (Figure 5.49). The latter species has no face pattern, the entire head being a uniform dull brown with tiny darker streaks overlaid. Cassin's shows a brown face patch (the margins of which may be slightly blurred, thus making the patch somewhat indistinct), that is set off from the brown crown by a broad whitish/tannish supercilium. This patch is bordered below by a slightly paler area that is separated from the lighter throat by a dark malar streak. This same facial pattern is even more pronounced in the Purple Finch, which has a darker, more defined cheek patch that is bordered above and below by cleaner white stripes, that are also broader. The dark malar line of the Purple is also broader, being more of a stripe than a streak. Eastern and midwestern Purple Finches have whiter stripes bordering the facial patch than do West Coast birds (which are buffier), and thus are all the more striking, being reminiscent of female Rose-breasted Grosbeaks.

The underparts provide another important clue to specific identity and are an especially vital consideration in the separation of Purple Finches from Cassin's. All three species are extensively streaked below with brown streaks against a light background. House Finches have an almost dingy look, with blurred streaks that are often somewhat indistinct against a dirty washed-out background. The other two species have streaks that are bolder, and crisper (not blurred at the margins) and much more evident against ground colors that are cleaner. Purple Finches have very bold, thick streaks that are usually somewhat blurred at the margins (this blurring seems slightly more pronounced in West Coast birds, whereas the streaking is less bold). These are set against a background color of clean white in eastern/midwestern birds or cream-buff in West Coast individuals. Cassin's Finches have thinner, crisper streaking

FIGURE 5.49. Female *Carpodacus* finches (top to bottom:
House, Purple, Cassin's). Note structural differences and
differences in face/head pattern and ventral streaking.
Artwork by Dale A. Zimmerman.

that is more reminiscent of a Pine Siskin, and this is set against a white background.

It is especially critical to note the extent of streaking on the underparts. Cassin's have streaking on the undertail coverts, while most Purples lack streaks in this region. Unfortunately, this fairly diagnostic character can be difficult to see.

Upperpart coloration can also be helpful, because Purple and House Finches have a darker ground color than does Cassin's. This makes the back streaking on Cassin's more visible than it is on the other species. Eastern and midwestern Purples are more contrastingly streaked on the back than are western birds, which are a dingier olive above.

Some of the best clues are provided by head, bill, and body proportions (Figure 5.49). House Finches have smaller bills than the other two species, and their culmens are slightly curved. In profile they appear symmetrical with respect to tail length versus head/bill size. Purple Finches have noticeably larger (but stubby) bills, in which the culmen is also curved. In profile they tend to look big-headed and short-tailed. Cassin's Finches have longer bills, and straight culmens. They also have longer wings, which extend nearly half the length of the tail. In profile they appear more robust and big-headed than House Finches, but longer and less sawed-off than Purples. They also show a marked tendency to erect their crown feathers, thus giving their heads a peaked or crested appearance that is usually absent in the other *Carpodacus* Purples and Cassin's also have distinctly notched tails, a character not seen in House Finches.

See also Dunn (1976).

·6·

Keeping Field Notes

One of the most productive exercises that a field birder can indulge in is the keeping of a field journal to chronicle his or her activities. Besides providing a record of what birds were seen where, a journal is an ideal repository for notes on identification, behavior, and other aspects of natural history.

WHY KEEP A JOURNAL?

There are numerous reasons for keeping a field journal. The most logical is the simple desire to have a record of all field trips taken. This is worthwhile if for no other reason than the pleasure derived from poring over the accounts of fun days in the field.

If you are list-oriented a journal is essential. Who knows when a geographically variable species may get split by taxonomists? Without a written record it may be impossible to recall whether or not you saw yellow-legged "Western Gulls" (now Yellow-footed Gull—a separate species) several years ago at the Salton Sea, after having seen thousands of pink-legged ones up and down the California coast on the same trip. A well-kept journal will also save much time and memory-searching when you are attempting to compile lists of any kind.

As an active birder you never know when you may be called upon to contribute information to an area checklist, an article, or even a book. Under such conditions memory is an unreliable tool, and there are few things more frustrating than trying vainly to recall the events of a day or an hour of birding that took place months or even years earlier.

Equally or more important, a journal provides a permanent record for others to use. Researchers routinely search the field notes of past birders to gain insight into population trends of birds. By maintaining a journal and insuring that photocopies are deposited with a local museum, library, or university, you may be making a significant contribution to our future understanding of bird distribution. Don't make the mistake of thinking that your records show nothing of value. Ornithology is more advanced as a science than are most fields of organismal biology, thanks in no small part to the contributions of an unparalleled number of active amateurs.

HOW TO KEEP A JOURNAL

Keeping a field journal is like choosing a pair of binoculars—it is a highly personal activity that must reflect the nature of the individual. Just as there is no one "best" binocular, there is also no absolute right and wrong way of keeping a journal. However, some methods are more desirable than others simply for their capacity for efficient information storage and retrieval.

The method that I suggest is essentially the same as that developed decades ago by Joseph Grinnell, founder of the Museum of Vertebrate Zoology, University of California at Berkeley. Almost everyone has their own minor modifications of this central theme, and you will no doubt wish to incorporate your own changes to reflect a style with which you are comfortable.

At the core of every true field journal is a chronological log of every field trip taken, with a list of species seen and locations visited (see Figure 6.1). The date should be listed somewhere at the top of the page (be sure to include the year) and should be repeated for as many pages as are necessary to write up the trip. This becomes vital in the event that pages get torn or separated from their proper sequence. I put a "continued . . ." following the date on each page subsequent to page one of a write-up to indicate that other pages exist. When recording the date, do it in a manner that will be clear to everyone (for example, June 9, 1999 or 9 June 1999). Dates written "6/9/99" may be read as June 9, 1999 by most people, but to some it may be read "September 6, 1999." It is also desirable to place your name at the top of each page, allowing lost or separated pages some chance of finding their way back.

Next comes a list of the localities and habitats visited, written in chronological order. Again, keep in mind that others may have use for your notes. Make locality headings as specific as possible. A locale such as "Hueco Tanks State Park" may need no further explanation, but names like "The Old Refuge" or "Randel's Pool" do. The primary concern is that others should at least be able to pinpoint all spots on a detailed county map. Accordingly, the county and state of all areas visited should be recorded in the locality section. If locations listed are not readily apparent on most maps, then detailed directions (for example, 5 miles north on County Rd. #450 from its jct. with U.S. Hwy. 70) are in order. Too much detail is almost always better than not enough. It is common practice to place bold wavy lines under all of the localities listed, in order to highlight them for quick reference.

After the locality section you should list other accessory details of your outings. Minimally, this should include

1. starting and finishing times
2. some summary of weather conditions
3. a list of field companions, if any.

The starting time and duration of a field trip is important information to consider when reviewing the results of a trip. For example, the fact that a formerly common species is missed during a fifteen-minute stop at noon means little. On the other hand, if that species is missed after a full day of birding that began at dawn, then you may put more stock in your discovery. Again, such information is of great concern to others who may be using your records.

Likewise, a statement of existing weather conditions for the day of a field trip is also critical for placing the results of the trip in proper perspective. Low numbers of birds seen may result mainly from high winds or some other

JOURNAL — K.J. ZIMMER

THURSDAY — August 23, 1984

Las Cruces → east on Hwy 70/82 to Holloman
Lakes (alkaline playa pond — "Lake Stinky" —
and adjacent sewage ponds for Holloman AFB,
located 3.5 miles east of White Sands
Natl. Mon.); Otero Co., N.M.

TIME — 7:00 a.m. — 12 noon
WEATHER — partly cloudy, warm, wind 0-5 mph
OBSERVER — Kevin J. Zimmer

Eared Grebe — 6
Cattle Egret — 1
** Little Blue Heron — 1 imm.
White-faced Ibis — 13
Mallard — 7
Blue-winged Teal — ±20
Swainson's Hawk — 2 along Hwy. 70
Prairie Falcon — 1 ad. (made pass at shorebirds)
Semipalmated Plover — 2
Snowy Plover — 1
Killdeer — ±35
Willet — 2
* Pectoral Sandpiper — 1 juv. (photos)
Baird's Sandpiper — 1 juv.
* Semipalmated Sandpiper — 3 juv. (photos)
Least Sandpiper — ±100 (actually counted 58 ad.)
                              (24 juv.
Western Sandpiper — ±60 (18 ad., 42 juv.)

CONTINUED →

FIGURE 6.1. Sample page from a field journal (see text for explanation).

Aug. 23, 1984 cont. →   pg. 2

Long-billed Dowitcher — 1 ad.
Stilt Sandpiper — 1 juv.
American Avocet — 40 (3 downy chicks)
Wilson's Phalarope — ≈3000+
[Meadowlark sp(?)] — 5 along Hwy. 70

TOTAL — 22 species

NOTES :

   Semipalmated Sandpiper — At least 3
individuals were observed, and at least 2
of the photos taken included all 3 birds.
They were studied for ≈ 20 minutes through a
15-60 × scope under good light conditions, at
distances of 25'- 30 m. All 3 birds were
juveniles. They were a uniform light brown
above, with neat, crisp, cream-colored edges
to the scapulars and other dorsal feathers.
There was no hint of rust to the scapulars,
and the overall color tone was very different
from the gray of nearby juv. westerns.
Whitish underparts and a broad, whitish
supercilium completed the plumage picture.
The legs were black, as were the bills.
The bills of all 3 birds were much shorter
than those of nearby westerns, and were tubular
in shape (thick to the tip, with little apparent
tapering).

FIGURE 6.2. Sample "Notes" section from a field journal.

SPECIES ACCOUNTS — K. J. ZIMMER

Semipalmated Sandpiper (Calidris pusilla)

1984

Aug. 23 Holloman Lakes (Otero Co., NM) : 3 juv. (photos)
Aug. 31 Holloman Lakes (Otero Co., NM) : 1 juv. (photos)
Sept. 7 Holloman Lakes (Otero Co., NM) : 3-4 juv. (photos)
Sept. 15 Holloman Lakes (Otero Co., NM) 2 juv. (photos)
Sept. 29 Holloman Lakes (Otero Co., NM) 1 juv. (KJZ, R. Hill)
Oct. 5 Holloman Lakes (Otero Co., NM) 1 juv.

FIGURE 6.3. Sample "Species Account" (see text for explanation).

weather condition rather than from a true paucity of birdlife. The reverse situation may also hold. Large numbers of migrants on a given day could easily result from some prevailing weather pattern such as north winds and cold fronts. These bits of information may seem trivial at the time, but when records are kept over a number of years, the cumulative total may reveal some consistent trends.

The list of other observers is of primary importance when submitting your rarities records for publication, or when others are doing research based upon your notes. The more witnesses to an unusual sighting the better, and there is always the chance that one of your companions may have included important details in his or her field notes that you neglected to mention in yours. By listing your companions, the outside researcher is given a lead on where to find further information. An observer list may also be helpful to you in recalling the events of a particular outing.

Some people combine all of this accessory information in one paragraph. I prefer to give each category a separate line and heading (for example, Time, Weather, Observers) to make the information easier to read at a glance. You may wish to include other types of introductory information such as miles traveled (by car and foot), elevation, habitat descriptions, or, if multiple sites are visited, a breakdown of how much time was spent at each spot. This type of information may also be included in a "Notes" section at the end of the write-up.

The introductory material is followed by the meat of the write-up, which is a list of all species of birds recorded on the day. This is typically done in taxonomic order, although some people prefer to subdivide by locality, and then order the birds taxonomically within that framework. Try to avoid using any ambiguous abbreviations in your listing (for example, "B.t. Hummingbird" could refer either to Broad-tailed or Blue-throated). This is especially important in light of the tendency for common names of birds to change over the years. The safest course is to avoid abbreviations altogether. Birds not identified to species but narrowed to family or genus should still be inserted in the sequence, with the designation "sp (?)" (read "species unknown") following the broader classification (e.g., "Buteo sp. ?" for an unidentified soaring hawk). Birds seen by companions but missed by you should still be cited with some symbol in front of the species name to indicate that you did not personally see the bird. Initials of the person(s) responsible for the sighting should be included somewhere after the name of the species.

A species list is the minimal amount of information that should be recorded regarding the birds seen on the day. If more than one locality is visited, then the specific locale of the sighting should follow each bird name. This locale should be spelled out the first time it is used and can be abbreviated thereafter, providing that the abbreviation is cited parenthetically after the full name (for example, "Killdeer—1 at Hueco Tanks State Park (hereafter HT)"). An alternative is to provide a key at the head of the list and then abbreviate throughout. If your notes for a given day require more than one page, then the full name of each locale should be used the first time it is cited on each page.

Some indication should be also be made of the numbers of individuals seen of each species. Preferably, this would take the form of exact counts or at least accurate estimates. When large numbers of a species are encountered throughout the day and no attempt has been made at keeping a running tally, then it is probably more honest to record a descriptive term (e.g., common or abundant) rather than a number. Even the most imprecise designations, such as "many" or "several" are better than no information at all.

Estimates of numbers may be indicated by a "±" sign in front of the figure. Estimates should be rounded to the nearest 10 for numbers under 100, and to the nearest 25 to 50 for numbers from 100 to 1000. Numbers over 1000 should not be estimated to a level finer than the nearest 100. If you have estimated 500 individuals in one flock, and then see 3 individuals of the same species at another location, it is misleading to record 503 as the total count. You may wish to indicate the occurrence of flocks parenthetically (for example, "Surf Scoter—250 (95 in one flock)").

It is often desirable to record the age and sex of a bird in your notes. This is essential information when detailing rarities, but it is also useful under other circumstances. It is well known that the different age classes of many migratory birds move south at different times in fall. This is particularly true of shorebirds, where adults migrate before juveniles. By recording the ages of the shorebirds seen on each trip, you can determine the typical timing and pattern of fall shorebird migration in your area. Likewise, in many species one sex will migrate before the other (for example, many adult male hummingbirds move south well ahead of the females). By carefully recording the age and sex of birds seen you may reveal patterns of differential movement that are still not known for a given species. Because raptors are always of special concern, it is useful to record ages for all birds seen. This may lend clues as to how well the populations are maintaining themselves. Large percentages of adults with few young birds may indicate low rates of reproduction.

As with total numbers of birds seen, age/sex breakdowns do not have to take the form of exact counts. Such a process would be extremely tedious when dealing with large numbers of birds, and would provide little incentive for even making the effort. However, it takes little additional time to note percentages or ratios of the different sexes/age groups seen (for example, "Western Sandpiper—150 [75% adult, 25% juv.]").

When various breeding behaviors are noticed it is useful to make a note of them alongside the bird's name (you may want to expand on this in the "Notes" section at the end of the write-up). Behaviors that should be noted include food carrying by adults, territorial singing/calling, nest building, mating displays, copulations, and so forth. Such information is vital in determining the true breeding status of birds at a given locale. It is always surprising to discover how many species that are assumed to breed in an area have never actually been documented to do so.

Rare birds listed in your account should be highlighted in some way so as to make them stand out. I usually denote unusual species with an asterisk in the left margin. Rare species merit two asterisks, and extremely rare ones receive three. Other people underline the names of rare birds and use a similar system of one, two, or three lines to denote differing degrees of rarity. I make note of unusually high numbers of individuals by underlining the number only. If numbers are unusually low, I indicate that parenthetically. You may wish to include a "heard only" comment for birds that were heard but not seen.

The species list is followed by a "Notes" section, which is the repository for more detailed information that does not conveniently fit into the preceding list (see Figure 6.2). You may find that on short outings to familiar spots you have nothing special to write up in such a section. On the other hand, when birding in unfamiliar places, you may end up making this section longer than the rest of the entry.

The most important item to include under "Notes" is a detailed description of any rare bird that is seen. You may be the best field birder in your area, but a future researcher or someone from another region may have no knowledge of your abilities. Therefore, the simple fact that you recorded a rare species in your journal is not enough. You also need to document it.

Documenting rare birds is an art in itself, and there are definite right and wrong ways to go about it. First of all, descriptions should be written in the field, either while viewing the bird or as soon after as is possible. I prefer not to take my journal into the field for fear of losing it, but I do take some sort of notebook from which notes can be transcribed later. It is preferable to write details *before* looking at a field guide, since our minds often subconsciously alter remembered details to fit those pictured in the book. No details are more tainted than those which forsake an original description for "looked exactly like the picture in the book."

Details should include time of day, light conditions, distance of the observer from the bird, optical equipment used, duration of the sighting, and the number of observers and their previous experience (if any) with the species or with similar species. This should be followed by a detailed description of the bird, including remarks on plumage, size, shape, bill structure, habitat, and any behaviors or vocalizations that were noted. This in turn should be followed by a discussion of how and why other similar (and/or more likely) species were eliminated from consideration.

Rarities should always be reported to the appropriate regional editor of *American Birds*, the journal of North American bird distribution. *American Birds* breaks up their records into four reporting seasons:

1. spring migration (March 1 to May 31)
2. summer (June 1 to July 31)
3. fall migration (August 1 to November 30)
4. winter (December 1 to February 28).

Reports are due on the editor's desk no later than ten to fifteen days after the end of a reporting period to ensure that publication deadlines are met. If you keep a field journal, complete with detailed notes on rarities, it becomes an easy task to report unusual sightings, and your observations will become part of the published record.

The "Notes" section of your journal should not be limited to details of rare birds. This is the place for detailed notes on behaviors or vocalizations of more common birds; remarks on previously unnoted field marks; discussions on apparent population trends, migration patterns, habitat changes, or ecological theories; maps and detailed directions to new birding spots; names, addresses, and phone numbers of birders met in the field, etc. As such, the "Notes" section often makes for both interesting and informative reading, and can be great fun to read back through at some future date.

SPECIES ACCOUNTS

Many birders maintain separate species accounts as a supplement to their field journals. Unlike the journal, which is arranged chronologically by field trip, species accounts are ordered taxonomically, with whole pages devoted to individual species (see Figure 6.3). Within a species account, sightings of that species are entered consecutively through time, with all pertinent locality and numbers data included. This makes for great ease of data retrieval on any species, because you need only to turn to the proper species account to retrieve all sightings of that species for the year. This has obvious advantages over having to laboriously page through several years of journals to extract the needed pieces of information. For this reason, many people prefer to place detailed notes on a given species under the species account rather than in the "Notes" section of the journal.

Because species accounts are maintained as running, cumulative lists for each species, it is best to keep them in a loose-leaf binder. This allows you to add pages when necessary, and you can always have separate years or groups of years bound at a book bindery at low cost.

SUMMARY

A final word concerning the maintenance of a field journal is appropriate here. While all of the foregoing may seem like too much work, if it is done regularly it can be easily incorporated into your daily routine. The most important rule is to write your notes while the experiences are still fresh in your mind. There is nothing like procrastination to turn note-taking into a chore. Trying to catch up on multiple field trips is not only time-consuming, but also leads to errors. This is particularly true in the middle of a long birding trip, in which every day is devoted to seeing large numbers of birds. Under these conditions the days tend to run together in one's mind, and if you allow your note-writing to slide for even a couple of days you may find yourself hopelessly behind.

Good note-takers learn to take advantage of "dead time" to write up their notes. The time spent driving from one location to another is an excellent time to at least jot numbers down on a field checklist from which they can be later transcribed. If you are the driver, have a companion do the actual recording. This provides a good chance for all observers to provide input concerning the numbers of individuals seen of each species. Field notes can be readily written while watching television, listening to the stereo, or relaxing in the heat of the day with a cool drink. This takes discipline, but you'll soon find that with practice, note-taking takes little time and provides many real rewards.

Bibliography

Bartol, Dominic A. 1974. Inserts: Mountain Plover. *Birding* VI (1). 17.

Binford, L. C. 1971. Identification of Northern and Louisiana Waterthrushes. *California Birds* 2 (1): 1–9.

Cade, T. J. 1955. Variation of the Common Rough-legged Hawk in North America. *Condor* 57 (6): 313–346.

Clark, William S. 1979. Communications. *American Birds* 33 (6): 909.

Clark, William S. 1981. Flight Identification of Common North American Buteos. *Continental Birdlife* 2 (5–6): 129–143.

Clark, William S. 1983. The Field Identification of North American Eagles. *American Birds* 37 (5): 822–826.

Davis, L. Irby. 1962. Songs of North American *Myiarchus*. *Texas Journal of Science* 13: 327–344.

Dunn, Jon. 1975. Field notes—The Identification of Immature Orioles. *The Western Tanager* 42 (4): 7.

Dunn, Jon. 1976a. Field Notes—The Identification of Pipits. *The Western Tanager* 43 (3): 5.

Dunn, Jon. 1976b. Field Notes—The Identification of Longspurs. *The Western Tanager* 42 (5): 4–5.

Dunn, Jon. 1976c. Field Notes—The *Carpodacus* Finches. *The Western Tanager* 42 (9): 4.

Dunn, Jon. 1977a. Field Notes—Female Grosbeaks. *The Western Tanager* 43 (6): 5.

Dunn, Jon. 1977b. Field Notes—The Genus *Empidonax*. *The Western Tanager* 43 (7): 5.

Dunn, Jon. 1977c. Field Notes—The Genus *Empidonax*. *The Western Tanager* 43 (8): 5,7.

Dunn, Jon. 1977d. Field Notes—The Genus *Empidonax*. *The Western Tanager* 43 (9): 4.

Dunn, Jon. 1977e. Field Notes—The Genus *Empidonax*. *The Western Tanager* 43 (10): 5,7.

Dunn, Jon. 1978a. Field Notes—The *Myiarchus* Flycatchers. *The Western Tanager* 45 (3): 4–5.

Dunn, Jon. 1978b. Field Notes—The *Myiarchus* Flycatchers. *The Western Tanager* 4 (4): 5.

Dunn, Jon. 1978c. Field Notes—The *Endomychura* Murrelets. *The Western Tanager* 44 (8): 8–9.

Dunn, Jon. 1978d. Field Notes—Plain-winged Vireos. *The Western Tanager* 44 (10): 9.

Dunn, Jon. 1979a. Field Notes—Immature Red-shouldered and Broad-winged Hawks. *The Western Tanager* 45 (8): 13.

Dunn, Jon. 1979b. Field Notes—Northern and Louisiana Waterthrushes. *The Western Tanager* 45 (10): 7.

Dunn, Jon. 1981. The Identification of Female Bluebirds. *Birding* XIII (1): 4–11.

Dunn, Jon, and Kimball Garrett. 1982. Field Notes—Horned and Eared Grebes. *The Western Tanager* 48 (5): 8.

Dunn, Jon. L., and Kimball L. Garrett. 1983a. The Identification of Wood-Pewees. *The Western Tanager* 50 (4): 1–3.

Dunn, Jon and Kimball Garrett. 1983b. The Identification of Thrushes of the Genus *Catharus*, Part One: Introduction. *The Western Tanager* 49 (6): 1–2.

Dunn, Jon and Kimball Garrett. 1983c. The Identification of Thrushes of the Genus *Catharus*, Part Two: Hermit Thrush. *The Western Tanager* 49 (7): 4, 9.

Dunn, Jon and Kimball Garrett. 1983d. The Identification of Thrushes of the Genus *Catharus*, Part Three: Swainson's Thrush. *The Western Tanager* 49 (8): 7–9.

Dunn, Jon and Kimball Garrett. 1983e. The Identification of Thrushes of the Genus *Catharus*, Part Four: Veery and Graycheeked Thrush. *The Western Tanager* 49 (9): 1–3.

Faanes, Craig. 1984. Inserts: Yellow Rail. *Birding* XVI (3): 118 I–J.

Farrand, John Jr. (ed.). 1983. *The Audubon Society Master Guide to Birding* (3 vol.). New York: Alfred A. Knopf, Inc.

Garrett, Kimball and Jon Dunn. 1982. The Identification of Common and Lesser Nighthawks. *The Western Tanager* 49 (1): 1, 3.

Grant, P. J. 1981. Identification of Semipalmated Sandpiper. *British Birds* 74: 505–509.

Grant, P. J., and R. E. Scott. 1969. Field Identification of Juvenile Common, Arctic, and Roseate Terns. *British Birds* 62: 297–299.

Harrison, Peter. 1983. *Seabirds: An Identification Guide*. Boston: Houghton Mifflin Co.

Hume, R. A., and P. J. Grant. 1974. The upperwing pattern of adult Common and Arctic Terns. *British Birds* 67 (4): 133–136.

Kaufman, Kenn. 1979. Field Identification of Hutton's Vireo. *Continental Birdlife* 1 (3): 62–66.

Kaufman, Kenn. 1983. Identifying Streak-backed Orioles: a note of caution. *American Birds* 37 (2): 140–141.

King, Ben. 1981. The Field Identification of North American Pipits. *American Birds* 35 (5): 778–788.

Lane, James A. 1976. *A Birder's Guide to Southern California* (3rd ed.). Denver: L & P Press.

Lane, James A. 1983. *A Birder's Guide to the Rio Grande Valley of Texas* (4th ed.). Denver: L & P Press.

Lane, James A. 1983. *A Birder's Guide to Southeastern Arizona* (4th ed.). Denver: L & P Press.

Lane, James A., and Harold L. Holt. 1979. *A Birder's Guide to Eastern Colorado* (3rd ed.). Denver: L & P Press.

Lane, James A., and John L. Tveton. 1980. *A Birder's Guide to the Texas Coast.* (3rd ed.). Denver: L & P Press.

Lehman, Paul. 1980. The Identification of Thayer's Gull in the Field. *Birding* XII (6): 198–210.

Mueller, H. D., D. D. Berger, and G. Allenz. 1979. The Identification of North American Accipiters. *American Birds* 33 (3): 236–240.

Parkes, Kenneth C. 1982. Further Comments on the Field Identification of North American Pipits. *American Birds* 36 (1) 20–22.

Parmeter, Benjamin D. 1974. Inserts: Marbled Murrelet. *Birding* VI (3) 125–126.

Peterson, Roger Tory. 1947, 1980. *A Field Guide to the Birds.* Boston: Houghton Mifflin.

Peterson, Roger Tory. 1961. *A Field Guide of Western Birds.* Boston: Houghton Mifflin.

Pettingill, Olin S. 1951. *A Guide to Bird Finding East of the Mississippi.* New York: Oxford University Press.

Pettingill, Olin S. 1981. *A Guide to Bird Finding West of the Mississippi.* (2nd ed.). New York: Oxford University Press.

Pough, Richard H. 1957. *Audubon Western Bird Guides.* New York: Doubleday and Co., Inc.

Ramsey, Fred L. 1978. *Birding Oregon.* Corvallis: O.S.U. Book Stores, Inc.

Remsen, Van. 1973. Inserts: Lawrence's Goldfinch. *Birding* V (1) 17–18.

Roberson, Don. 1980. *Rare Birds of the West Coast.* Pacific Grove, Calif.: Woodcock Publications.

Roberson, Don. 1982. The Changing Seasons. *American Birds* 36 (6): 948–953.

Robbins, Chandler S., Bertel Brunn and Herbert S. Zim. 1966, 1983. *Birds of North America: A Guide to Field Identification.* New York: Golden Press.

Russell, Will. 1976. Field Identification Notes (*Sterna* Terns). *Birding* VIII (6): 347–8.

Scott, R. E., and P. J. Grant. 1969. Uncompleted Moult in *Sterna* Terns and the Problem of Identification. *British Birds* 62: 93–97.

Scott, Shirley L. (ed.). 1983. *National Geographic Society: Field Guide to the Birds of North America.* Washington D.C.: National Geographic Society.

Simon, David. 1977. Identification of Clay-colored, Brewer's and Chipping Sparrows in Fall Plumage. *Birding* IX (5): 189–191.

Simon, David. 1978. Identification of Snow and Ross' Geese. *Birding* X (6): 289–291.

Starks, Donald S. 1981. Inserts: Black Rosy Finch. *Birding* XIII (2): 54 u–v.

Terrill, S. B., and L. S. Terrill. 1981. On the Field Identification of Yellow-green, Red-eyed, Philadelphia, and Warbling Vireos. *Continental Birdlife* 2 (5–6): 144–149.

Udvardy, Miklos D. F. 1977. *The Audubon Society Field Guide to North American Birds: Western Region.* New York: Alfred A. Knopf, Inc.

Wahl, Terence R., and Dennis R. Paulson. 1977. *A Guide to Bird-finding in Washington.* Bellingham: T. R. Wahl.

Wallace, D. I. M. 1974. Field Identification of Small Species of the Genus *Calidris. British Birds* 67: 1.

Wallace, D. I. M. 1976. A Review of Waterthrush Identification. *British Birds* 69: 27.

Wallace, D. I. M., and M. A. Ogilvie. 1977. Distinguishing Blue-winged and Cinnamon Teals. *British Birds* 70: 290–294.

Wilds, Claudia. 1982. Separating the Yellowlegs. *Birding* XIV (5): 172–178.

Wilds, Claudia, and Mike Newlon. 1983. The Identification of Dowitchers. *Birding* XV (4/5): 151–166.

Glossary

Allopatric. Refers to two or more species (usually closely related) which occupy disjunct geographic ranges, and which are therefore unlikely to be seen in the same place.

Auriculars. The region around the ear opening (covered by feathers) generally including the area between the eye and the malar region. Often referred to as a "face patch."

Axillars. Underwing feathers lying close to the body (in the "armpit" of the wing). These are longer than the surrounding coverts, and in some species are conspicuously different in color from the remainder of the underwing.

Brachium. The portion of the wing between the elbow and the body.

Carpals. The "wrist" of a bird, which creates the forward-pointing bend in the wing.

Crissum. See *undertail coverts*.

Culmen. The top ridge of the upper mandible of the bill, extending from the tip to the base of the feathers at the forehead.

Distal. Situated away from the point of origin.

Elbow. The proximal, posteriorly-directed angle of the wing.

Eye line. A contrastingly-colored line that extends through the eye, as in the dark eye line of an adult Chipping Sparrow.

Eye ring. A ring of contrastingly-colored feathers around the eye. It may be complete (as in *Empidonax* flycatchers), or broken (as in MacGillivray's Warbler). In the latter case, the term *crescents* may be used to refer to the upper and lower halves of the broken ring. When the ring is continuous with a line extending forward to the bill, the term *spectacles* is often employed.

Eye stripe. A contrastingly-colored stripe above the eye that is usually wider than an eye line (as in the white eye-stripe of adult Chipping Sparrows). The terms *supercilium* and *eyebrow* are synonomous.

Gape. The line along which the mandibles of the bill meet. May also refer to the area between the opened mandibles.

Gonys. The lowermost ridge of the lower mandible of the bill. Forms an angle (the *gonydeal angle*—very prominent in gulls, terns, loons, etc.) where the two sides of the lower mandible fuse towards the tip. In many gulls this angle is marked by a red or black spot (*gonydeal spot*).

Greater Coverts. The smaller feathers on the upper and lower surfaces of the wing which overlie the bases of the primaries and secondaries (one covert per flight feather).

Gular Region. The posterior continuation of the chin, usually devoid of feathers in such groups as cormorants, boobies, etc., thereby revealing a colorful patch of bare skin.

Inner Web. The broader of the two flexible vanes of feather barbs that extend from the shaft of a feather.

Lateral Crown Stripes. Obvious stripes running longitudinally along the sides of the crown. Located above the supercilium.

Lesser Coverts. Very small feathers overlying the median coverts of the wing.

Lores. The area between the eye and upper mandible of the bill.

Malar Region. The area between the lower bill and the angle of the jaw (the cheek). Bounded above by the auriculars.

Malar Stripe. A stripe of contrastingly-colored feathers through the malar region. Such stripes are sometimes referred to as "whiskers" or "moustache stripes" (although some authors use the latter term for a stripe between the malar stripe and the eye).

Mantle. The area between the scapulars, which includes the upper back. Typically used in reference to gulls.

Median Coverts. The shorter feathers overlying the greater wing coverts.

Median Crown Stripe. A stripe of contrastingly-colored feathers running longitudinally through the center of the crown.

Morph. Refers to any one of the color phases which exists in a polymorphic population (as in blue and white morphs of the Snow Goose, or light and dark morphs of many hawks).

Nape. The dorsal (upper) surface of the neck.

Orbital Ring. A ring of unfeathered skin (often brightly-colored) surrounding the eye (as in gulls).

Outer Web. The narrower of the two flexible vanes of feather barbs that extend from the shaft of a feather.

Post-ocular. Behind (posterior to) the eye, as in a post-ocular stripe or patch.

Primaries. The remiges (flight feathers) that attach to the manus (hand) of the wing. These are the outermost group of flight feathers, and are numbered consecutively from the inside out.

Proximal. Situated near the point of origin.

Race. See *subspecies*.

Remiges. The long, stiff feathers that project posteriorally from the wing, and which attach to the ulna and manus of the wing. Often referred to as the "flight feathers."

Retrices. The large, conspicuous feathers of the tail.

Scapulars. A group of feathers that originate at the shoulder and that vary in prominence from group to group. Swimming ducks and standing shorebirds often have a majority of the wing concealed by the scapulars, which are often conspicuously patterned. On most passerines the scapulars are short, dully-colored, and overlap little of the remainder of the wing.

Secondaries. The inner group of remiges (flight feathers) that attach to the ulna of the wing. They are numbered consecutively from the outside in.

Shaft. The central tube or quill of a feather (minus the webs or vanes).

Subspecies. Refers to one or more populations of a species that are morphologically distinct from other such populations of that species, and which are essentially geographically isolated from those populations. Synonomous with *race*.

Supercilium. See eye stripe.

Sympatric. Refers to two or more species (typically closely related) whose ranges overlap. The area of overlap is referred to as the area of sympatry.

Tarsus. The section of the leg between the toes and the heel (the joint that bends backward, and which is often erroneously thought of as the knee). This is the only section of the leg that is likely to be unfeathered (some species have feathered tarsi).

Tertials. The feathers growing from the brachium, between the secondaries and the scapulars. Like the scapulars, the tertials vary in prominence from group to group. The tertials of a standing shorebird may have bright edges and cover all but the outermost primary tips, while the tertials of many song birds are short and fairly inconspicuous, and are typically referred to as only inner secondaries.

Undertail Coverts. The small feathers which cover the ventral bases of the retrices. Frequently referred to as the *crissum*.

Uppertail Coverts. The small feathers which overlie the dorsal bases of the retrices (posterior to the rump).

Vent. The exterior opening of the cloaca lying between the lower belly and the crissum, and not readily distinguished in the field from the latter region.

Wrist. See *carpals*.

Index